AUBURN BASKETBALL

FROM BARKLEY TO BRUCE

Also by Van Allen Plexico and John Ringer:

We Believed: A Lifetime of Auburn Football, Vol. 1: 1975-1998

Decades of Dominance: Auburn Football in the Modern Era

Season of Our Dreams: The 2010 Auburn Tigers

More Auburn Football, from White Rocket Books:

Lorendo, by Ken Ringer

Edited by Van Allen Plexico:

Assembled! Five Decades of Earth's Mightiest

Assembled! 2: Earth's Mightiest Heroes and Their Foes

AUBURN BASKETBALL

FROM BARKLEY TO BRUCE

VAN ALLEN PLEXICO & JOHN RINGER

HOSTS OF THE AU WISHBONE AUBURN PODCAST

WHITE ROCKET BOOKS

AUBURN BASKETBALL: FROM BARKLEY TO BRUCE

Copyright 2022 by Van Allen Plexico and John Ringer

Cover design by Van Allen Plexico for White Rocket Books

All rights reserved, including the right to reproduce this book, or portions thereof, in any form, save for brief passages to be quoted in reviews.

A White Rocket Book
www.whiterocketbooks.com

ISBN-13: 978-1-962993-02-9

This book is set in Times and Calibri.

First printing: July 2022

0 9 8 7 6 5 4 3 2

- THE AU WISHBONE FAMILY -

Van and John extend their eternal thanks and appreciation to these fine members of the Auburn Family and the AU Wishbone Family (as of June 2022) whose support helps to make our podcasts and other projects (such as this book) a reality. *War Eagle!*

Samuel Salvatore
Carl Von Drunker
Chris and Clinton Stewart
Parker Neill
Bradley Blackmon
Daniel Odom
Gary Grant (aka AU_Fan@KSC)
Logan Chilton
Matthew Flowers
Michael Kirshner
Phil Amthor
Richard Stephens
Steve Trawick
Susan Trawick
Trombone Tiger
William Cardin (Willy)
'76 Tiger (Bob Sammons in Winter Haven, Florida)
Anne Khandjian
Ben Bloodworth
Chris Hilton
Chris Thrash
Clay Henson
Dan Thompson
David Hegler
Earl Ricks
Eric Morgan
Bobby
Jacob and Robyn Fleming
John Otsuki
Kathryn England
Kevin Smith
Mickey Bee
George Gaston
Ole Miss's Miracle Medical Staff

OwlGoRhythm and Blues
Paul Miles
Phil Davis
Reynolds Wolf
Rich Reimer
Robo-Harsin! (Ben Wamsley)
Rusty Owens
Sarah Brouns
Steve Harlan
Tank Hunter
Win Carroll
Theodore Gary
War Eagle Always
War Hammer 6 (Preston Settle)
WDERICHIE Butler
Wes Atkinson
William Morgan
Wilson Beard
Winston Boddie
Patrick Williams
Auburn Blue
Blake Herrin
Boris the Tiger
Brandon Smith
Carter Glaus
Cato the Barner
Colby Butler
Cory Smyer
Daris Benton
David Simpson
Dyebama
Helping Van upgrade his insulation
Hu Anderson
Josh Teal

Kevin Kennoy
Kevin Mahan
Lane Middleton
Melissa Blackstone
Mike Findley
Papa Todd
Randall Walker
Rob Morgan
Russell Milling
Sarah Hines
Sasquatch
Shane Bailey
Shannon Butson
Danny Flack
Snowdog
Steven Huston
Tim Pittman
Timothy
Tony Perry
WEGL87
In honor of Auburn Man and the Greatest Dad in the World, John Sandy
AJ Herrmann
Alex Nguyen
Ben Amos
Ben Rigas
Brian Albanese
c_brAUn
Charles Mauney
Chris Comeaux
Colonel Dad
Constructiontiger
Daniel Barnett
Elizabeth Donald
Gotta Get Better at Celebrating
I want early access to the basketball book
I'll buy this for a dollar!!!

James Taylor
Jason Alberich
Jeremiah Shuman
John Samuel Shenker
Jingleheimer Schmidt
John Stubbs
John Zavatchen
Joseph A. Miller
Joseph Iliff
JT Jarhead
Justin Bean
Kenneth Brent Raines (aka AuburnDad4Life)
Loving Auburn Means You Have to Smoke Weed Everyday
Mark Squire
MVP - Captivating Kathy Bright
Bill Minor
Paul Bankson
Richard Rider
Robert Drane
Royce Alvarez
Russell Suther
Ruth and Darrin Sutherland
Spanky
Sports Illustrated's Auburn Elvis
Stephen Thompson
The Slinko Family
The USFL- where the intro and outro are longer than the update
This name is brought to you by Bubba's Discount Tire and Tax Services
Trevor Johnson
Brant Rumble
Chris
Daniel Whitten
Plus 1-time & anonymous!

To join their illustrious ranks, go to www.auwishbone.com and click on the big orange button that says "Become a Patron!"
Thank you—and *War Patron Eagle!*

- CONTENTS -

PREFACE	9
INTRODUCTION	11
1: THE SONNY SMITH ERA: 1978-1989	15
2: THE TOMMY JOE EAGLES ERA: 1989-1994	131
3: THE CLIFF ELLIS ERA: 1994-2004	149
4: THE LEBO & BARBEE INTERREGNUM: 2004-2014	181
5: THE BRUCE PEARL ERA: 2014-LIFE	207
AFTERWORD	289
SOURCES	291

This book is dedicated to the Jungle, the Cliff Dwellers, and everyone else who has spent passionate hours inside the Arena and/or the Coliseum, cheering for the Auburn Tigers.

—Van and John

Note: The season won-loss records listed in this book do not include or reflect the outcomes of exhibition games.

PREFACE:
WHAT ABOUT TEAMS BEFORE 1978?

Auburn Basketball existed before 1978. We know this for a fact.

We know there were players like John Mengelt and Eddie Johnson and Mike Mitchell. We know there were coaches like Bill Lynn and Joel Eaves. We even know that Ralph "Shug" Jordan was the head basketball coach on the Plains before he left to take the same job at Georgia–only to return as Auburn's football coach a few years later.

We know those players and coaches existed. We know they all contributed mightily to the legacy of Auburn Basketball that would be inherited by Sonny Smith and Cliff Ellis and Bruce Pearl, years on down the line.

The thing is, we never saw them play or coach.

Their heyday was before we knew what basketball was–much less Auburn basketball.

It was also, unfortunately, before AU basketball received much (if any) coverage on television. There's precious little to go back and look at today.

So it should not be seen in any way as a slight against those earlier teams that we do not include discussion of them here. We just never had the privilege of seeing them in action. And that fact mattered to what we are about here.

When John and I decided to put together a book about Auburn Basketball, the first thing we recognized was that it should focus on the years we experienced as fans and as Auburn students, so that it could include and reflect the passion and emotion we have experienced along the way. We knew the structure of the book would be similar to how we assembled *We Believed*, our deep dive into Auburn Football history: We begin with the years we were old enough to pay the sport any attention. A good portion of that book, and this one, is a long conversation we had with one another about our memories and recollections of Auburn hoops teams we'd seen play. That dialogue is the foundation of the narrative, woven into its entire length and breadth. We simply couldn't present memories here of teams we never saw in action, because we don't have any memories of them.

In short–this is a book about Auburn Basketball from 1978, when Sonny Smith arrived on the Plains, to 2022, when Bruce Pearl received his "lifetime contract"–and beyond. (And when Sonny is still serving as color commentator for home games–completing the Auburn circle around those years.)

We hope you enjoy what you find in these pages. If someone wishes to go back and write a book about Auburn Basketball before 1978, know that John and I will be first in line to buy it.

–Van

- INTRODUCTION -

We almost called this book *The Road to Jungle City*.

"Jungle City" was one of the first names to crop up for the sea of tents erected by students outside Auburn (now Neville) Arena, the day before the Tigers played Kentucky during the 2021-22 basketball season.

Hey—it would've been a good name; the kind of name John Feinstein might use on one of his sports opuses. And it reflected in such vivid detail the passion we all felt for our Auburn Tigers basketball team during that magical season–a season of Jabari and Walker; of Wendell bombing from outside and K.D. going nuts; of spending the night in the cold outside the arena and then beating the (other) blue bloods the next day inside it; of peacocking and meme storms and "You just lost to…" A season of so many highs and just a few lows, and everything in between.

Alas, that title was not to be. Other names for the tent village were thrown out, from Pearlville to Bruceland; copyright violation was suggested. Ultimately, we decided to go with the much clearer, more descriptive and alliterative Auburn Basketball: From Barkley to Bruce.

But let's back up a minute. Why would we choose this moment to be writing a book about Auburn basketball?

That's easy to answer.

As we type these words, two Auburn basketball players have just been chosen in the first round of the NBA Draft—two in the first round in the same year, for the first time ever.

Jabari Smith, Jr, the silky-smooth and dynamic freshman forward, was picked third overall by the Houston Rockets. His towering teammate, shot blocker extraordinaire Walker Kessler, is headed to the Minnesota Timberwolves.

Someone watching only the most recent season of Auburn basketball would respond, "Well, of course they were. They're great players. What's the big deal?"

It's not that they weren't great players. They were.

It's that they were Auburn players.

It's that they were great players who wanted to come to Auburn to play basketball at all. And to help Auburn to be great at basketball.

"What's the big deal?" The big deal is this: Auburn basketball in the 2020s is great, but this is not the way Auburn basketball has always been. Not by a long shot.

For much of the last fifty years and more, Auburn basketball has tended to occupy a spot closer to the bottom reaches of the SEC than the top.

There is no question that Bruce Pearl has changed all that. He's changed the culture of Auburn basketball, he's changed its fortunes, and he's changed the way it is perceived by the country and by potential players. And in so doing, he's brought enormous success to the Plains.

And a good portion of this book reflects that.

But here's the other thing: Auburn winning at basketball didn't begin with Bruce Pearl. There have been other moments in recent decades when the Tigers excelled. Perhaps those moments haven't happened as often as we would all have liked, but they did happen.

And a good portion of this book reflects that, too.

After building slowly for several years, Sonny Smith was able to bring Charles Barkley, Chuck Person, Chris Morris and a number of other great players to Auburn. Consequently, the mid- to late-Eighties saw the Tigers win the SEC Tournament and play in the NCAA Tournament for five straight years, making it to the Elite

Eight along the way. And Cliff Ellis won the SEC Championship and took two teams to the Sweet Sixteen, including one that secured a number one seed in the NCAA Tournament.

It's not just the winning, though. There are other stories springing from the Auburn basketball program that we have also sought to preserve and present to you here. They are stories of triumph and stories of tragedy, and everything in between.

There's the story of Paul Lambert, who very well could've been the Tigers' head coach throughout the late Seventies and the Eighties, but for a shocking twist of fate.

There's the story of Tommy Joe Eagles, who left his dream job to come to Auburn and give it his all—only to remind us of how tenuous our grasp on this life can be.

There's the story of how Jay Jacobs, Auburn's athletic director at the time, made up his mind that Bruce Pearl was going to be his next head basketball coach—and then executed a full-court press, doing whatever it took to convince the controversial coach and his family that they needed to be on the Plains.

And of course there's the story of how one head coach was apparently more concerned about the quality of his office furniture than about winning basketball games.

Sprinkled in among those stories you will encounter figures of mythic proportions, like the one and only Charles Barkley, the seemingly overweight kid from Leeds who drove both Sonny Smith and Bobby Knight to distraction, before going on to become one of the biggest personalities and one of the greatest players in basketball history.

The authors would like to thank Coach Sonny Smith for doing them the great honor of sitting down with them virtually in early 2022 for a conversation that appeared both on the AU Wishbone Podcast and in pieces throughout this book. They would also like to thank his daughter, Sheri Wood, for her great kindness and help.

And finally, this book would not exist if not for the success of the 2021-22 Auburn Tigers. Working on a project this complex and demanding requires a lot of energy and a lot of enthusiasm and dedication from the authors. We had discussed creating something like this for several years, but it took the amazing run of the 2021-22 Tigers—and all the astonishing, overwhelming enthusiasm they created among the fans—to motivate your intrepid AU Wishbone duo to swing into action, start researching, and start writing. The outcome of all that effort is what you now hold in your hands—the result of months and months of work, hard work. And we loved every minute of it.

The subtitle of this book is "From Barkley to Bruce," but the story of Auburn basketball in the modern era really begins earlier than that.

Come with us now, along the Road to Jungle City, as we venture back to the summer of 1978–the year Auburn decided to hire the coach of... Southern Illinois?

That's just the first of many stories we have to share with you. But hurry now; the Arena is full, the players are ready, the ball is about to be tipped.

War Eagle!

–*Van Allen Plexico and John Ringer, Summer 2022*

-1-

THE SONNY SMITH ERA
1978 - 1989

DAVIS AND LAMBERT

The story of Auburn Basketball in the "modern era" begins with the year of three coaches—and of a shocking tragedy.

The five-year run of Dr. Bob Davis as Auburn University's head basketball coach came to an end following the 1977-78 season. Davis's final Tiger squad had compiled a record of 13-14 overall, 8-10 in the SEC, placing them fifth in the then-ten-team league. Davis finished up with an overall record at Auburn of 70-61. His best team, the 1975-75 squad, featured future NBA All-Stars Mike Mitchell and Eddie Johnson, and finished with a record of 18-8, earning Davis SEC Coach of the Year. He also served for a decade as vice-chair of the US Olympic Basketball Committee.

Interestingly enough, while Davis would not coach basketball again after 1978, he lived another forty-three years. He passed away in 2021, at age 93, in his adopted hometown of Georgetown, Kentucky. Consequently, and remarkably, he lived to see almost everything else that transpires in this book.

With Dr. Davis stepping down, the Tigers found themselves looking for a new head coach.

"In 1978, you say? That must have been when they ran right out and hired Sonny Smith!"

Well... sort of. But, as with many things related to Auburn Basketball, it's a little bit complicated.

You see, the coach Auburn initially hired was Southern Illinois head man Paul M. Lambert, Jr.

The Tigers had played SIU the previous year in an early-season tournament, winning 66-65. It is possible Lambert came on Auburn's radar at that time.

Accepting the job, Lambert sold his house in Carbondale and bought one in Auburn, then went right to work, recruiting and visiting high school coaching clinics in the South.

Wait–Paul *who?* Who's Paul Lambert? You may be asking yourself, "Why don't I remember this man?"

And that, unfortunately, is a very sad story.

Van Allen Plexico:
We hired Paul Lambert from SIU, which happens to be the alma mater of my wife and my older daughter. He'd been quite successful there, and might very well have worked out as a solid hire. But we will never know, because tragedy struck.

John Ringer:
I had never heard the story of Paul Lambert until Van did this research! A big "What might have been," if we had not been able to hire Sonny Smith!

Lambert left Southern Illinois with an eight-year record there of 126-84. While at SIU he coached the Salukis to their first Division I NCAA Tournament appearance and win, partly thanks to the efforts of star player Mike Glenn.

He never got the opportunity to coach a single game for Auburn.

While in Columbus, Georgia on June 6, 1978, for a high school basketball event, he was killed in an early-morning motel fire. Firefighters found him lying face-down on the floor of his second-floor room.

"It looked like he had attempted to find his way out, apparently groping his way through the heavy smoke," the Columbus fire chief told reporters.

"Smoke was billowing, and it looked like every room was on fire," added District Fire Chief Robert Ledford. "The only thing to do was to evacuate the people. We went from room to room waking everyone up. It was a hell of a holocaust at one time."

The lone fatality in the fire, Paul Lambert was only 43 years of age.

> "Forty years later the name of Paul Lambert is seldom mentioned in basketball circles even though he won 227 games at Pittsburg State, Hardin-Simmons and Southern Illinois. Most listings of Auburn basketball coaches go directly from Davis to Smith without even an asterisk.
>
> "Right now, as the (Columbus) Airport Holiday Inn is being turned into piles of rubble, local people are sharing stories about nights they spent on the dance floor at Ethyl's Gas House or the enticing buffets the hotel served on holidays.
>
> "Few people talk about the smoke-filled night that Paul Lambert died crawling across the floor of his hotel room in hopes of escaping. Nor do they talk about the coach they never got to know. He is a coach who never got to coach, one that fans never got to cheer but one who should not be forgotten."
>
> —*Richard Hyatt, AllOnGeorgia editorial, July 15, 2018*

Following the proper period of respectfully bidding farewell to Coach Lambert, Auburn once again turned itself to the task of hiring a head basketball coach. Whoever he turned out to be, he would be the third man to hold that title in the same year.

As it happened, that man's name was Charles H. Smith—better known to all as "Sonny."

John Ringer:
My first perception of Auburn basketball was with Sonny as our coach.

Van Allen Plexico:
Yes. Me too.
For me, Auburn Basketball begins with Sonny Smith.

SONNY SMITH COMES TO THE PLAINS

On June 27, 1978, Auburn AD Lee Hayley announced the school had hired 41-year-old Sonny Smith as the new men's basketball coach. He was chosen over sixty-eight other applicants for the position, although it was stated that Auburn contacted him, rather than the other way around.

Smith had just finished his second year as head coach of East Tennessee State. Prior to that job, he'd spent a year each at Pepperdine and at William and Mary, followed by five years as an assistant to Don DeVoe at Virginia Tech.

"I was mainly known as an offensive coach when I went to (Virginia) Tech," Smith said after being hired by Auburn. "I gained a knowledge of defense under DeVoe. I think we complemented each other very well."

Interestingly enough, DeVoe left Virginia Tech for the Tennessee head coaching job at the same time Smith took the Auburn job–and both men would go on to hold those jobs for the same eleven years, from 1978-1989.

DeVoe had flirted with leaving Tech before. As Smith told the story, around the time of his hiring at Auburn, "Don DeVoe was rumored to be heading for Ohio State a few years back. I got excited and one night I told my wife, 'Honey, tomorrow you will be sleeping with the head coach of Virginia Tech.' It was a longtime dream. Anyway, the next morning the Roanoke Times had a headline: DeVoe Remains. I really felt bad. I moped around. I came home and saw my wife had her bags packed. I asked where she was going. (She replied), 'Do I go to DeVoe's house or is he coming here?'"

Upon his arrival at Auburn, Smith discussed his approach to basketball with reporters. "We have always been an inside-oriented, power-type team, and I am a great exponent of the high-percentage shot. I like to get the ball inside, or to the most open man. I feel that taking the high-percentage shot wins basketball games. We'll fast-break, but we'll have a controlled fast break. We've been a high-scoring team in the past, and I don't see why that should change."

In terms of defense, Smith referenced what he'd learned as an assistant to DeVoe at Tech. "I'm strictly a man-to-man proponent, and I like to use pressure most of the time. We'll use half-court pressure and full-court pressure, whatever the situation calls for."

More recently, Smith spoke to 24/7 Sports about his arrival in Auburn. "I was not as familiar with Auburn basketball as I was with Auburn football... I knew Auburn was noted as a football school. That went on for years and probably still has that reputation. I was really surprised the facilities were as good as they were. I noticed the crowds weren't that big. If I'd been a hotter commodity, that might have been a sticking point. But we (had) played basketball in the football practice facility at East Tennessee State."

In 2020, Smith told Phillip Marshall, "The thing that jumped out at me (about the SEC) was everybody was good. You didn't have any teams that didn't have players. The requirements to get in school back then were a lot less. That was a plus for getting athletes in. As I look back at my first couple of years, everybody was pretty good. My first year we had an unbelievable game with Georgia, four overtimes in the SEC Tournament. Everybody had at least one player capable of being an NBA prospect. I had one in Bobby Cattage. If I could have kept him healthy, he would have been in the category of Barkley, Person, Chris Morris. He would have been in that category. Earl Banks was another one. Neither one of them could stay injury-free. If I'd been able to keep them healthy, we'd have gotten off to a better start.

"Bobby's appendix ruptured and nobody was there with him. He almost died before Jan and I got to him and got him to the hospital. He went from 240 pounds down to about 160-170. He gained it all back, but it was all fat. He had all the Barkley-type skills and could really shoot. He was going to be something special."

Prior to the press conference to introduce him as head coach, Smith had already met with and spoken with two Auburn assistant coaches, Herb Greene and Herman Williams, and had decided "through mutual agreement" to retain them at Auburn as members of his new staff. "I was very impressed with both. They were very positive about the program. From that conversation, I'm very positive. They are Auburn people. I chose them."

Actually, Herman Williams had not been an Auburn person prior to that year. A former SIU assistant, he had moved to Auburn along with the late Coach Lambert, and had survived the same fire that claimed his previous boss's life. Herb Greene was a veteran Auburn assistant who had been retained by Lambert as well as by Smith.

The Seventies were a different time in terms of transfer players. When asked if he would bring any of his East Tennessee players with him to Auburn, he reacted as if the mere suggestion were an affront. No, he replied, "I just won't do that."

He did, however, bring someone else of note aboard his administrative team: the late Paul Lambert's wife, Carol. She had gone ahead with moving her family to Auburn, and Smith hired her as his secretary.

(In a comment on an online article posted in 2018, Lambert's daughter, Jill, noted that her mother continued to live in Auburn for the next forty years, until her second husband—whom she met at an Auburn basketball game!—passed away earlier that year. At that point, Carol moved to Kansas City to be with her family.)

Meeting the Alabama sports media for the first time, Smith told them, "I've spent eleven years as a high school coach, seven years as an assistant coach and two at East Tennessee State, preparing for this day." He had accepted the Auburn job despite returning all five starters from his 1977-78 team and even though East Tennessee had just constructed a new basketball arena in Johnson City.

As small as Auburn still was in 1978, Smith felt it represented a major move up from his own childhood experience growing up in Roan Mountain, Tennessee. "It was so small, the highlight was once every ten years someone would paint their house and we'd all watch."

"Everybody talks about the Auburn Family and I like that kind of thing," he added. "I'm looking forward to being part of the Auburn Family."

Smith finished up his introductory remarks with, "My only promise to Auburn fans and alumni is total dedication and loyalty to the job. I will work as hard as possible to get the job done."

For the next eleven years, few could question whether or not he did just that.

RAMPING UP TO SONNY'S FIRST SEASON

After the first few practices with his new team, Smith expressed concerns. The team had just lost Mike Mitchell and several other solid players from the 1977-78 squad. Smith had liked to use a "nine-starter" system in his previous coaching stops, but recognized that his first team at Auburn lacked the personnel for such an approach.

"We not only don't have nine kids who can start, we don't have four. Depth-wise, we are hurting." Additionally, "(Our players) don't have the quickness that is necessary to play the man-to-man defense like it should be played."

Asked about how the team was responding to his approach to coaching, Smith replied, "There very definitely has been a reluctance of the players to accept us, based on the pre-season running program. But there has been more conforming than non-conforming. On a whole, however, young players are all looking for discipline. All won't accept it immediately. It's a gradual thing."

He added that he had set a three-year timetable for his team to begin playing in a truly competitive manner, allowing time for him and his assistants to recruit players who would excel in his system.

When asked how his team would stack up against the rest of the SEC, he said, "We're the small game, the food that everyone in the conference is waiting to partake of."

In the days leading up to the start of his first pre-season basketball practice on the Plains, Smith was asked about the possibility of scheduling a game with UAB, which was about to field a team for the first time that year, under former UCLA coach Gene Bartow.

"We can't be worried about our non-conference schedule right now," Smith replied. "We've got to make our team competitive in the conference or they'll try to hang old Sonny Smith from the nearest tree around here."

Was the honeymoon already over on the Plains, before his first season had even started? Smith met such questions with his usual homespun humor: "I called over to the motor pool for a car to be used on a recruiting trip. I asked the guy what kind of cars he had. He had a Pinto for professors, a Fairlane for the football coaches, and a beat-up LTD for the 'stupid basketball coach.' I asked him, 'Do you know who this is?' The guy replied, 'Do you know who THIS is?' I said 'No.' He said, 'Well, so long, stupid.'"

As Smith's first season on the Plains and the Tigers' opening game against Southwestern Louisiana drew near, Smith expressed what he called "cautious optimism."

"We have improved in practice because of the play of Bobby Cattage. In the last ten days he has dedicated himself to becoming a basketball player of SEC quality."

Joining Cattage on that first Smith team were Earl Banks, Bubba Price, Benny Anthony, Eric Stringer–playing the critical role of point guard in Smith's offense–and Roy McGrew, as well as Lewis Card and Kirk Powers. One other player Smith inherited that had him excited was Rich Valavicius, a junior 6-5 wing who had transferred from recent national champion Indiana. Valavicius had strained an arch in practice, but Smith felt confident the injury wouldn't slow him down. "Knowing Val, he will play. He's one of the most hard-nosed players I've ever seen."

John Ringer:
We had no strong history in basketball, and no expectations to do that much better.

Football also was a distraction at this time, taking attention away from basketball. Maybe in some ways that was a good thing–it meant less pressure for Sonny while he was trying to build up the program.

Van Allen Plexico:
That's true. But we also heard from a number of players over the years–particularly Chuck Person, when he was a player–that the players seemed to resent the football team getting so much attention on campus and from fans, compared to the basketball team. I think they would've happily settled for being the second most important sport on campus, but they felt like they weren't even that, most of the time.

THE 1978-79 SEASON
13-16 (5-13, 9th in the SEC)

Earl Banks (C)
Bubba Price (G)
Rich Valavicius (F)
Benny Anthony (F)

Eric Stringer (G)
Lewis Card (G)
Bobby Cattage (F)

Smith's squad managed a one-point victory over Southwestern Louisiana in Smith's first game as Auburn coach, on Friday, December 1, 1978, in Birmingham-Jefferson Civic Center. Three days later, however, the Tigers fell to Florida State before six thousand fans on a rainy evening on the Plains. In both games, the Tigers rallied from behind to take the lead, but against FSU, they came up short at the end. Bubba Price took a shot with seven seconds to go, and Cattage was called for a pushing foul in attempting to rebound the miss. FSU made the free throws and pulled out the win.

"We found out something about our young team," Price said afterward. "We've got to play both halves and we've got to play defense."

"Our team should be praised for the comeback, but our young team will make a lot of mistakes," Smith told reporters. "When they learn what effort it takes to win, I'll be more pleased. This is tough on a young team to come back and then have this happen to them."

Following the loss to FSU, the Tigers went on a tear. They won the next five games in a row, including wins over Iona, Richmond, Oklahoma and Navy.

The fifth and last win of the streak came over Georgia Tech in Birmingham, behind strong efforts from Earl Banks and Bobby Cattage. Unfortunately, Cattage twisted an ankle late in the game and wasn't as effective afterward.

Auburn now stood at 6-1 on the season, and fans were very pleasantly surprised, given the modest pre-season predictions for the team. SEC play would begin with the next game, but unfortunately it would bring with it a downturn in the Tigers' fortunes. They went .500 over the following four contests, beginning with a loss to Vanderbilt and then sandwiching wins over Florida and Georgia around a loss at Oral Roberts. And then the wheels came completely off.

Beginning with the game at Ole Miss on January 13, the Tigers dropped the next seven games straight. Oddly enough, the closest of those losses was a home tilt against Kentucky that went to overtime. The last game of the losing streak was the return match at Rupp Arena, just four days later. The Tigers had played three games in four days, two of them against Kentucky–a tall order for anyone. All told they'd played eleven games in the month of January (!!) and finished 2-9 during that span.

By the time the SEC regular season had ended, the Tigers had completed sweeps of Florida and Georgia, but had otherwise fared poorly. They headed off to Birmingham for the SEC Tournament with a 5-13 record in the conference.

And there things got a little crazy.

This would be the first SEC Basketball Tournament to be held in twenty-seven years. It had been canceled after the 1953 tournament in Lexington, Kentucky, and was allegedly only brought back in order to obtain an automatic bid for the winning team to the NCAA Tournament, along with the added revenues the tourney would surely bring.

Sonny Smith, as it turned out, had picked a good year to take a job coaching in the SEC.

Auburn limped into Birmingham coming off a home loss to Tennessee, and little was expected of the Tigers in the newly-restarted tournament. But things didn't go as expected.

The Tigers opened against highly-favored Vanderbilt, a team that had swept Auburn in the regular season and had gone on to tie Miss State for a third-place finish in the conference. Defying the odds, the Tigers beat the Commodores by six, 59-53, in the BJCC on Wednesday, February 28. Vandy never led in the game.

"We had been working on a (delay game approach) for a couple of months but never had a chance to use it," Smith said afterward, "because we never had a lead and the ball at the same time."

"This tournament has given us new life," added Auburn wing Rich Valavicius. "Late in the season we didn't have anything to play for."

The win put Auburn into the quarterfinal round, where they would face Georgia–a team they'd swept during the season. Facing a team they knew they could beat, one had to speculate that the Tigers would have an easier time of it on Thursday night.

Again, however, expectations would be turned on their head, and the game was anything but easy.

On the same night fans in the BJCC were getting to watch Alabama lose in a blazing, 101-100 shootout with Kentucky, they also got to witness a long and drawn-out war between the Tigers and the Bulldogs.

Auburn won, finally, to reach the semifinals of the tournament—and a date with Tennessee—by pulling out a 95-91 victory. But it took a lot longer than anyone would have expected: the game lasted through four overtimes. *Four overtimes!*

The win was Auburn's third in four overtime games that season.

Prior to the first-round game, the Tigers had visited a children's hospital in Birmingham, where a young patient gave Bubba Price a patch and promised a victory if he wore it. Price wore it against Vanderbilt, and for the Georgia game the entire team wore copies of it on their warm-ups.

"It's not that we're superstitious," Smith said afterward, "but if you had been with us (at the hospital), you would have worn something they asked you to."

After the game, Smith said, "That was a very tired two teams out there, which was why the game lasted four overtimes. The last two games our battle cry has been to push ourselves beyond the limit, which is what we did tonight and what I think we will do tomorrow night."

On Friday night, in the semifinals of the SEC Tournament, an exhausted Tigers team that had already played twice in two days–including a four-OT thriller the night before–faced a fresh Tennessee team that had sailed in with a bye. A Tennessee team coached by Smith's old boss at Virginia Tech, Don DeVoe.

Despite their fatigue, the Tigers actually led by one, 57-56, with 4:15 left to play in the game. But then a turnover and a quick score gave the Vols a lead they would not relinquish the rest of the way. The final score was 75-64, Tennessee.

"The final score was no indication of the game," DeVoe said afterward. "Auburn could have been playing for the championship, or even won it, if it had put a few more things together."

Auburn had played an effective zone defense for the first twenty-five minutes of the game, but the referees forced the Tigers to abandon that defensive approach on a technical point that Smith disagreed with.

"It's my understanding that you have to have somebody within three to six feet of the ball, which we did. But official Ben Dunn came over and warned us that we had to come out of the zone. After that, it became a Reggie Johnson game."

The Vols' Johnson scored fourteen points in the remaining 14:30 of the game, making the difference.

"I'm very proud of our team," Smith said. "They gave great effort."

Though they finished just 13-16, the strong showing in the tournament left Auburn's players and fans feeling positive about the direction of the program.

"I believe next year is going to be different," said guard Eric Stringer. "Everybody is back, and we have a good coach that everybody believes in."

Stringer added, "Last year, we played more run-and-gun, a fast tempo. This year, we are slowing it down, trying to get a good shot every time down the court. Last year on defense, you were responsible for your man. This year, everybody is responsible for everybody else's man. It's a helping kind of defense."

Referring to Stringer, Smith noted, "Point guard was our biggest problem, but now it's not quite as big as it was. Eric has temporarily put it on better footing this year."

"On the surface, you wouldn't know how far this team has come," said Smith. "It has been a slow learning process. I don't think you can ever pick up the type of defense we run in a year."

He also pointed out, "We didn't have one situation all year where a member of the team embarrassed the school."

Smith and all the players talked after the game about the need to bring in more quality recruits, to give the starters more opportunity to rest.

"We're down to the final two with so many kids," Smith said.

THE UAB CONTROVERSY

Meanwhile, the Tigers also found themselves caught up in a controversy brewing among all the major basketball programs in the state. Both UAB and South Alabama had hoops teams now (with South Alabama coached by future Auburn head man Cliff Ellis), and they wanted to be included on the schedules of Auburn and Alabama. For various reasons, neither of the two more established programs had a lot of interest in adding them. Particularly Alabama.

Amid talk of a general hostility between the administrations of the two Alabama campuses, there were also rumors that Paul "Bear" Bryant—then AD in Tuscaloosa as well as head football coach—was angry about some major Alabama donors giving large sums of money to UAB to help get their program going. He wasn't particularly interested in doing anything to help UAB athletics rise in prestige and divert any attention or money away from the Capstone. Additionally, resentment was building in Tuscaloosa over a general lack of fan support for the Crimson Tide basketball program. Head coach CM Newton had brought them solid success over the past several years, but the fans were not responding. Coleman Coliseum stood half-empty through most games. Sports writers speculated that Alabama fans were simply too spoiled by Bryant's football success to care anything about the basketball program. The last thing Bryant and Tuscaloosa wanted to see was Birmingham's campus and its sports program attracting more money and more fans than what they had going on the home campus.

At the conclusion of the 1979-80 season, it looked as if both Alabama and UAB could be extended invitations to the NIT—the National Invitation Tournament, which had become secondary to the NCAA Basketball Tournament, but which still represented acknowledgement of a team's success. Alabama officials went so far as to suggest they would give the NIT an ultimatum: either take Alabama or invite UAB, but not both. And certainly don't have them play each other in the opening round. (As it turned out, both teams received NIT invitations, and they did not have to play one another. Their first, and to this point only, meeting came in the NIT on March 18, 1993, in Tuscaloosa, with UAB prevailing over the Tide, 58-56.)

As the other major and established basketball program in the state, Auburn was drawn into this controversy. "It's only a matter of time" before Auburn and Alabama would have to start scheduling UAB and South Alabama, observed Sonny Smith. "I've already gotten a letter from the Lt. Governor suggesting such."

Auburn did schedule UAB beginning in 1982, in just their fourth year of existence as a program. The two teams have played on-and-off twenty-one times in the years since and, as of this writing, Auburn leads the series against the Blazers, 11-10. Alabama has still only played them once.

John Ringer:
It made sense to play UAB from a recruiting perspective. Lots of Auburn fans could go to the game when it was in Birmingham. It was also good to build up other programs in-state, especially since UAB could become a thorn in Alabama's side. It made sense to play them, but of course they were well-coached and dangerous.

Van Allen Plexico:
Agreed. I'm glad we played them. But all parties concerned should've found a way to play the game in Auburn sooner.

THE 1979-80 SEASON
10-18 (5-13, 9th in the SEC)

Earl Banks (C)	Darrell Lockhart (C)
Bubba Price (G)	Alvin Mumphord (F)
Rich Valavicius (F)	Frank Poindexter (F)
Benny Anthony (F)	Byron Henson (G)
Eric Stringer (G)	Bobby Cattage (F)

For the 1979-80 season, the Tigers brought in six-foot-nine Parade All-American and future NBA player Darrell Lockhart at center. He made an immediate impact as both a scorer and rebounder.

"I had so many colleges coming in," Lockhart later told a reporter. "I had three or four letters from major colleges a day. One time, I had Jerry Tarkanian (from UNLV) sitting down in the office wanting to talk to me and I just flipped. I said, 'This guy flew all the way out from Las Vegas to come to Thomaston, Georgia just to get me to go to school there.'" Fortunately, Lockhart chose the much closer Auburn.

AUBURN BASKETBALL

Unfortunately, the Tigers did not enjoy the success they had hoped for this season, ending up with a record of 10-18 overall, 5-13 in the SEC, and another next-to-last 9th place finish in the conference. They suffered a losing streak through parts of January and February lasting one game longer than the awful one they'd faced during the previous year, losing eight games straight; seven of them to SEC opponents and one a bitter loss in a rematch with Florida State. They did manage a win over hapless Georgia in the first round of the SEC tournament in Birmingham, giving them a three-game sweep of the Bulldogs for the season, before falling to Kentucky in the quarterfinals, 69-61.

The highly-ranked Wildcats had beaten them in both previous games that season, but each had been extremely close, coming down to a single basket on both occasions. This game was not as close, and could've turned into a blowout.

"Kentucky is a much different team," Smith said afterward. "They're playing at a faster tempo (than in the two previous meetings). That plus (freshman star Sam) Bowie's improved rebounding makes the others play better. I don't fault our (players) as much as I applaud (Kentucky's) play in the first eight or nine minutes of the second half. We got the (slower) tempo we wanted and our shot selection was good, but we just didn't hit our shots."

Bubba Price and Eric Stringer played well down the stretch for Auburn, scoring 16 points between them in the final four minutes and keeping the game closer than it otherwise would have been.

With Sonny Smith's second season behind him, attention turned to the future.

Results this far had not been what Auburn fans or players had hoped for, yet the Tigers continued to pull off the occasional unexpected win here and there—just enough to give the fans hope and to show promise of better things to come.

Unfortunately, 1980-81 would prove no more successful.

THE 1980-81 SEASON
11-16 (4-14, 9th in the SEC)

Earl Banks (C)
Darrell Lockhart (C)
Alvin Mumphord (F)
Greg Turner (F)

Frank Poindexter (F)
Byron Henson (G)
Bobby Cattage (F)
Mark Cahill (F)

The 1980-81 season started out well enough for the Tigers. They won six of their first seven games and finished the calendar year of 1980 with a win over Columbia in the consolation game of the Blade Glass Tournament on December 30. Surely the remainder of the season would yield much better results than the previous two years had.

Well...not quite.

Following that December 30 win, the Tigers would not taste victory again until February 11–a losing streak of eleven games. And every one of those losses came against an SEC opponent. If not for a strangely out-of-place early December victory over Tennessee at home, the Tigers would've found themselves winless in conference play with only seven games remaining.

But on February 11, the losing streak came to an end as abruptly and unexpectedly as it had begun.

The Tigers hammered Vanderbilt, 69-55, in Nashville. They took the lead for the first time at 44-42 with sixteen minutes remaining in the game, then poured it on. Frank Poindexter led the way with 21 points, 19 of which he scored in the second half. It was Auburn's first win in Nashville since 1977.

"This was the most patient we have ever been since I've been at Auburn," said Smith after the game. "We took our shots with confidence and we hit the backboards well. We did not commit any foolish fouls. The key, though, was our shooting in the second half. We shot something phenomenal like seventy percent.

"I thought somebody's attitude would slide during this 11-game losing streak. Nobody's did, though, and I think it's a tribute to this bunch of guys."

The win improved Auburn's conference record to 2-11, but they remained at the bottom of the standings. They closed out the remainder of the season with two more wins and three losses—but one of those wins was over Alabama in Coleman Coliseum, which certainly helped morale.

It seems somehow fitting that the win in Tuscaloosa came on the same day that word was leaked that Pat Dye would be named Athletic Director at Auburn. Dye would be known just under two years later as the man who ended Alabama's winning streak over the Tigers in football. That night in Tuscaloosa–February 25, 1981–Smith and his team ended the Tide's streak against Auburn in basketball.

"I don't feel it now. It'll take a while to sink in. But I'll feel it by the time I get back to 418 Joy Street," said Smith, giving out his home address to the media after the big win over Alabama.

The 56-54 win ended a six-year losing streak to the Tide.

"I'm just so happy for our kids. They've had to go through so much, and now, they get a big one like this. I'm just thrilled for them.

"I got on them pretty bad before the game. I was almost unmerciful. I told them I was tired of us being the laughing stock of the league. I told them it was time we played basketball instead of (making) foolish fouls."

Said guard Alvin Mumphford, after making two big steals in the closing minutes, "This is somewhat like winning a national championship."

Added forward Frank Poindexter, "I'm just going to lay back, celebrate and think about how sweet it is."

"There's always a reason to smile when you beat Bama," said center Earl Banks, a senior who'd been winless against Alabama before that night.

Banks was asked how this win compared to his record-setting rebounding performance in the Alabama state high school tournament, where he made an amazing 32 rebounds.

"Yeah, I remember that, but this is even better than that. I think this tops it."

The Tigers had to play one more regular season game, which turned out to be a 75-63 loss at Tennessee. They followed that by dropping the first game of the SEC Tournament to Florida in Birmingham, 50-48, in overtime.

Just like that, the 1980-81 season was over. The Tigers finished up with a record of 9-16 overall, 4-14 in the SEC. Not great numbers by any measure. It was also the end of Sonny Smith's third year as basketball coach on the Plains. High hopes at the start of his tenure had given way to cold reality: Auburn had consistently finished near the bottom of the conference all three years. What—or who—could turn things around for the Tigers in 1981-82?

The answer, as it turned out, was a somewhat overlooked high school player from Leeds, Alabama, who would show up on campus a short time later. He didn't reverse the Tigers' fortunes instantly, but he definitely made an immediate impact on Auburn and the SEC. And his three seasons on the Plains would leave behind a trail of myths and legends to rival those Vincent "Bo" Jackson was creating at the same time only a short distance away, on the grass of Jordan-Hare Stadium.

CHARLES BARKLEY

Along with the 1981-82 season came the arrival of a very noteworthy recruit. A young man from the Birmingham suburbs who would one day be an NBA All-Star and Olympic Gold Medalist. A larger-than-life personality who wolfed down pizzas and kept a mini-fridge in his dorm room. A player destined for all of the basketball Halls of Fame, with a statue of himself outside Auburn Arena.

We are of course talking about the Renowned Round Mound of Rebound, Charles Barkley.

One has to see Barkley play to fully appreciate what he brought to the game. His signature move was to dart into a passing lane—moving much more quickly than someone of his size should be able—and intercept a pass (sometimes physically wrestling the ball away from its intended receiver), then race to the other end of the court, usually with very little thought toward passing to anyone else, to deliver a thunderous slam dunk. And in between the steal and the dunk, his transition from one end of the court to the other transfixed the viewer: Barkley would fly down the court like an elephant with a hotfoot, the ball not so much being dribbled as smashed into the floor along the way, a good distance from his body. Perhaps someone could've reached over and stolen it, since he transported it so seemingly recklessly—but who on God's green earth would have the guts to try? It would be like trying to snatch the ball out of a tornado funnel—you probably wouldn't come away with the ball and you might just lose an arm in the process.

How did Auburn wind up with this remarkable player and person?

To a degree, Barkley had been an obscure prospect up until that point because of his sheer uniqueness. He doesn't look like one would expect a future NBA All-Star to look. He's not particularly tall in basketball terms, and his heavy build belies his true athletic abilities, muscular frame, remarkable nimbleness and leaping ability. Probably because of these factors, he was only fifth or sixth on the list of most coveted recruits coming out of the state's high schools that year. Alabama coveted Ennis Whatley and Bobby Lee Hurt, and didn't pay Barkley much attention at all.

And it wasn't just Alabama that was overlooking him. He nearly passed under Auburn's radar, too. Maybe he would have, if not for Herbert Greene.

It's a story told many times in many places: an assistant coach visits a high school or junior college to scout one player, and ends up smitten by another.

Smith had dispatched assistant Herbert Greene to Leeds High School to recruit a player (probably Travis Abernathy). Once he got to the game and started watching the action, however, Greene quickly found himself fascinated by one of that guy's teammates.

As Smith tells the story, "(Greene) had gone to see another guy, and saw Charles and realized what great potential he had and how good he could be. He came back (from Leeds) and said, 'They've got this kid on that team who's 6-3 or 6-4, probably weighs 280 or 290, and he can jump out of the gym. You need to go see him."

So Smith visited Leeds. What did he witness there?

"The ball bounced off the board for a rebound. (Barkley) jumped up and caught it and threw it to midcourt before he ever hit the floor. And I said to myself, 'We've got to have this guy.' Fortunately, we ended up with him, and got one of the greatest players to ever play here."

All thanks to Greene, who left Auburn shortly thereafter—but not before making a great impression on Barkley.

"I have always had great admiration for Herbert because he was the first guy who actually thought I could play. ... (He was) actually the first person who thought I could play major college basketball. I will always be in debt to him for that. He will always be a special person in my heart."

John Ringer:
There are recruitments that are program-defining. Charles Barkley changed what Auburn basketball was and what it could be, and he laid the foundation for later, when more talent came in behind him.

Charles was the kind of player who, if he had been six inches taller, would've gone to Kentucky or UCLA. But we were able to recruit him because, in high school, nobody knew how good he could be yet.

THE 1981-82 SEASON
14-14 (7-11, 8th in the SEC)

Charles Barkley (C)	Frank Poindexter (F)
Odell Mosteller (G)	Byron Henson (G)
Darrell Lockhart (C)	Paul Daniels (G)
Alvin Mumphord (F)	Mark Cahill (F)
Greg Turner (F)	

Several excellent prospects emerged from the high school ranks in the state of Alabama in 1981. Bobby Lee Hurt and Ennis Whatley chose Alabama, while Charles Barkley signed with Auburn. Barkley was asked in the fall of his freshman season how he felt he stacked up against those other great high school players coming into the college game that season.

"I know Bobby Lee and Ennis were thought to be the top players in the state, but I don't feel I have to prove myself against them. College ball is a lot different from high school and anything can happen. I'm just going to try to be the best I can be. Charles Barkley can play like everyone else. You can't rely on what you did in high school."

Barkley received scholarship offers from UAB and Alabama as well as Auburn. What caused him to want to become a Tiger?

"I first thought about coming here because I thought I would have the best chance to play right away. That was a big factor in my coming here."

Sonny Smith was asked how Barkley stacked up as a freshman coming in and competing with the players already in place.

"Greg Turner is our most improved player at the forward position, but Barkley has the ability to dominate the game at times. I've heard he's done that in some of the preseason games. Barkley is more suited to playing with his back to the basket and as soon as he learns the defense needed in this league, he'll be a big factor for us."

Defense was something Barkley struggled with at first.

"The toughest thing for me when we first started was the defense. It was something new I had to learn. My offensive rebounding and my shot blocking are pretty strong, but my defense and conditioning have to improve. This is a great (conference). You never get a break and nobody is a pushover. It's a lot different from high school."

He added, "It doesn't make me nervous knowing what I'm facing (at Auburn and in the SEC). Really it just makes me want to play harder. I'm just a rookie now and I have to start all over and leave everything else behind."

The Tigers only lost one starter from the previous season—center Earl Banks. The excellent Darrell Lockhart and Frank Poindexter returned at forward, along with guards Byron Henson, Alvin Mumphord and Paul Daniels.

"We feel like we're going to have a better basketball team without a doubt... I feel we're a team that can pass it, catch it and shoot it as a unit better than any team we've had since we've been here. We're a little bit quicker...(and that) gives us the opportunity to do some things we have not been able to do in the past."

Fortunes didn't reverse immediately, no—but the games got a lot more interesting with Charles Barkley on the floor, and the scores got a lot closer.

Barkley came off the bench at first, but that didn't last long. He moved into the starting lineup on December 19 for a win at Florida State, and things would remain that way going forward. Freshman or not, he was simply too valuable to keep on the bench.

The Tigers would compile a record of 11-2 at home and 3-12 on the road, including an 83-81 overtime win at home against Kentucky in which Barkley finished with 18 points and 12 rebounds.

"Just say we played good," instructed Sonny Smith to reporters after the Kentucky game. "The most important thing for us was the change to the half-court trap. We made the steals. Another key was our free throw shooting. We were 31 of 38."

The Tigers forced nineteen turnovers on Kentucky with the use of the trap.

Auburn came from 11 points down in the second half to take the game to overtime.

It was the Tigers' first victory over Kentucky in thirteen games.

"If I had to give credit to anyone," Smith said, "I'd give it to Henson, Cahill, and the others who came off the bench and did a great job."

"The bench wins it for Auburn!" shouted backup forward Greg Turner in the locker room after the game. "Let that be the headlines: Super Subs Do It Again!"

Charles Barkley, Odell Mosteller and Byron Henson each scored four points in OT, leading the Tigers to the win. Auburn moved to 11-8 overall and 5-6 in the SEC—not great, but much better than Auburn's record the previous three years of the Smith regime.

The game nearly went Kentucky's way in regulation. With 27 seconds remaining, Charles Hurt tied the game with a layup, and Barkley was called for a flagrant foul on the play by official Roger Paramore. Hurt made both shots, putting the Cats up, 68-66.

"I recommended we get (Paramore) into the league," Smith said after the game. "Now I'm going to recommend that he read the rule book. I've seen some weird calls before, but as they say in Roan Mountain, Tennessee, that was the weirdest."

"It wasn't (an) intentional (foul). If it was, then he would never have gotten the shot off," said Barkley later. "I could have sent him up in the stands if I wanted to."

"And those guys have the nerve to call themselves Wildcats," said Alvin Mumphord.

Frank Poindexter chimed in, "More like MILDcats."

"But I'll bet they're over there purring now," Mumphord retorted. "Here kitty kitty. I'll have to bring them some milk over."

As a true freshman, and coming off the bench prior to the SEC portion of the season, Barkley had led the team in rebounds in nearly every game. Only Darrell Lockhart gave him any real competition in that category, leading the team in rebounding seven times to Barkley's twenty-three.

Following the Kentucky win, the Tigers stood at 5-6 in the SEC–a drastic improvement over previous seasons under Smith. Unfortunately, they finished out the remaining seven games of the SEC regular season with a record of 2-5. Four of those losses were on the road.

So many of this team's losses were by just a point or two. They lost by 1 at Duke, by 1 at LSU, by 2 to Alabama in both games, and by 1 at Georgia. They finished the regular season eighth in the league.

The SEC Tournament that season was being held in Rupp Arena, home of the Kentucky Wildcats. As one of the bottom four teams in the conference, the Tigers had to begin play on Wednesday. In the first round, they matched up with Mississippi State. In a bizarrely low-scoring affair, the two teams needed overtime to get to a final score of 38-36.

After Mississippi State ran a drastically slow offense for the entire game against Auburn—resulting in a 36-36 tie at the buzzer of regulation—Auburn turned the tables on the Bulldogs and held the ball for the entire five-minute overtime. They ran down the clock without Miss State ever touching the ball, and then took one final shot. Auburn forward Frank Poindexter knocked down the game-winner from the left side of the key with three seconds left. Those two points were the only ones scored by either team during overtime. Charles Barkley was not a factor in the OT period after fouling out before the end of regulation.

Van Allen Plexico:
This had to be the basketball equivalent of that infamous 3-2 football game we had with the same school—Miss State—during the Tuberville years. It's like when Auburn and MSU get together, they try to set the sport back a hundred years—no matter which sport it is!

"They were not stalling," said Miss State coach Bob Boyd of Auburn's play in overtime. "They were just using the clock to take the last shot. I don't use the word 'stall.'"

"We didn't intend to hold the ball that long in overtime, but we couldn't get the layup," Smith said afterward. "That's what we were playing for. If we keep this up (holding the ball so long)," he added, "the shot clock may be coming."

The shot clock did indeed arrive in college basketball at the start of the 1985-86 season, followed by the three-point shot in April of 1986.

Van Allen Plexico:
I can remember when the three-point shot was coming in, Sonny was against it just like he was against the shot clock. I remember him saying that whoever was in charge of the rules was putting it in just so he could have made a mistake every single year.

John Ringer:
The "four corners" offense that college basketball teams would play before the shot clock came into existence was painful to watch. A team would get ahead six points and then basically play keep away with the ball for the rest of the game—it was boring. The game was also getting too clogged up near the lane and the three-point shot helped with that.

For their quarterfinal matchup with Kentucky, Smith was asked about playing the Wildcats on their home court.

"Everybody has been talking about Kentucky having the home court advantage," he said. "I just don't see it that way. I just don't see 23,000 fans in here pulling for Kentucky. There's a mixture of fans. We'll have some of our own, and maybe if I wear the right color coat, some of the other fans will pull for us."

"They might not have 23,000 fans pulling for them," responded Poindexter, "but I'll bet they'll have about 20,000 fans pulling for them."

Alas, Kentucky didn't seem to need massive fan support in order to win. They handled the Tigers easily, 89-66. Auburn made only 7 of 30 shots in the first half.

"We lost our poise, we lost our confidence, we lost everything associated with the cliches of basketball," Smith said afterward. "We just lost it all. They destroyed us." He noted the massive ratio of

Kentucky fans in the arena. "I feel like the Christians with the Lions—if that (the Roman Coliseum) was what you'd call a neutral arena... Their fans gave them a great advantage. I thought there would be enough mixture among the fans to help us along, but it wasn't that way. I was wrong about that."

Auburn trailed 42-22 at the half. "I told the team I didn't know if we could catch them or not. All I could ask of them was that they not give up, that they go back out and try to regain their poise and their confidence—regain everything that we had lost in the first half."

Charles Barkley fouled out once again, but not before putting up decent numbers. Held to only four points and six rebounds in the first half—along with picking up three fouls—Barkley improved in final minutes. He scored fourteen points and grabbed five more rebounds in the second stanza.

Kentucky coach Joe B. Hall noted, "There's no question (playing the SEC Tournament in Rupp Arena) is an advantage (for UK). But because of the tradition of Kentucky basketball, that adds pressure on us. I will accept that kind of pressure for the advantage the home court gives. You have to remember that the tournament itself was created for economical reasons, and having it here will have good economic results."

With the 1981-82 season completed, Auburn saw the departure of Frank Poindexter to graduation, but nearly everyone else was coming back. With a more experienced Charles Barkley now as a sophomore, there was every chance to believe the next season could be special. Unfortunately, the next year's team would play the second-hardest schedule out of all 274 teams in college basketball– and the Tigers would end up with a very similar set of outcomes as the ones they'd just experienced.

Even so, in his first four seasons at Auburn, Sonny Smith had won 21 SEC games and lost 51. It's hard to imagine, in today's high-pressure sports environment, how he could've survived beyond his fourth or fifth season. Fortunately for Auburn, he did.

THE 1982-83 SEASON
15-13 (8-10, 8th in the SEC)

Charles Barkley (C) Alvin Mumphord (F)
Chuck Person (F) Greg Turner (F)
Odell Mosteller (G) Paul Daniels (G)
Darrell Lockhart (C)

The 1982-83 team was as loaded as an Auburn basketball team had been in quite a few years. It featured sophomore Charles Barkley along with Odell Mosteller, senior Darrell Lockhart and freshman Chuck Person. And it entered the season with high hopes and higher expectations.

In 2020, Smith told Phillip Marshall about how Chuck Person, and a little later, Jeff Moore, came to be Auburn Tigers: "What turned the program here into a better program was when we got Jeff Moore and Chuck Person out of the state of Alabama. Before he broke his wrist at Georgia Tech as a junior, Jeff Moore was an outstanding player. If he doesn't break his hand, I think he would have been one of our better players. He was much more highly recruited than Chuck. Chuck was mostly recruited by Mississippi State, Tennessee and Auburn. Alabama wasn't in it. I don't think they knew how good Chuck was. Chuck was going to Tennessee until I talked Coach Pat Dye into going down and speaking to his mother. She loved Auburn football. She didn't care about basketball much at all. Pat Dye walked into that living room, and we had Chuck Person that day."

Auburn started the season with a 63-61 win over UAB in the Birmingham-Jefferson Civic Center, in the first-ever matchup of the two programs. The Blazers had made the Elite Eight of the NCAA Tournament the previous year, finishing as Sun Belt Conference champions, with a record of 25-6. But Auburn caught them at the right time, because only one starter—guard Luellen Foster—returned from that squad's starting lineup.

The game was broadcast over a small television "network" that reached parts of Alabama, Georgia and Florida.

"We're happy to see this much interest in our game with UAB," said Sonny Smith prior to tipoff. "Creating more interest in basketball in this state is one reason Gene Bartow and I got together. It will help everyone concerned.

"TV is just another way of exposing our product. At first I was hesitant about putting the game on TV because (it might hurt) ticket sales. But that's going well. I think it was a good idea now."

Indeed, the game was played before almost 17,000 fans in the Civic Center. This was described in Auburn's game notes afterward as the "second-largest crowd to watch a regular season basketball game in the state of Alabama."

Darrell Lockhart led the Tigers with 20 points, and Charles Barkley led in rebounds with 9.

"This is the start of a great cross-state rivalry," said Foster before the game.

Following the UAB game, the Tigers went on to record a 6-2 mark in the remaining early, non-conference portion of the schedule. Then the Tigers got things rolling in a big way when SEC play began.

They opened conference play with a 77-66 home win over Mississippi State, then two days later beat fifth-ranked Alabama by 11 before 12,542 in Memorial Coliseum. This came as a shock to fans of both teams; this highly-regarded Tide team had just days earlier beaten Patrick Ewing's Georgetown by 21 on a neutral court to begin their season 8-0.

The 19-year-old Charles Barkley scored 21 second-half points, including two huge dunks, and helped Darrell Lockhart hold the Tide's Bobby Lee Hurt to only 10. The Tigers held on to win despite Alabama's All-American guard, Ennis Whatley, going for 31 in 39 minutes of play.

"We beat a good team. We had a great team effort and I guess you would have to call this a team victory," said Sonny Smith afterward.

"It hurts real bad to lose to an intrastate school," said Whatley afterward. "I hate losing, especially to the other school in the state."

"It was the first time I really played with emotion," said Barkley. "I'm a slow starter and it takes me time for me to warm up. Tonight I stayed out of foul trouble and it gave me a chance to get started."

When asked about a possible feud with Alabama's Hurt, Barkley rejected the notion. "I respect him. He's a good player." The two congratulated one another for their play on the court after the game.

"Barkley plays very physical and he got away with a lot of things," said Alabama's Terry Williams. "I'm not taking anything away from Auburn. They beat us fair and square."

After an away loss to Florida, who possessed a very strong inside game that season and was able to neutralize Barkley somewhat, the Tigers traveled to Lexington and shocked Kentucky, 75-67.

"Our team played super," said Sonny Smith afterward. "Usually I'm over there on the bench trying to settle them down, but tonight with about thirty seconds left they're having to tell me, 'Settle down, Sonny. Settle down. We've got it won.' This is real thrilling for me."

Auburn jumped out front early and kept the Wildcats at bay by using a 1-2-2 zone defense that Kentucky struggled to overcome. The Wildcats led only once, at 4-3, and after that the Tigers dominated.

Senior center Darrell Lockhart scored 14 points in the first half, and Odell Mosteller knocked down two long shots at the start of the second half to keep things going. Charles Barkley was called for his third foul with 18:50 remaining in the second half and his fourth foul with 6:43 to go, before fouling out with 3:20 left. He finished with nine points and nine rebounds—far below the numbers he'd notched in Rupp Arena the previous season. Lockhart soon followed him to the bench with five fouls, forcing the Tigers to close out the game without their two powerful inside players. Moesteller's free throw shooting helped Auburn pull it out late.

Freshman Chuck Person unexpectedly added 20 points to the mix, and hit both shots of a one-and-one in the final minute to keep Kentucky at bay.

"When I first came in I was a little afraid," Person said, "It's a very intimidating place. Even though I missed my first two shots, I wasn't going to shy away. If I had the shot I took it."

"This win tonight will help us the rest of the year," Barkley said. "It means we have confidence we can go anywhere in the league on the road and win. If we win up here it kind of makes our whole season."

With the win, Auburn moved into sole possession of first place in the SEC at 10-3 and 3-1 in the league.

Unfortunately, the good times wouldn't last.

They alternated losses and wins back and forth over the next eight games, then dropped three straight. As of February 26, their record had fallen to 13-10. The season didn't end any better, as they finished the regular season with an 86-78 loss to Alabama in Coleman Coliseum, followed by another loss to the Tide four days later, 62-61, in the first-round matchup of the SEC Tournament in Birmingham. There would be no postseason play beyond that.

Charles Barkley had certainly come into his own in this, his sophomore season. He shared the "scoring leader of the game" column that year with a number of his teammates, but he dominated the rebounding statistics all season. He was no longer a big surprise; great things were expected of him in the year to come.

In what was Sonny Smith's fifth season at Auburn, the Tigers finished eighth again, the same as the previous year, with a record of 15-13 overall and 8-10 in the SEC. They had yet to post a winning record in conference play under Smith, nor finish higher than eighth out of ten teams.

Interestingly, the highly regarded Alabama team of Wimp Sanderson finished ninth that season, with the same 8-10 conference record as the Tigers. The Tide, however, turned it on in the SEC Tournament and beat Auburn, Kentucky and Miss State to make the title game–where they lost to Georgia, 86-71. By dint of their SEC Tournament run, the Tide received an invitation to the NCAA Tournament (despite being the ninth-ranked team, finishing below Auburn), and were promptly blown out in their first-round game by Lamar, 73-50.

Auburn Basketball in the five seasons from 1978-1983:
13-16 (5-13, 9th in SEC)
10-18 (5-13, 9th in SEC)
11-16 (4-14, 9th in SEC)
14-14 (7-11, 8th in SEC)
15-13 (8-10, 8th in SEC)

The Tigers had won a total of four SEC Tournament games during that five-year stretch, two of which came in the first season. In the four seasons that followed, their tournament record stood at 2-

4. Perhaps it was the promise of players like Barkley and Person on the roster that kept Smith's job secure at that point.

Darrell Lockhart was a senior on the 1982-83 team, and that loss to Alabama in the BJCC marked his final appearance in an Auburn uniform. He finished his career with 1,236 points scored and 54 blocks, and was named to the third-team All-SEC team.

Following this season, Lockhart was chosen in the second round of the NBA draft by the San Antonio Spurs. He would only play two games there before transitioning to the European leagues the following season. For the next fifteen years he would play for ten different teams there, mostly in Spain and Italy.

"I remember my first time playing basketball in Rome," he said in 2019. "We were playing on the road and we walked into the gym. The gym was full and they had a rag doll hanging on a stick and they burned it. They were lighting it on fire. It was crazy, smoke everywhere. We had to pause the game for a while until the smoke cleared. It was crazy.

"Stuff like that, that stuff went on all the time. After a while, you just begin to expect it."

Lockhart later earned a Master's degree from Albany State and went on to coach his hometown high school in Thomaston, Georgia, to two state titles. As of 2019, he was head coach at Valdosta High in Georgia.

Interviewed after he'd taken the Valdosta job, Lockhart was asked what it was like playing with Charles Barkley.

"He was crazy. To see so much talent, it's just crazy. Three hundred pounds, jumping and running like he did when he first came to Auburn, it was just amazing to me. I haven't seen it since.

"It was just God-given talent, the things he was doing out there on the floor. You could tell he was going to be one of the greats. He was a good guy, he just can't stop talking. He says what comes to mind and sometimes it hurts you and sometimes it doesn't, but he was that way and he's still that way. I wish I'd had more years, but it was fun to play with him at Auburn."

> **John Ringer:**
> Chuck Person looked like a power forward; a back-to-the-basket kind of player. But he was a pure shooter, at his best facing the basket from twenty feet away. As he improved, he

became even more dangerous. He became a guy who could take over games. We saw flashes of it early, when he served as a good complementary piece to Charles, inside and outside.

His emergence took scoring pressure off of Charles. Person could score in a hurry.

It's a sad part of the story that he later does what he does as an assistant coach at Auburn.

Van Allen Plexico:

In a day when there was no 3-point line, and despite being a bigger-body guy, Person was a player who thrived at taking longer-range shots. He would later transition quite well to the NBA, where they had a 3-point line already, because he'd been practicing that kind of shot his whole career, even though it didn't count any more than a layup back then.

THE 1983-84 SEASON
20-11 (12-6, 2nd in the SEC)
First Round of NCAA Tournament

Charles Barkley (C)	Vern Strickland (F)
Chuck Person (F)	Carey Holland (C)
Frank Ford (G)	Greg Turner (F)
Gerald White (G)	Paul Daniels (G)

Auburn's fortunes finally took a turn for the better in the 1983-84 season, though that might not have seemed likely given the outcome of their opening game–an overtime loss to UAB in Birmingham.

In the second-ever meeting of the two in-state programs, a tight game dissolved into blown opportunities for both teams late. UAB missed two free throws after a technical foul on Auburn, and then UAB was called for a foul on the final play of regulation, but Auburn wasn't in the bonus and didn't get to shoot free throws, so the clock expired and the game went to OT. There, ironically enough, UAB won essentially a free-throw shooting contest to prevail, 69-62.

Charles Barkley played limited minutes due to a bad back, and the Tigers relied on a number of freshmen and transfer players for substantial minutes. New guards Frank Ford and Gerald White saw considerable playing time, along with Vern Strickland and Carey Holland. Each contributed, but Chuck Person was the only Tiger in double figures in scoring, with 23.

Asked about his team's low shooting percentage–just 34 percent–UAB's Gene Bartow replied, "You have to remember who we were playing."

"He could get rebounds, but we needed him to play defense," Smith said of the injured Barkley and his limited playing time. "I thought it was a great effort on his part just to try to play."

Three games later, the Tigers faced another new, in-state program–and were defeated again. Traveling to the University of South Alabama, they lost badly to the Cliff Ellis-coached Jaguars, 95-73. Ellis, of course, would become Auburn's head coach a decade later.

"Auburn was beaten inside and out, end to end, like a drum," wrote Mike Land in the *Montgomery Advertiser*. Referring to Charles Barkley's hurt back, he added that after the game, "Barkley's feelings were hurt as well."

Barkley played 16 minutes, but was largely ineffective due to his injury. Chuck Person had another strong game, but the team overall shot only 36 percent from the field.

"I'll tell you what, they killed us with everything they did," said Smith afterward. "They whipped us in every phase of the game... It was just a complete domination of the game by them."

South Alabama's Terry Catledge was not impressed with Auburn overall. "I didn't expect it to be that close... I guess they must have took us too lightly. They weren't playing with a lot of intensity."

With the loss to USA, the Tigers fell to 2-2 (not counting exhibition games). The conference schedule hadn't even started yet, and already Auburn had lost to two brand-new in-state rivals. The season was not starting out the way anyone could've wanted.

Barkley's aching back was causing pain for the entire team.

Fortunes turned a bit beginning on December 28, when Auburn defeated Villanova in the second game of a tournament. Returning from that event, the Tigers reeled off three more victories in a row: Alabama, Florida and Kentucky. Kentucky was ranked number 1 in the country in at least one poll, making it Auburn's first victory over a number 1 team.

Kentucky raced out to an early 8-0 lead, but the Tigers came back to tie it. Then, with Charles Barkley in the game and serving as a dominating presence inside, the Tigers took the lead and more or less pulled away, ultimately winning by 19. It was a shocking turn of events for the top ranked team in the country–and a team surrounded by so much hype–to go down to Auburn by almost 20 points.

Indeed, the press had been playing up the potential of this Wildcat team for weeks. They featured the "Twin Towers," 7-1 Sam Bowie and 6-11 Melvin Turpin. They were coming off a 16-point win at LSU. There was speculation of them perhaps going undefeated in the conference.

Sarcastically referring to them as "the world's greatest basketball team," as some in the media had with all seriousness, Phillip Marshall wrote in the *Montgomery Advertiser* the next day that Kentucky was "unmercifully tortured, played with like an injured rat trying to escape a stalking cat." He added, "They got their tails kicked.

"It was Auburn that looked confident, Auburn that controlled the tempo. It was Kentucky that got flustered, Kentucky that played like a team waiting to get beat."

"I know this has got to be an understatement, but this is our greatest win of all time," said Sonny Smith after the game. "It was a great victory over a tremendous team."

Auburn played what Smith described as a "gimmick defense." When Kentucky tried to force the ball inside to Bowie or Turpin, three Auburn players would surround them. Refusing to settle for the outside shot, the Wildcats came away frustrated, possession after possession.

"They were 8 for 22 against us in the second half," Smith noted. "Another big factor was we didn't give them any second shots."

"Our local press has a way of getting our opponents ready to play," growled a clearly angry Joe B. Hall, the Kentucky coach. "It's just a shame our kids set goals and the press uses them to sell papers."

"I'd be lying if I said I thought anybody could beat us by 19 points," said Sam Bowie after the game. "I never would have believed that. They went straight out and whipped our tails. There are no excuses. Auburn just beat us all over the floor, and we'll be waiting for them when they come to Lexington.

"For the first three minutes, we were into our game plan real well. Then it just fell apart. I'm sure Charles (Barkley) had a lot to do with it. He's a great player and he's going to get his no matter who he is playing against.

"We knew they felt like they could match our talent and that they thought they could run up and down the floor with us. They went at us with much more aggressiveness and intensity than most people we have played."

Bowie guarded Chuck Person most of the night. Person finished with 25 points, along with 9 rebounds.

"He's as good a forward as you can find," said Bowie. "As good as any in the SEC."

Barkley had 21 points and 10 rebounds, and his powerful presence inside disrupted the Wildcats from the moment he took the floor.

"It was a joy to watch him operate and perform on such a big stage," Chuck Person said a number of years later, looking back on that Kentucky win. "After that game, I knew he was one of the best, if not the best, college basketball players in the country."

> **John Ringer:**
> We drove down from Atlanta and attended this Auburn-Kentucky game and though I was young I remember the game and the crowd. The two centers for Kentucky were so big and talented, but Auburn did an amazing job defending them that day.

The elation of beating big, bad Kentucky only lasted four days. Then the Tigers welcomed Vanderbilt to Memorial Coliseum and suffered the first of what would be back-to-back losses–first to the Commodores, then to Georgia.

Auburn recovered from those two hiccups and ran off six more wins in their next seven games, the only loss being when they visited a still-angry Kentucky at Rupp Arena. The Wildcats were indeed lying in wait, and extracted a little revenge for the earlier whipping on the Plains. They beat the Tigers by one point more than Auburn's margin of victory in the first matchup. The final was 84-64, Cats.

Aside from that loss in Lexington, Auburn's 6-1 run from late January to mid-February included revenge victories over Vanderbilt and Georgia. The Tigers would not be swept by anyone this season.

Their chance of winning the conference evaporated in the face of three straight losses to close out the month of February, the last two of which came by a single point each, and all three together by a total of only five points. Still, that was enough to deny them the title and to encourage critics to whisper that the Tigers lacked mental toughness and were folding under the pressure of the season's end. Backup point guard Paul Daniels in particular was singled out for criticism by some, after committing key turnovers that contributed to the losses.

The Tigers rallied, however, and knocked off Mississippi State, 68-53. After that, only one game remained on the schedule: the traditional season-ender against Alabama.

In what would be Charles Barkley's final game in Memorial Coliseum in Auburn, the Tigers defeated the Tide, 83-70. It was the first time since 1971 the Tigers defeated Alabama twice in the same season.

Barkley scored 28 points, shooting 9-for-9 in the second half. He put the finishing touches on the win with a massive reverse slam-dunk. Phillip Marshall described it as "a great artist applying his signature to a finished painting."

Barkley had led the Tigers to an 18-9 record overall. After five straight seasons of finishing eighth or ninth in a 10-team league, the Tigers this time around finished second, at 12-6 in the SEC. It was Auburn's best finish in the conference in twenty-one years.

Senior guard Paul Daniels was one of the happiest Auburn players in the locker room after the game. After struggling in previous games, he'd single-handedly broken Alabama's full-court press on numerous occasions, finishing with 6 assists to just one turnover.

The man who had taken Daniels' starting job, freshman point guard Gerald White, finally came into his own with this game. He scored 20 points and connected repeatedly from long range.

"We've been waiting a long time for this," White said afterward. "We're starting to play up to our ability. I've got my confidence and I'm finally relaxed in the things I'm doing. I'm starting to play like I can." A mainstay in the lineup going forward, the Tigers would rely heavily on White in the seasons to come.

Sonny Smith addressed the issue of the team's recent losses: "There's some frustration in that all everybody wanted to dwell on (coming into this game) was us folding up. It bothers me that people wrote about it and didn't understand that Charles has been hurt, that Greg Turner couldn't even practice. This team wasn't going to fold up. I knew that."

They did not fold up. They whipped the Tide, then turned their attention to the SEC Tournament, being played that year in Nashville.

With the number 2 seed in the tournament, the Tigers did not have to play on Wednesday for once. Instead they faced tournament hosts Vanderbilt, winners over Ole Miss the night before, in the Commodores' own Memorial Gymnasium. Auburn prevailed in the quarterfinal matchup, 59-58.

"I want to compliment Sonny for the way he's handled himself and his basketball team," said C.M. Newton of Vanderbilt afterward. "Sonny really struggled for four years in this league and you find out a lot about the people around you and yourself in situations like that. Sonny hasn't changed a bit. He's the same guy now when he's winning as he was then. That tells you something about the kind of person he is."

Auburn moved on to the semifinals, where Tennessee awaited them, coached by Sonny Smith's old boss, Don DeVoe.

Auburn's 60-58 win over the Vols was described by some as "heart-stopping." Charles Barkley delivered another epic performance. He had to step up even more than usual after Chuck Person left the game three minutes from the end with a sprained knee. Barkley swatted away Tennessee's last-gasp shot attempt that would've sent the game into overtime.

Afterward, Vols coach Don DeVoe remarked, "When it came down to the nitty gritty and they wanted to get the ball inside to Barkley they were able to do it. They handled the pressure well and made the big play when they had to... Auburn was just a stronger team in the last five minutes. They were able to dictate the tempo, we weren't, and that's important late in the game."

He also had warm thoughts for his former assistant. "Sonny Smith fortunately came into my life at the right time. He was very instrumental in bringing me a lot of good players while we were at Virginia Tech. I didn't even know him when I hired him."

The victory put Auburn, now at 20-9, into the SEC Tournament finals for the first time ever. It was also seen as guaranteeing the Tigers a spot in the field of the NCAA Tournament for the first time, as well.

First up, though, was Kentucky–and after the UT game, there was concern Chuck Person would not be able to play at all, due to injuring his knee during a collision late in the game.

"We can win with or without Chuck," Barkley asserted that evening. "We want him out there, but if he's not we can get the job done."

Person's injury turned out not to be as severe as first thought. "I'm going to be out there (tomorrow) unless this thing falls off," he stated.

It was no surprise who awaited Auburn in the finals. The game would match up SEC number 2 Auburn against Kentucky, now number 1 in the conference and number 3 in the country. The Wildcats were coming off a narrow 48-46 win over Alabama in the other semifinal.

Meanwhile, the Friday night after the Tennessee semifinal game, there came a situation that only seems to happen in the SEC, where—as we are constantly reminded—"It just means more." A large group of Auburn, Alabama and Tennessee cheerleaders were arrested by Nashville police and carried off to jail. It seems they were all congregated in a Krystal across from the Vanderbilt campus, and they started cheering and good-naturedly shouting at each other. The restaurant owner warned them to quiet down, which only prompted them to get louder. Next thing anyone knew, the police had rolled up and carted the cheerleaders away to the pokey. They were eventually freed after the charges were dropped.

Asked afterward if she knew they were college cheerleaders, the owner replied, "It don't make no difference."

Apparently, to her, it did not, in fact, mean more.

The SEC Tournament Final against Kentucky was a close affair from start to finish. With the game tied, 49-49, Auburn had possession of the ball and was set to play for the final shot and the win. Unfortunately, Gerald White's inbound pass to Chuck Person was picked off by Winston Bennett. The Wildcats ran the final two minutes off the clock (it was two years before the shot clock would be instituted) and Kenny Walker scored on a jumper from fifteen feet away to give the Cats the win and the championship.

Kentucky's win marked their first SEC Tournament title since the event was resumed in 1979, and they became the sixth different team to win it. Additionally, it marked the first time the top-seeded team won it since that first season.

"I don't know what else we could've done," Smith said afterward. "I thought we did a great job of taking them out of their final play. Walker just made a great shot when he got it. I'm just so proud of these people for showing the ability and the courage to get here. The disappointment was the worst ever when (Kenny Walker's final shot) went through and then waiting for Kentucky to cut down the net. But this has to be the best feeling I've ever had about a team as a coach. It's a team that gained confidence when it didn't have any. It's a team that stayed together and gained the ability to get to the finals of this tournament." As he shook hands with his players and assistant coaches, he repeated a mantra: "Our time is coming. Our time is coming."

"All I kept saying and all I kept thinking is we never gave up," said Auburn's senior guard Paul Daniels. "People doubted us. They never thought we'd be here. If I was rich I'd buy the people on this team rings myself. We are champions. Even though we lost and I'm hurting, I'm proud. I never knew how much the fellows on this team meant to me and how much I love them. We played with all our hearts today."

"We don't have anything to be embarrassed about," said Chuck Person, who scored 14 along with grabbing 7 rebounds while playing with an ailing knee. "I am proud of our team. We did a heck of a job. We played hard and had a chance to win the tournament. It just didn't happen. We did everything we could. You have to give Kentucky credit."

Auburn placed two players on the all-tournament team, Chuck Person and Charles Barkley. Barkley also took home the tournament MVP award.

After the game, thoughts turned to the upcoming NCAA Tournament, which featured a smaller field than it does today, meaning invitations were harder to come by back then. Even very good teams had to sweat until they got word they were officially in—or out.

"Sure they'll get a bid to the tournament," said the Wildcats' Sam Bowie. "How are you going to keep a team like Auburn out of it? They beat us once and played us to the wire today. They have a great team. They deserve a bid."

"Auburn will make the tournament, and I think they will surprise some people," said Melvin Turpin.

Unfortunately, Turpin was more accurate than he knew. The Tigers would go on to surprise people—though not in a good way.

But first, they had to get invited.

"If we don't get an NCAA bid, I'm gonna shoot somebody," Smith summarized.

They needn't have worried. The Tigers had indeed earned their very first appearance in the NCAA Basketball Tournament, as a 5 seed in the East Regional in Charlotte, North Carolina. There they would face the 12 seed Richmond Spiders in the first round—which, at that time, was the Round of 48.

Auburn's record under Sonny Smith at that point stood at 83-87. The record would not improve that evening. As Melvin Turpin had predicted, some people were surprised.

Auburn fell behind early to Dick Tarrant's Spiders and trailed by 17 at the half, then by 20 early in the second half, at 48-28. Surely they were done. There could be no coming back from such a drastic deficit, right?

But then Charles Barkley went to work on the inside and brought Auburn roaring back. The Tigers racked up 43 points in the game's final 14 minutes—a blistering total in the days before the three-point shot. Auburn pulled within three as the game turned into a foul-and-free-throw-shooting contest. Chuck Person fouled out with less than a minute remaining, but the Tigers kept fighting, cutting the lead to 1 on a Barkley rebound and put-back with 10 seconds to go. Out of timeouts, however, Auburn couldn't stop the clock and the final few seconds drained away as Richmond inbounded the ball. The Spiders held on to win, 72-71. It was a disappointing finish for the SEC's number 2 team, especially in losing to a 12-seed.

"It's been a great year for us, but I hate to see it end this way," said Smith after the game. "I don't think we played hard at all in the first half. We stood around a lot."

Barkley had a statistically dominant game, scoring 23 points along with 17 rebounds, 4 assists, 2 blocks and 2 steals.

"What happened to us didn't have anything to do with being nervous," he told reporters. "Richmond just kicked our behinds."

Barkley was asked to compare this loss to the defeat by Kentucky in the SEC finals.

"It doesn't hurt as bad because we didn't play well. It wasn't because we weren't trying. I don't care what anybody says, this team deserved to be here and we played hard. I just thank God for the opportunity."

"Our kids weren't the least bit intimidated by Auburn or by the 14,000 people here," said Richmond's coach, Dick Tarrant.

The Spiders' Bill Flye, who was charged with guarding Barkley for much of the game, came away impressed. "He's much stronger than I thought. I knew he was big, but I didn't realize how strong he is. We just packed the zone in there in the first half and I think he got frustrated. In the second half, they just started lobbing the ball over us."

Sonny Smith was named SEC Coach of the Year following the 1984 season. The Tigers had ended the year 20-11, 12-6 in the SEC, and second only to Kentucky in both the regular season and the conference tournament. Quite a turnaround after those first five seasons of struggle.

(For their part, Kentucky went on to reach the Final Four that season, where they led Patrick Ewing's Georgetown team in the first half of the national semifinal. But they shot an abysmal and frankly astonishing 3 for 33 in the second half and fell to the Hoyas, who then went on to defeat Hakeem Olajuwon's Houston Cougars in the national championship game.)

Charles Barkley was named SEC Player of the Year and MVP of the SEC Tournament. After teasing reporters and fans all year long about his intentions of returning to Auburn for his senior season or turning pro, he declared for the 1984 NBA Draft. He was taken by the Philadelphia 76ers as the No. 5 pick overall. Picked ahead of him were some remarkable names, with Hakeem Olajuwon first, to Houston; Sam Bowie of Kentucky second, to Portland, Michael

Jordan of North Carolina third, to Chicago; and Jordan's UNC teammate, Sam Perkins, fourth, to Dallas. Coming just after Barkley at sixth was the other Twin Tower from Kentucky, Melvin Turpin, who went to Washington. Future fellow Dream Team member John Stockton of Gonzaga fell all the way to 16 in this draft, going to Utah.

Said Smith of Barkley in 2020: "If I'd known how to coach superstars, I might have won a national championship. You have to treat those people different. Their personalities have to be managed. I admire Charles Barkley for doing as well as he did after taking the abuse from me trying to make him better. Instead of making him better, I probably held his career back a little bit. He wasn't about to handle too much discipline."

Van Allen Plexico:
Auburn has never lost in the Round of 64. This was the only year we lost in the first round of the Tournament, but the Tournament that year only included 48 teams.

John Ringer:
That was the beginning of Richmond's reputation as a giant-killer.

They did it again this year (winning in an upset in the first round of 2022).

This outcome was also disappointing because we wanted Charles to be successful on the big stage, on the big platform.

This game might not even have been televised. Probably not many people saw it.

Van Allen Plexico:
I actually found it on YouTube. Apparently it was shown on a regional sports channel or network, sort of like the old Jefferson Pilot football games. So, no, I doubt many people saw it.

Thinking of how Charles's NCAA opportunity was cut short by this upset, it reminds me of something from a few years later. Charles was on the Arsenio Hall talk show—I'm not sure if he was even a guest; he might just have been in the audience—and Arsenio went over to talk to him for a minute.

After introducing him as a member of the Sixers, Arsenio looked at Charles, appearing sort of confused, as if he didn't know something he felt he should know. He asked Charles, "Where did you play your college ball?"

"Auburn," Charles replied.

"Ahh. Auburn," Arsenio said back to him, the tone in his voice indicating he was searching his memories for anything he might remember about Charles and Auburn–and clearly finding nothing. It seemed like he was expecting himself to suddenly go, "Oh, yeah! Auburn!" But he didn't. He couldn't remember anything about Auburn basketball. Another second, and Arsenio moved on to other topics.

It was depressing in a way, because it meant the national audience–even folks like Arsenio, who seemed interested in basketball and apparently followed it pretty closely–had no idea about Charles's Auburn career and didn't even know where he'd played.

That contrasted sharply with Bo Jackson, who emerged as a big-time star just a couple of years later. People always seemed to know Bo played for Auburn and always associated him with it. With Charles, people only tended to think of the NBA and the Dream Team, and later with his broadcast work.

In recent years, though, I think he's done a lot to show his connections to Auburn and his love for it.

John Ringer (to Sonny Smith, 2022):
What is your favorite story about coaching Charles Barkley? And did he change over time? Or did you change how you coached him over his time at Auburn?

Sonny Smith:
No, but I wish that I had. I'll tell you why. When you were a guy that coached at Auburn, coached at other schools in the SEC, very rarely did any of you have a superstar. You had good players. You had SEC type players, but you didn't have a superstar. I had a superstar and didn't know how to coach superstars. If I had been able to coach Charles Barkley by turning my head (looking the other way), letting him loaf a little, letting him do what he wants to do. Because he's going

to win the game for you. If I had used that attitude, Charles would have been better, quicker. And he was going to be good. I knew he was going to be good.

I'll give you a good example of how good he was. This is to give you how other people think. Billy Cunningham was the coach of the 76ers and Charles was drafted. And when he decided to go pro, Billy says to me, he says, "Sonny, how do you handle Charles?" That's not exactly what he said. I said, "Well, you're going to have a hard time, you're going to have a hard time because I treated him like (I treated) all the rest of them. And, you know, it was like an old school approach. Treat them all the same, work them all the same, get on them all the same, I said, "I didn't coach Charles properly." And he said, "Well, I'll tell you one thing. I'm going to coach him properly." I said, "Billy, I'm going to call you one year from today. And I want you to tell me how you properly coached Charles Barkley."

I met him, it wasn't even a year (later). He said, "I can't get (Charles) to do anything. I want him to do something (but) I can't handle him". He put his hands up like this. I said, "See, I told you!"

If I had left Charles Barkley alone, we might have won a national championship with him, because not many people know how to coach superstars because they don't have them. They never had one. And I looked back at the thing and I said (to myself), "Who coached a superstar better, me or Pat Dye? Pat Dye had Bo Jackson. I had Charles. Well, I'm not going to tell you how Coach Dye coached Bo Jackson. But it's totally different than the way I coached Charles. And you see the success that Bo Jackson had. Whether that had anything to do with it or not. But if I had it to do over, I would know how to coach a superstar now as opposed to how you would have back in the day. That's about as much as I can say about it.

John Ringer:
Did you know when he walked onto campus that he was a superstar?

Sonny Smith:
No, because I didn't think I'd ever get him in shape to be what I thought he could be. I said, he's gonna be really good. He's gonna be undersized. He's gonna always be out of shape. And I don't know if I'm getting him to do what I need him to do. I was totally wrong on all of those things. He could play. He could have played at the weight that he was—he could do it. And I didn't believe he could. So I was thinking, if I ever wrote a book, I would say how to coach superstars. And I didn't know because I had not had any. Well, Charles Barkley could play at any weight, and do what he wanted. Once the game started, weight didn't mean anything to him. (He was) just a straight ahead, win the game type of guy. And I wish I had known that. And so, not that Charles will tell you today that I did for him what he needed to have done, with the discipline-type things, but I disagree. I think I should have coached him. I should have been a head-turner, ignored his weight, ignored his loafing a little bit in practice—you know, I'd be all over him. And it was not the way to do it, even though I made him a better player, taught him moves and things like that. But you've got to learn how to coach superstars if you are going to have one.

Van Allen Plexico:
I think he said that he had to learn to play defense at all, basically, from you.

Sonny Smith:
He did. He didn't want to play defense. He made me have to play more zone than I really wanted to play. I've had people criticize me: "Oh Sonny, all you want to do is play a zone." I played a zone because of things like that. (With the zone defense) I could keep him in the game and he wouldn't foul out. If I were to let him guard a guy, he beat that guy to death and fouled out. So this is the thing about it: I played zone even though I didn't want to. But I had nine players that played and seven of them could really play, you know, so I couldn't afford for him to foul out. I couldn't afford to play strong man-to-man (defense) and look like we were really are getting after

them. Because I didn't have the bench, (so) I had to keep Charles in the game. And the zone was the best way to do it. And if people today are still curious, (saying), "Sonny, he didn't know much about defense,"— but I really did. And I knew I would rather have a player stay in the game, than show that I was playing the right kind of defense. And that kind of makes sense. But I had to keep Charles in the game. So I played a zone all the time or he would foul out. He would. He was so aggressive. I don't think people ever gave him credit for how aggressive he was.

Van Allen Plexico:
I just dug that up in my research about the poor Angolan guy that he basically beat up, mugged and scared to death (in the Olympics).

Sonny Smith:
I was lucky Charles didn't beat me up. He tells everybody about that I hit him one time. It wasn't a hard lick though, I hit him in the stomach a little bit. He says that was the right thing to do. I doubt that.

BARKLEY AND THE 1984 OLYMPIC TEAM

A 16-year NBA career, 11 All-Star game appearances, MVP of the NBA in 1993, MVP of the NBA All-Star Game in 1991, and two Olympic gold medals followed Sir Charles's career at Auburn. And it all started with a discerning assistant coach—Herbert Greene—who had come to Leeds to recruit an entirely different player.

After Auburn, Barkley was considered a near-certain lock to make the 1984 US Olympic Basketball team. Michael Wilbon, writing in the *Washington Post*, assumed it would be a done deal.

"Barkley is the story at these trials. It will be a major surprise if he is not one of the eighteen players who survive Monday morning's cut, and he is a good bet to make the final 12-player team. Many people here, playing against Barkley or just seeing him in person for the first time, can't stop talking about him. He dunks, passes, rebounds, runs the break and knocks the hell out of people. Unintentionally, of course."

One player who felt the wrath of Barkley was Joe Dumars. The future Pistons star stood in Barkley's way, attempting to draw a charge. Barkley knocked him into the stands.

"I said, 'Joe, I can't believe you tried to do that.' He rubbed himself and said, 'I can't believe it either.'"

Kenny Fields of UCLA noted, "When you're running back down court (after Barkley knocks you around), Charles always says, 'I'm sorry.'"

Tim McCormick of Michigan observed, "Barkley has been dominant. Three or four times a day, you see the backboard shaking. You look back and you see Barkley walking away."

John Williams of Tulane described Barkley as "the toughest I've ever played against. You see the guy driving toward you and you just say, 'Oh, no, anybody but him.'"

This was still in the era when the pros were not eligible to play– although "pro" always seemed to have a different meaning when applied to players from the Communist Bloc nations. The players available to USA Basketball that year, however, were virtually a who's who of future NBA stars and All-Star games. Whoever the head coach would be, he would have his pick of some great ones.

Unfortunately, the coach turned out to be one Robert Montgomery Knight.

Bobby Knight was unquestionably a great coach. However, he also happened to be the absolute worst fit as a coach for someone of Barkley's personality. He always treated his players like they were in boot camp, and he demanded military-level discipline from them. That was never going to fly with Sir Charles.

Knight describes his first telephone conversation with Barkley: "He called and asked how much I wanted him to weigh when he came in. I didn't tell him, because I wanted him at about 215 pounds."

Wilbon asked Knight if he had ever coached a "fat player." "Not for long," Knight replied.

Sonny Smith knew exactly what Charles was walking into with Bobby Knight in charge. "I was afraid (Charles's) reputation would hurt his chances for making the team, which is why I was reluctant to join in the talk about his weight and his eating. His attitude has improved. He was never a bad kid—just a kid who wouldn't work. This year is the first time we reached any kind of understanding. Earlier, Charles and I had some very hard times.

"I wanted to coach the hard-line, disciplined way: shirt tucked in, short hair, mouth shut. But after a while, I realized it was stifling him. He played harder when he didn't have to worry about his shirt, when he was giving high fives and blowing kisses to the fans."

Smith described some of the changes he'd persuaded Charles to make in his third and final year on the Plains: "Not taking outside jumpers, playing defense the way (Smith) wanted and concentrating for more than five minutes at a stretch."

"I think Charles boosts his weight if it improves the interview," Smith told Wilbon.

"I really don't eat that much," Charles responded. "I just, more or less, tend to eat all the time. If I could go into a room and peel some of this stuff off of me, I'd come out looking like Hercules."

Coming into the Olympic trials, Barkley had attempted to lose weight. At one point he went on a crash diet of just juices, but that landed him in the hospital.

Northeastern forward Steve Halsel tried to block a Barkley dunk in practice. Charles easily dispatched Halsel with one hand while slamming the ball home with the other. "After that, me'n Charles, I been trying to be his friend."

Barkley dominated the practices for the next two weeks, going up against some of the best players in basketball history.

"If they cut Charles Barkley, they'd better mail it in," said Jim Boeheim of Syracuse, after the second day of practice.

Bobby Knight cut him anyway.

"Bobby Knight had a hidden agenda against me," Barkley said later. "Because I was the second-best player there, I kinda felt like he didn't want me there. He didn't want me on the team. It was a joke." Later he would say of Knight, "I love to hate him."

Alvin Robertson, later of the Spurs, attempted to explain. "Charles didn't like anything about Coach Knight. There were a lot of confrontations with Knight. (For one example, the coaches) would talk about being on time. (Knight) was telling us all to be punctual and then he showed up about 10 minutes late.

"Charles got up and said, 'It's 10 after 5, where the hell have you been?' And Knight just went off. `Let me tell you something, you fat s.o.b., there's only one leader in this army' - he just went totally nuts."

Leon Wood, later Barkley's teammate at Philadelphia, put it this way: "Charles' whole idea was to make the top five in the draft. So he kicked butt (at the trials). To me, he was the best player the first week. After his stock went up and it was known that he was going to be in the top five, he pretty much coasted. I don't think he really wanted to play."

Barkley later described himself as the second-best player at the Olympic trials, behind only Michael Jordan. His Auburn teammate, Chuck Person, agreed.

"When he pretty much dominated everyone there, I knew at that point that he was probably gone (from Auburn), but before that, I didn't have any indications he was going to leave. He was clearly the second-best player at that Olympic Trials behind Michael Jordan.

"There is no doubt that we would have had the opportunity to compete for a national championship (in 1984-85). Had he stayed, we would have dominated our respective SEC class, although Kentucky would have had something to say about that.

"We were all set to jockey for a national championship. (Barkley) left, but it was a good decision he made for himself. It turned out great."

Speaking of Sonny Smith, Charles remarked, "My coach sent me (to the Olympic trials) to get better, and he said, 'I think you're the best player in the country. I want you to go there and prove it.' When I got back, I said, 'Coach, we're pretty damn close. I'm the second-best player in the country. But there's this damn guy ... from North Carolina, who's the best I've ever seen."

Eight years later, Charles finally got his chance to prove himself as an Olympian, as a member of the original Dream Team of 1992. That team, taking advantage of rules changes that allowed NBA players to participate in the Olympics, brought an absolutely loaded roster to Barcelona. With the cream of the crop of NBA All-Stars at every position, they absolutely dominated all competition. And Charles Barkley was possibly their most visible and talked-about player.

"Barkley would say things that (the rest of us) would think about but never say," Michael Jordan noted afterward.

One much-discussed incident came when the USA played Angola. Before the game, Charles was asked about the opponent.

"I don't know anything about Angola," he said, "but Angola's in trouble."

During the game, the USA went on an eye-popping 46-1 run. Also during the game, Barkley punched an Angolan player in the chest, drawing the ire of the international media. His defense was that the player had been elbowing him the entire game.

"People always say, 'Turn the other cheek.'" Charles observed. "If you turn the other cheek, I'm gonna hit you in the other cheek, too."

Barkley's Team USA cruised to the Finals and won the gold medal game over Spain, who was just happy to be there. Barkley was the leading scorer on that team of teams. Four years later, he'd be on the US squad again, and they'd do it all over again in Atlanta.

In the 1992 Barcelona Olympics, Barkley averaged a team-high 18 points a game, along with 4 rebounds, while shooting 71% for the Dream Team. In the 1996 Atlanta Olympics, his scoring average fell to 12.4%, but his rebounds went up to 6 per game, and he shot an astonishing 81.6% from the floor–a US Olympic record.

John Ringer:

I remember being mad about this, and disappointed. There were lots of really good players in that camp. Coaches had to decide who to assemble for the Olympic team. Barkley was one of the best players in the country, but Bobby Knight was old-school. He wanted discipline, not talking back. He wanted players who would do exactly what the coaches asked. That was not Barkley's game. Plus Charles was unconventional as a player. Coaches at that time in his career weren't sure how to use him best. Knight wasn't creative as a coach in that way; he wasn't going to try to find the best way to use him. So Knight, for all those reasons, wasn't going to put up with Charles, regardless of his talent.

BARKLEY IN THE NBA

In his first season with Philadelphia, Barkley was named to the All-Rookie First Team. But he almost ate his way out of being chosen by the Sixers—on purpose!

In 2018, appearing on ESPN's "The Russillo Show," Barkley described his efforts to avoid being drafted by Philadelphia.

Wait–*avoid*? Why wouldn't he want to go to the team that had just won the NBA title the previous year? The team that included on its roster the great Dr. J, Julius Erving, and the NBA MVP, Moses Malone?

As it turns out, the Sixers had asked Barkley to slim down to a mere 285 pounds prior to the Draft. If he did that, they told him, they would choose him fifth overall.

Being picked in the top five sounded good to Charles, so he worked hard and got his weight all the way down to a svelte 282.

But then his agent told him something deeply disturbing: Because of the NBA salary cap, the Sixers would only be able to pay him the league minimum of $75,000 for his rookie season.

"I said, 'I didn't leave college for $75,000.' So I said, 'Well, we got to make sure the Sixers don't draft me then.' So we went on a two-day binge."

What followed was an epic two-day eating fiesta, focused largely on multiple Grand Slam breakfasts at Denny's and lunch at KFC. Over the space of 48 hours, Barkley gained twenty pounds. "So the next day, we fly to Philly, I get on the scale and I'm 302."

Unfortunately for Charles, this turned out to be insufficient grounds for the Sixers to pass on him. They took him after all, at number 5.

"If people take a good look at the tape, when he said, 'With the No.5 pick, the 76ers take Charles Barkley', the look on my face is, 'Are you kidding me?'"

It all worked out, however. Barkley so impressed the Sixers higher-ups that they worked out a four-year, $2 million contract for him.

Charles didn't start for Philly until twenty games into his career there. "I was lazy," he told reporters later. "First of all, you don't know you're lazy until you move to the next level. Your level of laziness is dictated by your level of success. Think about it. I'm 300 pounds, but I'm leading the SEC in rebounding. So, like, I don't (expletive) think I'm lazy."

Then he asked teammate Moses Malone why he wasn't playing as much as he thought he should be. Malone replied, "You're fat and lazy." That seemed to light a fire under Barkley. He soon had worked his way down to 245 and began to emerge as a true superstar.

Sixteen seasons later, he retired as a legend. He was just the fourth player in NBA history to amass 20,000 points, 10,000 rebounds, and 4000 assists.

The closest Charles came to an NBA title was in 1993 with the Phoenix Suns. They worked a massive trade with Philadelphia to bring him in that season, and he nearly delivered for them right off the bat. His team finished with the best record in the NBA's regular season, at 62-20, winning the Western Conference. He took the Suns all the way to game 6 of the Finals before falling to Michael Jordan's powerful Chicago Bulls. This marked the third straight title for the Bulls, and the last before Jordan's two-year self-imposed exile to minor league baseball.

In 2022, as part of the NBA's 75th anniversary, Barkley was named one of the NBA's 75 all-time greatest players.

"I got emotional. I'm not going to lie," he said after being introduced as part of that group. "It hit me a lot harder than I thought it was going to, seeing some of the guys. These guys mean a lot to me. Basketball means a lot to me. I've never had a real job because of that stupid basketball, and all those guys out there made my life great. I just want to thank the older guys because if it weren't for the older guys, we wouldn't be who we were. But it was really emotional.

"I was glad to be a part of it, and I just want to thank everybody. And the fans are important. The fans are real important to the whole picture. But there are so many people who have helped me in my life. This goes to everybody in my life who has helped me."

Charles Barkley remains the most famous and celebrated basketball player in Auburn history. In 84 games with the Tigers, Barkley averaged 14.1 points and 9.6 rebounds. Beginning with Barkley's final season, Auburn made five consecutive NCAA Tournament appearances.

"To the basketball program, he brought it back from the dead," Sonny Smith would say, years later. "Before he got here, we were wallowing around in the bottom of the league. He took us to heights. He put us on a trail that we had never been on before. And it was all because of him."

John Ringer:
That was an exciting time. Charles was with the Sixers, playing with Moses Malone, Dr. J, Maurice Cheeks, and more.

They had a big rivalry with the Bird/Parrish/McHale-era Celtics. They had some big playoff games.

Philadelphia loves players who play hard and give their all. They loved Charles.

He became a great rebounder. He improved his game over time. Changed his body. Became a better shooter and a better ball handler. That led him to become an all-star, All-NBA player and one of the best in the league, when the NBA was as good as it's ever been, with Bird and Magic and others.

I watched a good bit of the NBA back then and enjoyed watching Charles play there. They were competitive.

When things got really fun was when he went to Phoenix. That was a fun team. He got to play with a bunch of other good players in a dynamic, explosive offensive system.

Van Allen Plexico:
That year at Phoenix was the closest he came to winning a title. They made it to game 6 of the Finals against the Bulls. Before the game, Charles said he told Michael Jordan, "You're having dinner at my house tonight," meaning, "You'll still be in Phoenix for a game 7 tomorrow." Unfortunately, the Suns lost game 6, and that was that.

John Ringer
Barkley's teams lost in the Western Conference Finals to the Rockets (with Hakeem Olajuwon) and then in the NBA Finals to the Bulls (with Jordan).

That really was a fun Suns team, though. Dan Majerle, Steve Nash–and even Wesley Person as a reserve at one point.

NBA PLAYERS AND COACHES ON BARKLEY

During the 1987 season at Philadelphia, Barkley grew unhappy with the rest of the team and how those players were approaching the games.

"We've got guys who have complained, complained and complained," he said. "That's why we haven't moved ahead.

"We have so many wimps and complainers on this team, that's one of the problems. If the guys we have played every night, we can beat anybody."

The team's general manager, John Nash, responded: "It shows he cares. I find him refreshing. He thinks he's as good a player as anyone and I wouldn't argue with that."

The team's head coach, Matt Guokas, had this reaction: "I don't like criticism of any kind unless it's constructive, but if this brings us closer together, then it's good."

Boston's coach, K.C. Jones, said of Barkley, "He's very emotional and he shows it through the work ethic. To me, he's a total player."

Barkley's teammate, guard Maurice Cheeks, observed, "The boy's crazy. There's got to be a reason why he's acting like he does. He's crazy off the court, too."

And legendary Sixer Julius Erving said the following: "When he first came here, his body proportions were a lot different. He's like a statue now. He's like (Michelangelo's) David, and before he was like Dom DeLuise.

"The only thing that's fat now is his head."

BARKLEY ON BARKLEY

On future retirement from the league:
"I want to win at least three (NBA) MVP trophies. At the age of 30, I'm going to retire and never get out of bed before noon again."

On money and endorsements:
"I try to keep a lid on my endorsements. The only reason I do endorsements is to make money. I feel like basically I have enough money for me and my family.

"There's no sense in being greedy. I don't want more money than I can spend. My family has everything they need--my mom, my grandmother and my two brothers, my girlfriend and my future kids.

"I don't need no more money. I don't want to die and have $50 million. That's just greedy.

On how to treat people:
"I don't care if people like me. They don't know nothing, just like the media. They can't bother me. I'm getting paid for the next 80 years.

"I have one basic rule, I treat the person how they treat me, whether it's good or bad. I'm a nice guy but I don't mind being a jerk.

"I can get along with anybody, but I'm not going to take nothing off nobody. When I was growing up, we didn't have anything. There are so many snobby people in the world. They don't have time for people who don't have anything. I've always felt if I had a lot of money, I wouldn't treat people like I was treated because they didn't have anything.

On success:
"I don't think I'm better than anybody unless I'm on the court. I don't think anybody can play basketball like me.

"That's one of the screwed-up things about our society. If you have something, everybody treats you good. If you don't, everybody treats you bad. It's very unfortunate, and I've been on both sides of it. Most people I know who have money are jerks. They think they're better than everybody else."

(The above quoted by Chris Baker in the LA Times, February 22, 1987.)

THE 1984-85 SEASON
22-12 (8-10, 8th in the SEC)
NCAA Tournament: Sweet Sixteen

Chuck Person (F)	Gerald White (G)
Frank Ford (G)	Carey Holland (C)
Chris Morris (F)	Terrance Howard (G)
Jeff Moore (C)	Johnny Lynn (G)

Auburn's climb to almost the top of the SEC lasted exactly one season. The following year, with Barkley gone to the NBA, the Tigers fell to their seemingly customary spot near the bottom, finishing 8th in the ten-team league, with a record of 8-10 in SEC play.

While they did ring up a satisfying 61-59 win over 13th-ranked UAB in Birmingham in November, the conference schedule turned into a lackluster, back-and-forth affair. They managed back-to-back SEC wins only once all season, when they defeated Florida and Tennessee within four days in early February. The Tigers were swept by Kentucky, Alabama, Georgia and LSU. The disappointment was palpable. One could certainly be forgiven for expecting this Auburn team to make a quick exit from the SEC Tournament and not even qualify for a second NCAA appearance.

Given that disappointing showing across the 1985 season, coupled with the Tigers' early exit from the previous year's NCAA Tournament–and possibly a sense of too little support from the fans and from the administration–Smith decided he had had enough. On February 8, 1985, he announced he would be stepping down as coach when the season was over. Most likely that would be after the first or second game of the SEC Tournament.

At that point it looked as if the Tigers would miss the rest of the postseason entirely, lacking the necessary resume for the NCAAs and probably even for the 32-team NIT field.

If Auburn was to make some noise in Birmingham, they would have to charge all the way from the opening night game on Wednesday. No team in SEC history had ever won the tournament when playing all four days.

The Tigers got things rolling by knocking off 9-seed Ole Miss on Wednesday. The next day they faced the number 1 seed in the conference, LSU—a team that had swept both regular-season games against Auburn.

LSU might have been a prohibitive favorite, but they'd suffered terrible and nigh-inexplicable fortunes in tournaments in recent years. Coming into the game against Auburn, they'd lost eight of them straight, all the way back to 1981. Auburn added to their woes, beating them 58-55.

Kentucky had only the four seed in this tournament, and the Tigers were spared a date with them on Friday in the semifinals, as the Wildcats fell to Florida, 58-55, that same day.

Florida had yet to make the NCAA Tournament and wanted a win over Auburn badly, to burnish their credentials. It didn't work out that way. The Tigers defeated the Gators for the third time that season, 43-42.

For the second year in a row, Auburn had made the SEC Tournament Finals. The previous year, their opponent had been intimidating Kentucky, where they'd lost by a single basket. This year would be different. This time, they faced old rival Alabama. And they knew what to do.

The Tigers had been swept by the Tide in the regular season, losing 60-55 at home and 74-72 at Coleman Coliseum. Auburn was still reeling from that second loss to the Tide. The Tigers had chances to win at the end of regulation and at the end of the first overtime, but missed shots both times—first by Gerald White, then by Frank Ford—sent the game into double overtime, where Alabama pulled out the 74-72 victory.

In their third matchup, played before 14,500 in the BJCC, the two rivals again went to overtime. This came after Alabama squandered a 48-44 lead with nearly six minutes left. Alabama coach Wimp Sanderson's plan was to take advantage of the lack of a shot clock against the weary Tigers, who were playing their fourth game in four days. (The SEC had chosen to not use the shot clock in the tournament since it was not going to be used in the NCAA Tournament later that month). Sanderson's Tide played keep-away, forcing the Tigers to chase the ball and, it was hoped, wear themselves completely out.

Unfortunately for Sanderson, his plan did not work.

In an age when teams played slowly and deliberately, and when every point loomed huge, Alabama's poor free-throw shooting late kept Auburn in the game. When Chuck Person hit two foul shots with around four minutes left, the lead was cut to 48-46.

Alabama ran nearly three minutes off the clock before Bobby Lee Hurt made a free throw to push the Tide's lead back to three. It would be the last point Alabama scored in the game and in the tournament.

Frank Ford made one free throw, followed by a jump shot, tying the game with nine seconds left. Neither team could score from there and the game went to OT.

Auburn ran two minutes off the clock in overtime, but then turned the ball over. They got it back when Alabama's Jim Farmer missed a shot, and with just eleven seconds left, Gerald White was fouled by Terry Coner. White made both free throws, and Auburn finally had the lead, 51-49. Alabama inbounded the ball to their future coach, Mark Gottfried, who was called for traveling, giving the ball back to Auburn. Chuck Person inbounded the ball to White, who narrowly avoided a steal and hit Frank Ford for a slam-dunk punctuation mark at the buzzer. The Tigers had beaten Alabama, 53-49. They had won the SEC Tournament for the first time—and become the first team to win it while playing four games in four days. And now their season wasn't over; they'd locked down an automatic bid to the NCAA Tournament.

John Ringer:

What is your single favorite Auburn victory from your time as coach?

Sonny Smith:

Not the NCAA wins, it was when we beat Alabama to win the SEC Tournament. Auburn needed that—they needed that so badly to get some validity towards the basketball program. And I thought that win gave us a real boost. That was one of the biggest for me. Winning the SEC Tournament, and winning it over Alabama.

Van Allen Plexico:

And that was the year you came from the first night!

Sonny Smith:
Yes, I think it was four games in four days.

Van Allen Plexico:
You were the only team for fifteen years to do it, until Arkansas in 2000. So, from the time the SEC Tournament started in 1978 until 2000, you were the only team to do it.

Sonny Smith:
One of the games I remember in the SEC Tournament (was when) we beat Georgia in four overtimes. You won't see a four-overtime game these days. That jumped out at me. I cannot remember how we won it, but neither team could shoot. We held the ball. I thought that went a long way towards establishing what we could do.

Van Allen Plexico:
That was when overtime was basically just "try to run the clock down and get a good shot" instead of back-and-forth (scoring).

Sonny Smith:
That is true. I cannot remember who held it the longest. Whoever got the ball put it behind their back and held it.

The league was awfully good from top to bottom in those days. And it will never be mentioned because of the amount of television coverage the league gets now compared to back then, but if you think back to the time I coached here in the Eighties, everybody had really good players. Everyone had a pro prospect or two on their teams. Well, you get one or two out of the league now. It is different. And the league is great now – the style of basketball has something to do with it. But that league back then was stocked full of players. And someone asked me, "Why would you say those players were better?" Because we could get a living person into school; they just had to be alive. Academically they just had to be alive (back then). And you cannot get them in academically like that today. That sounds crazy but it is true. If a guy does not have the academics now, he has to go to a junior college. If he did not have the academics he could still play back in those days.

Van Allen Plexico:
I remember you saying when the shot clock came in and the three pointer came in, you told a reporter, "They want to make a mistake every single year." Did you really not like the shot clock and the three-point shot at the time, and have you changed your position since then?

Sonny Smith:
It made the game better. So I was wrong. (But) you have to give a team that does not have a chance a chance to win, and when you put those things in you took away some of the chances for upsets. Before that you could create an upset with the way you played. When they put those in you had to play a style according those rules and still win. It made the better teams better, in my opinion, and took away some upset potential.

Think about it—we don't have many of those huge upsets in the SEC today. Big upsets, we just don't have them, like we had them back then. And I think a lot of that has to do with those changes. They took those things away.

Auburn received an 11-seed in the Southeast Regional of the NCAA Tournament, where they would face 6-seed Purdue in South Bend, Indiana.

Auburn never trailed in the game, leading by as many as 9 in the first half. The Boilermakers did manage to tie the game with less than a minute to go, but Chris Morris made a free throw to put the Tigers up, 59-58, and then grabbed a rebound on a missed Purdue shot that would have won the game at the buzzer. While Chuck Person led all scorers with 20 points, Chris Morris came in just behind him with 19. Person and Frank Ford played 39 minutes each in the win.

This game marked Auburn's first-ever NCAA Tournament win, and it sent them to the second round, where they would face 3-seed Kansas, coached by Larry Brown and starring freshman Danny

Manning—the same Manning who would go on to be the hero of the 1988 tournament.

Auburn led most of the game, but fell behind after an 11-2 Kansas run when Chuck Person picked up his fourth foul and had to take a seat. With the Jayhawks up 45-42, Person came back in and immediately delivered. He pushed the Tigers back ahead, 59-52, with less than two minutes remaining. Kansas charged back once more, until Person made a free throw with four seconds left to give Auburn a two-point lead, 66-64. The Jayhawks had one last chance to tie the game, but Manning missed his final shot and the Tigers held on for the win. Ford and Person combined for 44 of Auburn's 66 points. Calvin Thompson of Kansas led all scorers with 21 in a losing effort.

"This was a tremendous win over a great basketball team," Smith said afterward. "And I mean it. Kansas has a great team. They put a clinic on us on how to win in the last minutes of a game, and we withstood it to win. That makes it a very satisfying victory."

Somehow, some way, an Auburn team that had finished with a losing record in the SEC had made it to the Sweet Sixteen. Now they were headed back to Birmingham—the site of their improbable conference tournament victory—to face mighty North Carolina. The Tarheels, a loaded team that featured future NBA stars Brad Dougherty and Kenny Smith, were the number 2 seed in the region.

Auburn played well but eventually fell to the Tarheels, 62-56. The Tigers outscored the Heels in the second half, behind 17 points from Frank Ford and 16 from Chuck Person, but couldn't recover from a ten-point halftime deficit. Kenny Smith led all scorers with 22 points. Smith would, of course, go on to play the role of Charles Barkley's foil on future NCAA Tournament television broadcasts, after both players had long retired.

As the *New York Times* noted about the game's finish, "Auburn, which shot only 33 percent in the first half, cut the North Carolina lead to 3 points five times. With 18 seconds left, Carey Holland hit a layup to cut the margin to 58-56. Holland was fouled on the play and missed the free throw. Chuck Person grabbed the rebound for Auburn and fell to the floor but was called for traveling."

Said Person afterward, "I was pressing too hard. I was trying to score 6 points on one shot and that can't be done."

While the Tigers made the short trip home from Birmingham, that North Carolina team lost in the following round to 8-seed Villanova–the team that went on to shock the world and win the entire tournament. Villanova defeated Patrick Ewing's Georgetown in the finals, 66-64, by shooting a miraculous 79 percent.

Sonny Smith:
My biggest "what if" is we're playing North Carolina. And the winner is going to go to the (Elite Eight). And it's a tie game. They called timeout. I drew the play that North Carolina was going to run as we come out of the timeout, and I drew how we're going to stop it. And so we go out on the court, and they throw the ball in and they're running the exact play that I drew.

What happened, Gerald White was guarding Kenny Smith, who was a great North Carolina player, and Jeff Lebo, you remember that name, was the guy with the ball. Jeff dribbled the ball over towards Kenny Smith, he reverse-dribbled and started back towards the middle of the court. And he threw a behind the back pass to Kenny Smith, who banked it off the board and won the game for Carolina. And they went to the Final Four and we didn't.

Well, the problem was - we knew the play was coming. We had talked about it in the huddle. Gerald White's foot flew out from under him and he fell down, and Kenny Smith lays the ball up. And I bet everybody's thinking "Ol' Sonny didn't know what to do in that play", but Ol' Sonny *knew* what to do and so did Gerald White. And, you know, they say, "Well, somebody from the backside could have got there," (but) he shot a bank shot right before he got to the help side. And they won the game on that play.

And the "What If" for me was, I think, I think that team was good enough to win a national championship.

John Ringer:
It was a young team. Chuck Person, a junior, was the only real upperclassman. There was a lot of talent and balance.

Person was the leading scorer, but there were others that could chip in, about 8-11 points each per game, while Person was the star.

Person was on fire in the NCAA Tournament run. He was explosive at times. He scored 39 against Florida (with no three-point shot in the game yet). That's the kind of player he could be on a given day.

Van Allen Plexico:
I have few memories of this tourney. I remember hearing on the news that they lost and being disappointed, but somehow I must not have seen any of the games.

I do remember watching every minute of the SEC Tournament title game–I remember that game like it was yesterday–and being super-happy we beat Alabama in it.

John Ringer:
UNC had Dean Smith. They had lots of talent; a ton of great players. We outscored them in the second half and came back, but they played good defense. Person was 8-for-25– not a good scoring game for him. We needed him to be awesome all the time for us to have a chance against those kinds of teams.

WILL HE STAY OR WILL HE GO?

Even as the team was enjoying such success on the court, questions were mounting over whether Sonny Smith would still be the Tigers' coach after this postseason run concluded.

To this day, it remains unclear how much of the issue was truly Smith wanting to move on from Auburn, and how much of it was the Auburn higher-ups (including athletics director Pat Dye and university president James Martin) wanting to move on to a new basketball coach. Rumors indicated Auburn officials had approached Eddie Sutton (later the Kentucky coach) and Pat Foster at Lamar about the job, to little interest. Meanwhile, the Auburn players and fans were rallying around Smith, and for obvious reasons: the team was suddenly playing lights-out.

"All Pat (Dye) has said is that the door is still open," Smith said at the time. "We will sit down and talk after this weekend. But there's been no money discussed or anything. We're just going to talk."

On March 22, 1985, national sportswriter John Feinstein, writing in the *Washington Post*, addressed the issue of Smith's impending retirement:

"It was the feeling that basketball would never make it at Auburn, no matter how much the team won, that led Smith to quit in the first place. But the Tigers have since won the conference tournament and two NCAA tournament games.

"Smith says it is difficult to look at his players, many of whom wept when he told them he was quitting, and not be swayed."

Feinstein quoted Smith as saying, "You cannot look at a Chuck Person and be cold and just say, 'No, I won't think about it.' When you get emotional, you can change your mind 400 times. But when you step back, the reasons for the resignation (mainly lack of support) are still there."

Feinstein also quoted Auburn's Frank Ford: "If people want to say we're winning one for Sonny or we're doing it for the coach, that's fine with us. It's all true. We do want to win for him. We don't want him to leave."

When asked about Auburn's matchup problems against UNC, Smith replied, "Five. Six if you count coaching."

Said Feinstein: "Smith is one of those naturally funny men who seems to have a line for every situation. But like many funny people, Smith, who is 48, burns inside. Dean Smith, the North Carolina coach and a friend, said he never understood that until Sonny Smith resigned.

"'He's so funny all the time you don't realize how important all this is to him,' Dean Smith said. "I never thought about him being frustrated by things until I heard that he resigned. It surprised me.'"

Feinstein quoted Smith as comparing himself to Alabama's coach: "Inside, I'm just like Wimp Sanderson and he never smiles. Sometimes when a person is funny, people don't understand that he may not get as much enjoyment out of being funny as they do. I don't know if that makes sense or not but I've never laughed at what I say the way other people seem to.

"I've always been good at being funny on the outside but the last few years, I've gotten very frustrated on the inside."

Chuck Person was asked about the source of his coach's frustration. "At Auburn, we're about the fourth-most popular team on campus," Person said. "There's football, there's the High-Fives (an intramural basketball team made up of football players), there's women's basketball and then there's us."

Smith summed it up thusly: "Three years ago, when Pat Dye talked me out of quitting, he was right, it wasn't time. But this time, I thought it was right. It was not an emotional decision. I had thought it through."

He was asked if he was certain that this time, the decision was right. "I think so," he said. "I think so."

"The frustration level was high," he told Phillip Marshall in 2020. "I thought we should be doing better than we were. Winning the SEC Tournament was one of the highlights of my career. Being in Birmingham, beating Alabama in the championship game, that was a great day. To me, the season had been disappointing, but when you look at the overall talent in the league, I'm not sure it was."

As the question of whether Smith would remain at Auburn lingered on, a subtle change seemed to come over the broader conversation. With the Tigers winning the SEC Tournament and then making the Sweet Sixteen in the NCAAs, the conversation morphed from Sonny retiring because he couldn't get it done at Auburn to Sonny perhaps moving to a different program because he wasn't receiving enough support from Auburn. In short, as the team kept winning, he went from having little leverage in the equation to having most of the leverage. At that point, he could exert pressure on Auburn, rather than the other way around, to try to get some of the concessions he believed he needed for Auburn basketball to be more successful going forward. It helped his cause that Eastern Tennessee, the school he'd left to come to the Plains originally, was asking him about returning to that job.

"There is a strong move that's getting stronger to persuade me to stay at Auburn," he told reporters after the win over Kansas. "I don't know what is going to happen. It will depend on how I'm approached. Certain things have to happen (at Auburn, for me) to go somewhere or stay somewhere."

He denied rumors he had been offered a new deal at Auburn worth $170,000 per year.

For several days, nothing more was said. Then, three days after the loss to North Carolina that ended the season, he announced that the issue was settled and he was remaining at Auburn.

The reasons he decided to stay have never been made entirely clear. Did he get more money? A promise of more support from Dye and the Athletics Department? From the university administration? Was it simply that Auburn couldn't let him walk away, given the remarkable success his team was enjoying at that moment? Why exactly did he decide to stay?

"I am convinced that this is the right thing to do," he told the media at the time. And there it remained.

It surely didn't hurt that he would return all five starters from his Sweet Sixteen team for 1985-86.

Sonny Smith:
I was beginning to think that because of the probation that we'd taken over under and because of the slow start we'd gotten off to, that I might not be able to turn it around here (at Auburn). And I was being offered a job in another field, that was pretty good money. And I was thinking, "Well, maybe I ought to take this (other job, because) maybe this is not going to be the place that I can get it done." But all that was a "maybe" and should never even have been in my mind, but I was considering heading out (because of) that.

Van Allen Plexico:
It was interesting to learn about this during our research, because I don't remember it at all.

John Ringer:
It makes sense Sonny might do this, because he had a good run at the end, and this would be the time for him to try to market himself, especially if players are leaving soon. It would be him saying, "Let's capitalize on this (success)."

THE 1985-86 SEASON
22-11 (13-5, 2nd in the SEC)
NCAA Tournament: Elite Eight

Chuck Person (F)	Gerald White (G)
Frank Ford (G)	Terrance Howard (G)
Jeff Moore (C)	Johnny Lynn (G)
Chris Morris (F)	Vern Strickland (F)
Mike Jones (F)	Melvin Haralson (G)

The 1985-86 Auburn season was one of the more memorable and successful years in Auburn basketball history.

> **Sonny Smith (in 2022):**
> The 1986 team was fully capable of winning the national championship and that was probably my favorite team. Gerald White, Frank Ford, Chris Morris, Jeff Moore, Chuck Person. That was the time that I thought that if you were ever going to win something big here, those are the people who are going to have to do it.

The season was also stranger than you might remember.

The Tigers started off by losing badly to, and then beating badly, the same team in back-to-back games.

They played West Virginia in the first round of the Big Apple NIT in Hartford, Connecticut, on November 22, and were beaten soundly, 75-58.

"You can't pin this one on the players. This one's my fault," Smith said afterward. "West Virginia was ready for everything we did, and we weren't ready for anything they did."

"I guess I was just too anxious to get the season off to a good start. If anybody should take blame for this, it's Chuck Person," said Chuck Person. "This was the worst game I've played since, well, sixth or seventh grade."

Oddly enough, Auburn had an opportunity for revenge in their very next game, and took advantage of it. They welcomed the Mountaineers to Memorial Coliseum on December 3 and absolutely crushed them, 83-59.

AUBURN BASKETBALL

The Tigers led 45-26 at halftime, and never looked back. In the second half they pushed the lead to 57-28 and never looked back.

"I'm very happy tonight," Smith said when the game was over. "We recognized their defenses, while in the first game we didn't."

Chuck Person had a rather pedestrian night, compared to his usual standards, and the other players more than picked up the slack.

"I don't think our kids thought they could play without Chuck, which is why we got beat the first time," Smith said. "They did it tonight, so now they know."

"West Virginia knocked us around pretty good before," said Person, "so we wanted it bad tonight."

At the same time Auburn was beating the Mountaineers, Smith was also talking about bringing the series with UAB to an end. Note that this was at a time *before* Alabama was coming to Auburn to play football every other season. This was a time when all Iron Bowls were still played in Birmingham's Legion Field.

"I have to look at what's best for the Auburn program, and I'm not sure playing UAB is at the moment. I think it has to occur where we have to depend on a football crowd," Smith said. "It's putting too much pressure on us to have to play on their court all the time. If I thought I could fill up the Auburn coliseum with the UAB Blazers, it would be a different matter."

A week later, on December 10, the Tigers fell to the Blazers at the BJCC, 62-56, evening the record between the two schools at 2-2.

The home win over West Virginia was the Tigers' only victory thus far. Auburn's record stood at 1-3, and after a win over Stetson and a loss to Louisiana-Lafayette, it wasn't much better, at 2-4. The season was not unfolding the way Smith or his returning players had expected.

On December 23, the Tigers overcame previously-undefeated Boston College, 89-85, to win the Red Lobster Classic in Orlando. They had knocked off Central Florida the day before. It was Auburn's first regular-season tournament win since 1982.

"Santa Claus came early tonight by turning us into a very good basketball team," said Smith of the victory.

Chris Morris led the way with 25 points, despite playing with ten stitches in his jaw from a collision in the previous game. He was named to the all-tournament team. New addition to the team, freshman Michael Jones, scored ten.

After the holiday break, the Tigers on January 4 traveled to Gainesville–always a tough place for Auburn to play–and dropped their SEC opener to Florida, 62-59. They were now 4-5 overall, 0-1 in the SEC. What had happened to the Sweet Sixteen darlings that had been expected to make a run for the SEC title and maybe more?

"I think it's a confidence level thing," Smith said later. "That's killing us more than anything else. We've been having good effort, but our confidence level is so low. We played so tight tonight."

It didn't take long for the Tigers to correct that situation in a big way. They welcomed 11th-ranked, 10-1 Kentucky to the Coliseum two days later, and beat the Wildcats, 60-56.

Before the game, Smith challenged his players to return to the form they'd displayed at the end of the previous season. They responded, surging to a 34-20 lead at the half.

With Chuck Person injured at the end of the first half, the Tigers faltered in the second half but shot free throws well enough to hold on for the victory.

"I'm upset with my team even though we won," Smith said. "We're losing because that little extra we reached for last year hasn't shown up yet. I thought the killer instinct wasn't there when we needed it. I told the team I didn't want to be associated with the team I was associated with now. I wanted to be associated with the team I came back for."

"I don't think they would have lost five games if they'd played like this (earlier in the season)," said Kentucky coach Eddie Sutton. "They played (tonight) like they did late last season."

Chuck Person scored 18 points in the first half, before straining his back and becoming more limited in the second. Kentucky's Winston Bennett, who guarded him, described Person's play as "in another world... I just don't know what you can do when he plays like that."

"I wasn't fired up so much because it was Kentucky," Person said. "It was 6-5 Auburn (counting two exhibition wins). We've got too many good players to be .500."

The Tigers carried the momentum from that game forward for wins over Tennessee and Mississippi State. Following a loss at Alabama, they knocked off Georgia and Ole Miss. They then alternated wins and losses back and forth through the rest of January and early February, until a 1-point loss at Tennessee on February 8.

After that, they didn't lose again the rest of the regular season. They beat Miss State, Alabama, Georgia, Ole Miss, LSU and Vanderbilt in a streak of six consecutive wins.

On the night of the Vanderbilt win, Auburn set a school record for most conference wins in a season, with 13, against only 5 losses. Chuck Person scored a career-high 40 points in Vandy's Memorial Gymnasium.

"I don't think I've seen a player in a long time who just took charge like Person did tonight," said Vandy coach C.M. Newton. "I don't know what you do to defense that—an NBA three-point shot."

"Sonny was yelling, 'Get it to Chuck.' I felt I had great confidence from anywhere tonight," Person said. "I had the adrenaline flowing. I would have put it up from (anywhere)."

Sonny Smith was certain that win had locked up a third consecutive berth in the NCAA Tournament for the Tigers. "I don't want to hear anything about this (needing) one more or two more (wins). We're there."

A SHOCK IN RUPP

All signs pointed toward the Tigers roaring into the SEC Tournament in Rupp Arena in Lexington and making some serious noise, as they'd done the two previous seasons.

Auburn, coming in with the number 2 seed, didn't have to play until Thursday, the second day of the tournament. There they would meet 10-seed Mississippi State, the lowest-seeded team in the field, with a record of 8-20. The Bulldogs had advanced from Wednesday night by virtue of a 62-54 upset win over 7-seed Vandy. Beat State and Auburn would likely face Alabama in the semifinals, for another shot at Kentucky and another conference title.

Shockingly, the Tigers never got that chance. They didn't advance beyond their first game, in fact. They fell to the cellar-dwelling Bulldogs, 65-63. They were out of the SEC Tournament before they'd barely begun.

Miss State, meanwhile, became the first last-place team to make it to the semifinals. They would lose there to Alabama, who would in turn lose to Kentucky in the finals.

Auburn had led, 36-31, at halftime. But long scoring droughts in the second half allowed the Bulldogs to seize the lead. After that, the two teams traded the lead back-and-forth. Auburn had a chance to tie the game and force overtime at the end. With Chuck Person having just fouled out, however, the task of nailing that shot fell to Frank Ford, who missed.

"I felt like it was up to me," Ford said afterward. "But that might have been a mistake. There are four other players. But I feel like when the game is on the line, I can hit the shot."

Chris Morris, who wore a mask after suffering a broken nose in practice earlier in the week, scored 14 points, as did Person. They were the high-scorers for the Tigers.

Van Allen Plexico:
Poor Chris Morris! In just this season alone he'd suffered stitches to the jaw and a broken nose. Yet he kept going, kept playing hard.

He certainly put the lie to the notion that basketball isn't a contact sport!

"I drew exactly what Mississippi State was going to do in the locker room before the game," Smith said afterward. "It was like I was in the Mississippi State dressing room. They gambled. They gambled that Gerald White couldn't score (from long range). They gambled that Terrance Howard (the young Auburn point guard) couldn't score. They gambled right.

"This was exactly how Mississippi State played us in Auburn (a 69-64 win by the Tigers). After that game, (Coach) Bob Boyd came to me and said it was a heck of a thing to coach for six years and finally figure out how to beat you. They did it better this time because of a great offensive game from (guards) Robinson and Brown.

"We try to get the fast break going when we can't get inside, but they stopped our fast break, too. And we never got the ball inside."

"That was the lowest part of the season," said guard Frank Ford later. "We took a couple of days off, and we knew it was time to go out and bust our tails and redeem ourselves for that."

THE ELITE EIGHT RUN

Now all the Tigers could do was wait and see if they had done enough prior to the SEC Tournament to still make the NCAA field– or if their woeful showing there had ruined their chances. Assuming they would make it to the big dance, they also wanted to know what their seed would be, who they would be playing, and where they would be going.

As it turned out, the Tigers would be traveling all the way to Long Beach, California, as the 8-seed in the West Regional. There they would open up against the 9-seed, traditional PAC-10 power Arizona, coached by the legendary Lute Olson, in a game that, due to being in the Pacific time zone, wouldn't start until nearly 11 pm Central time.

"We were sitting around before the announcements and I said I'd like to go to Long Beach," Smith said after the field was revealed. "It just sounded more exciting. But I'm not tremendously excited about playing in that region now (after seeing the competition there). It seemed that the other teams in our conference that went were treated better. ... I'm very happy to just be going, though."

Auburn won their first game in Long Beach by double-digits, handing Olson's PAC-10 champion Wildcats a shocking 73-63 loss.

The victory gave Auburn its third 20-win season in a row, and the 10-point margin of victory represented the Tigers' largest in their three years of NCAA Tournament appearances.

Chuck Person began the game by shooting only 4 of 11, and Arizona pulled into the lead.

"I came in at halftime and the guys said to keep putting it up," said Person after the game. "They said, 'You can get the job done.'"

Michael Jones and Gerald White added 12 points each, while Jeff more scored 11 and Chris Morris added 10.

Auburn took the lead for a time in the second half. Then, with 6:50 to go in the game, the Wildcats' star player, Sean Elliott (a future All-American and NBA All-Star), scored to tie the game at 54-54.

The Tigers responded by going on a 19-9 run. From that point, they didn't look back.

"We got on the boards a whole lot better in the second half," said Smith. "Rebounding and our position defense were the keys."

Elliott led the Wildcats with 20 points. Steve Kerr scored 10. Arizona finished the season 23-9.

Next up for Auburn would be the Round of 32, and a date with the number 1 seed in the West Regional, the St John's Redmen. St John's was led by their star forward, Walter Berry, the national player of the year, as well as future NBA player Mark Jackson. Surely Auburn's run would end here, against so powerful an opponent.

As Lee Corso likes to say, "Not so fast, my friend!"

Auburn outrebounded St John's by *sixteen*, 38-22. They limited Berry to 4 points in the second half. And, shockingly, they outscored the Redmen, 81-65.

At one point in the second half, the Tigers led by 19. When the Redmen cut into that lead briefly, Auburn went on a 12-4 run to push the margin back out to 75-59 in the final four minutes.

"Auburn threw everything but the kitchen sink at us in the first half," said St John's legendary coach, Lou Carnesecca. "We tried everything to stop them—man-to-man, half-court trap, matchup. Nothing worked. Nobody belted us the way Auburn did today. It wasn't an upset. They were in charge."

After the win, Auburn's record was 21-10, while St John's was 31-5. Not hard to see why this game was considered a huge upset by most observers.

"I doubt if we could play any better than we did today," Smith said. "Winning this game is probably the best feeling I've had since we won the Southeastern Conference Tournament championship game last year."

The usually-reserved Person was breathing fire during and after the game, having outdueled the John Wooden Award-winning Berry.

"I had fire in my eyes. I was going to test Berry's strength. I thought I was stronger than he was."

Berry had the early lead in the contest between the two. "I bumped into him and he said, 'I'm an All-American.' I said, 'You're right, but I'll catch you before it's over.'"

Indeed, Berry faded in the second half and finished with only 4 points after halftime, to finish with 24. Person racked up 27, along with 15 rebounds.

Frank Ford offered a slightly different take on the static coming from Berry: "He told Chuck, 'You can't check me. I'm the Player of the Year.' He kept telling Chuck he couldn't do that."

"It was one of the few times I've never had to quiet (Person) down," said Smith. "He was saying, 'Get me the ball, get me the ball!' This is a fulfilling thing for Chuck. When he didn't make any All-American teams, he came here with something to prove."

"For us to have won that game, Berry would have had to score 130 points," said Carnesecca.

"We were like horses on the boards," said center Jeff Moore. "This was a total team effort."

Van Allen Plexico:
I remember one national sportswriter after the St John's game being quoted as saying, "Auburn runs the floor like Bo Jackson and crashes the boards like Charles Barkley."

It was just a tremendous upset and a spectacular win for Auburn Basketball and for those players and coaches.

On the same day Auburn defeated St John's, Alabama beat Illinois to also advance to the Sweet Sixteen. LSU and Kentucky were also still alive, to give the SEC *four* teams in the last sixteen standing. Meanwhile, the Big East—who had dominated the event in recent years, including having both Finals participants the previous year—had been entirely eliminated.

Having knocked off Arizona and St John's, the Tigers traveled to Houston for the Sweet Sixteen. There they would face yet *another* legendary coach, Jerry Tarkanian, and his 4-seeded UNLV, who were coming off a win over Maryland on the other side of the West bracket.

Auburn fell behind early and went into halftime trailing the Running Rebels, 34-25. In the locker room, Sonny Smith made a prediction.

"I told them we were going to make adjustments and, if they did what I told them, we would win the game. I knew they would do what we told them."

In the second half, Chuck Person rang up 17 points, giving him 25 overall, along with 11 rebounds. Gerald white scored 12, Jeff Moore added 11, and Chris Morris had 8.

Armon Gilliam of UNLV managed 21 points, and Freddie Banks added 20.

"We said we could give it all we had or we could go home," said Ford later. "We dug deep and got it. Coach Smith had confidence in us. He came in here and told us we were going to win the game."

The Tigers chipped away throughout the second half, finally overtaking the Rebels at 50-49 with just under eight minutes remaining. The two teams swapped the lead briefly, with UNLV taking their last lead at the 4:37 mark. After that, the Tigers went on a 10-2 run to put the game away.

Auburn started the game in a zone defense, but that led to the Rebels taking an early 30-16 lead. At that point, Smith changed to a man-to-man defense, which made the difference.

"We felt like we had to play them zone because we didn't feel we matched up with them inside. That turned out not to be true. That was a coaching mistake."

UNLV meanwhile ran a 1-1-3 zone that disrupted the Tigers early.

"You can't prepare for the zone they play in two days," Smith noted. "We made the adjustments to their zone at halftime and went out and got it done. We started swapping baskets, then we got the defense going. When we did that, it was over."

"The big thing was the second and third shots Auburn got," said UNLV's Tarkanian afterward. "They jumped over us to get the rebounds and made some clutch shots. They went and got it when they had to have it. You've got to give Auburn credit."

"I think we are a better team than they are," said Gilliam after the game. "It's just that they outplayed us down the stretch. I definitely think we are a better team, but we let them take the game away from us in the second half."

Van Allen Plexico:
It's always fun when opposing players still claim their team is better than yours, after you've just beaten them and ended their season. If only we'd had Twitter back then!

AUBURN BASKETBALL

That UNLV team was good, and they would only get better in the next couple of years. This was a very satisfying win, and a huge one in terms of getting us to the Elite Eight for the first time.

"I'm not thinking about (being left off the All-American teams) anymore," said Person. "I'm just thinking about helping our team get to the Final Four."

UNLV became yet another 30-plus game winner to be sent home by the 22-10 Tigers.

After the win over UNLV, Phillip Marshall wrote, "The nucleus of this team was built over a three-year period. Person signed in 1982, Frank Ford and Gerald White in 1983 and Jeff Moore and Chris Morris in 1984. None of them could see anything in Auburn's history to indicate what was ahead. But they believed and they made it happen."

"Sure I could imagine (this success) happening. That's what I wanted to do when I came here. I wanted to help build a great basketball program. I wanted Auburn to be known as a football and a basketball school," said Frank Ford after the win. "I think maybe we've passed spring football now," he added.

"I went to Auburn because it was building," explained Jeff Moore. "I wanted to be part of an up-and-coming program."

"This is a good basketball team," said Smith. "A very good one. We can play with anybody when we do what we're supposed to do."

Now only one thing stood between Auburn and its first Final Four appearance: the Louisville Cardinals, and their freshman star, Pervis Ellison.

Coming into the game, the *Birmingham News* featured a headline: "Auburn is a Win Away from the Final Four."

Alas, that was as close as the Tigers would get that season—and for the next 33 years.

Louisville won, but the game was far from a blowout. The lead swapped hands seventeen times, and was tied five times. Neither team could ever manage to pull away from the other, until the very end, at the free throw line.

Chuck Person finished with 23 points in the final game of his Auburn career. Sophomore Chris Morris added 17. Person played 38 minutes. Morris, White and Ford played 34 each. Moore played 31.

Louisville featured a full cast of players who could score, and they did; all five of their starters finished in double-digits.

"Their balance made it tough," said Person. "It's hard for one guy to ease off on his man and help out with another when everybody they put on the floor can put it in the hole."

Louisville outrebounded Auburn 37-27, and that made the difference. "Auburn did everything else well enough to win," said Phillip Marshall afterward–except win the rebounding battle. It was only the seventh time all season Auburn had been out rebounded.

"They kept us from getting the second shot," Smith observed. "Ellison was tremendous in there. He'd keep the ball alive, get it to Crook. Keep the ball alive, get it to Thompson."

Auburn was never able to increase their lead to more than 3 points.

"We couldn't make a run on them," said Jeff Moore. "They wanted it as bad as we did and played like it. They were a real good team and had to play a damn good game to beat us the way we're playing now."

With nine minutes left, Louisville switched to a zone defense—something they had rarely done that season—and it disrupted Auburn a bit, forcing the interior-loving Tigers to play more from the perimeter.

"We don't use the zone a lot," said Louisville's Billy Thompson. "We use it late in the game when we don't have a big league but are up by a few."

"I think the zone upset the tempo of the game, like we wanted it to," said Cardinals coach Denny Crum. "Auburn plays best at a steady, fast tempo. It was a pretty fast-paced game until then."

As Tracy Dodds described it, writing in the *Los Angeles Times*, "Louisville Coach Denny Crum knew he had to make a move, try a new strategy, do something to change the pace that was keeping Auburn in the basketball game. Eventually he was going to leave his tried-and-true man-to-man defense and go to that crazy zone. The question was, when. Timing is everything."

Crum wanted to hold off on that change as long as possible—and preferably until Louisville had the lead.

"I was remembering what Coach (John) Wooden always used to say. 'Be quick, but don't hurry,'" Crum said later. "I didn't want to hurry and do something too soon out of anxiety. I wanted to stay under control and not do it so soon that they would have time to adjust."

With the Cardinals' star forward, Billy Thompson, having picked up his fourth foul, Crum knew it was time to make the move. in addition to wanting to disrupt the Tigers, he also needed to relieve Thompson from having to guard Chuck Person in man-to-man defense.

"We don't even practice a zone, because I don't really like it," Crum said. "But sometimes it's the change itself that messes up the other team. I didn't do it so much to protect Billy—because I knew he would play smart—as much as to take Auburn out of what they were doing."

Crum took Thompson out for a time, but reinserted him with 10:27 remaining.

"I gambled putting him back in that early, but we needed the lead going down the stretch. If you're behind them coming down the stretch, there's no way you beat them. Not with the way they shoot free throws. If we had to foul them, we wouldn't win."

Despite the disrupting effects of the zone defense, Auburn trailed by only 3 points very late, and the Tigers were inbounding the ball with a chance to cut it to 1. The ball went to center Jeff Moore, who was supposed to pass it to Person but instead took the shot himself. Pervis Ellison blocked it and Louisville got a Jeff Hall fast-break bucket the other way, putting them up by 5 with less than two minutes to go.

Smith described it to Phillip Marshall this way in a 2020 interview:

"It came down to one play. I drew the play up. Louisville had played a zone the whole day, something they hadn't done all season. The ball had to go to Jeff Moore. He was supposed to skip it up to Chuck. It worked perfectly. But we threw it in to Jeff and he didn't respect (Louisville center) Pervis Ellison. He thought he was open. Normally, he would have been, and he was a great shooter.

"Pervis knocked it into the backcourt, Jeff Hall grabbed and it laid it up and that was it. That was our chance. We were good enough to win it. We had guard play and had the rebounding. We didn't have as much depth as some, but we managed it by playing zone. We had the formula to win it all."

After that, Auburn was forced to foul to stop the clock. Louisville made 7 of 9 free throws to seal the win.

"They had to dig deep down inside to beat us," said Frank Ford. "We weren't going to give them anything and they knew it. We gave it our best shot. They got the rebounds over the square and we didn't. We needed some more people who could jump like Chris Morris. We were a foot over the square, but they were two feet over the square."

"Yeah, we played well, but it still hurts," said Gerald White. "It meant so much. This was the biggest game of my career. I would swap any other game I've ever won, anything I've ever done, to have won this game. It's so hard because you came so far. You know you were just a couple of bad breaks from being in the Final Four."

The next day, Phillip Marshall summed it up this way: "The Tigers, who brought huge hearts and tremendous dedication to Houston, heard for two days that they couldn't beat Louisville. They never believed it. They fought their proud hearts out. They planned on winning the game."

"This has been the best year for me," said Smith afterward, "because I've handled basketball and I've handled Sonny Smith. I've had no uppers and no downers. I was down when they were crying in the dressing room, but I'm not now. I'm proud."

"He said for all of us to look him in the eye," said White. "He told us he loved us."

Chuck Person was named MVP of the West Regional, ahead of Walter Berry and Pervis Ellison. Yes—ahead of the National Player of the Year and the freshman phenom. Person averaged nearly 24 points per game in the tournament.

An *LA Times* reporter asked Person if this team would be remembered at Auburn. "We'll be remembered until about the second week of spring football practice," Person replied.

Van Allen Plexico:
That is *definitely* not true. They are *absolutely* remembered.

Louisville would go on to win the national championship, beating Dale Brown's Cinderella LSU squad in the Final Four and Duke in the Finals.

John Ringer:
I remember this team mostly for this NCAA run. They played a bunch of major basketball powers and won.

Losing in the first round of the SEC Tournament just before this didn't portend well, but then they went on the big run in the NCAA Tournament.

Van Allen Plexico:
I remember listening to Jim Fyffe calling the UNLV game on the radio. I'm not sure why I didn't see it on TV. I remember Jim talking about (UNLV coach) Jerry Tarkanian and the towel.

John Ringer:
Him chewing on the towel, yeah. (Tarkanian was notorious for chewing on towels as he paced the sidelines of basketball games.)

I either saw or heard that game. They had Gilliam and other really good players, just before they became the power they were about to become.

Auburn was the better team at that time. UNLV was winning by 9 at halftime and Auburn outscored them by 16 in the second half. The Tigers turned it on and pulled away.

Van Allen Plexico:
I can't remember now if I watched or listened to the Louisville game, or if I just heard about it later. For some reason, I wasn't able to watch the basketball team back then as much as I would have liked. Maybe it was just the limitations of television at the time—not everything was always available like it is now. But we always had Jim Fyffe!

John Ringer:
The 1986 team was a really good team. Very balanced. Athletic. We were down 1 at halftime to Louisville, but we

didn't play as well in the second half. Person had a good game but he took a lot of shots. He went 11 for 24. We needed him to hit a few more shots. Morris had 17 points, four steals, and 9 rebounds. That's pretty good against a team like that.

Sonny Smith:
We couldn't stop Louisville's play. Because Herman Crook made the winning shot, and he couldn't shoot a lick. And he made the winning shot. We had everybody else covered. And they had a great team, a great team. But we didn't cover old Herman and he made a shot to beat us.

But we were there a number of times. I was fortunate. I had really good players. I think if we could've ever gotten to the Final Four, gotten to that game, we might have won it all, because I had a really good team, really good team. It was deep, had good guards and had good size inside. And they could really play.

Van Allen Plexico:
And it seemed like we drew the eventual national champion three years in a row in our region (or close to it).

Sonny Smith:
That's funny you mention that. I mentioned that on another show. And I think they thought I was making an excuse. But the people that won it (all) are the people that beat us three times. Yes. And the best team we played in that bunch was probably that Louisville team. I mean, they were stocked from top to bottom. And their bench was really good. And we thought we had the team to beat them.

Van Allen Plexico:
I remember, after the loss to Louisville, Kevin Scarbinsky wrote a column about the current state of the Auburn basketball program in the *Birmingham News*. This was the first time I became aware of him as an individual, rather than just reading the various articles and not paying attention to who wrote what. Here's why I noted him: I was ecstatic that the Tigers had made it to the Elite Eight, after making the Sweet

AUBURN BASKETBALL

Sixteen the year before. It seemed like Auburn was getting farther and farther into the Tournament each season. So, naturally, I was already looking forward to the following year, when surely we would make the Final Four.

And then I saw Scarbinsky's *Birmingham News* Sports section headline: "Auburn's Roller Coaster is Heading Downhill."

I was shocked.

Scarbinsky was right, though. While Auburn would appear in the NCAA Tournament the following two years–and advance beyond the first round both times–the Tigers' fortunes weren't trending upwards anymore. They dropped off, leveled out, and then trended downward.

The reason, of course, was recruiting.

Van Allen Plexico:
It's been a few years since I read that column, obviously, but I believe the reason he gave was recruiting. He argued that at least one Auburn assistant had made the difference in the Tigers bringing in several top players. That coach was Tevester Anderson.

John Ringer:
The next wave of great recruits wasn't coming in. Anderson left for Georgia. You can clearly see a difference in the recruiting talent coming in after this.

Sonny had hired Anderson from Towers High School in Atlanta before the 1982 season. During his five years on the Plains, Anderson helped bring in Charles Barkley, Chuck Person, Chris Morris, Jeff Moore, Frank Ford, Gerald White, Michael Jones–the absolute key players on all of Auburn's NCAA Tournament teams under Smith.

Anderson left Auburn for Georgia after the 1986 season, and it would be at least a decade before the Tigers consistently brought in talent at anything approaching that level again.

Van Allen Plexico:
In two years of NCAA Tournament games, Sonny Smith's Auburn teams had beaten opponents coached by Gene Keady, Larry Brown, Lute Olson, Lou Carnesecca, and Jerry Tarkanian. That's practically a hall of fame of great coaches knocked off by Smith and his Tigers.

John Ringer:
That's pretty good, because nobody ever thinks of him alongside those coaches. But he beat them all.

He'd beaten some great coaches indeed. And it wouldn't be long before he'd have a shot at at least one more.

THE 1986-87 SEASON
18-13 (9-9, 5th in the SEC)
NCAA Tournament: Round of 32

Frank Ford (G)
Jeff Moore (C)
Chris Morris (F)
Mike Jones (F)
Gerald White (G)
Aundrae Davis (G)

Terrance Howard (G)
Johnny Lynn (G)
Melvin Haralson (G)
Derrick Dennison (F)
John Caylor (F)

The 1986-87 season was momentous for all of college basketball, for at least one reason: It was the year the 3-point shot came to NCAA basketball.

For Auburn, the season began in extremely promising fashion. The Tigers ranked 12 nationally to start the season, returned everyone except Chuck Person from the starting lineup. Sophomore Mike Jones moved into the starting lineup in place of Person. Senior Gerald White remained the starting point guard (and was looked-to as possibly a 3-point shooting specialist among the starters), with juniors Terrance Howard and Johnny Lynn spelling him occasionally. More of the scoring responsibility fell on the dynamic duo of Jeff Moore and Chris Morris.

Van Allen Plexico:
This year we also welcomed a 6-6 freshman from the same area of Tennessee as Sonny Smith—big man John Caylor. We'll have more to say about him later, but for now I'll note that Sonny used to say he needed Caylor to translate his Tennessee accent or dialect for the other players.

Another big freshman addition that season was forward Derrick Dennison.

We never seemed to have a lot of depth during Sonny's years, and even the 1986 team had the starters playing a lot of minutes. But as long as we could keep rolling a couple of star players out there, we did okay.

John Ringer:
When you say John Caylor, I think of his mustache and of that one game at Kentucky when he carried the team to victory in Rupp Arena. An Auburn icon for that one game.

Van Allen Plexico:
I think of him shooting threes and theatrically taking charges, going down to the floor and drawing the fouls. "OOOF!"

John Ringer:
Yes. He may have put a little flourish on there, but he got the job done.

That game was on Saturday, Jan 9, 1988. At Rupp. The final score was 53-52. Kentucky was the number 1 team in the country. Auburn was without some good players. John Caylor made it happen.

The Tigers defeated UAB, 68-58, in the BJCC on Friday, November 28—the day before the Iron Bowl in Birmingham. The two wouldn't play again until January of 1989, and the Tigers wouldn't beat the Blazers again until February 9, 1993.

Following that win, Auburn ran off six more victories, rising as high as fifth in the AP Poll, before suffering their first loss at UTEP on December 29.

The Tigers opened league play at home against Kentucky on January 3, losing by three, 63-60. They regrouped and took down Georgia, Mississippi State and Tennessee before dropping back-to-back games to Vanderbilt and 13th ranked Alabama. The Crimson Tide had one of their strongest teams of the Wimp Sanderson era that season.

The Tigers alternated wins and losses during the middle of the season, including scoring a big, 81-68 win over the 19th ranked Florida Gators in Memorial Coliseum. Nine days later, Auburn traveled to Gainesville and swept the Gators for the season, winning 84-70, and knocking Florida out of the top spot in the conference. In between those two wins, however, they dropped three straight—beginning with a home game against the last team they'd beaten the previous season.

Yes, the Running Rebels of UNLV paid a visit to the Coliseum, just a day after the Tigers had knocked off the Gators, in what was billed as the biggest basketball weekend in Auburn history.

Unfortunately, the weekend didn't end as big as it had begun. The third-ranked Rebels beat the Tigers soundly, 104-85. It was the first time an opponent scored over 100 points on Auburn since LSU in 1978. Under Jerry Tarkanian, UNLV was in the process of building a powerhouse program that would crank out NBA stars and go undefeated all the way to the national championship game, only a couple of years later.

"If they are number three, I'd sure hate to play one and two," said Frank Ford afterward.

In the first season with the three-point shot, UNLV's Freddie Banks made 9 of 14 from beyond the arc.

"They kind of sagged off on me," said Banks, of Auburn's defensive approach to him. "They should have known I was capable of hitting that shot. I was very surprised. Sonny Smith is a good coach. I was very surprised he let his players do that.

"This was revenge time for last year," he added.

"We went to a party with the Auburn guys last night, but we kind of just went on and did what we wanted. We said, 'They're all drunk now, so we're going to go out there tomorrow and beat them good.'"

Frank Ford quickly corrected the record. "No, no, no. We saw their guys and went to a reception. I know Freddie Banks personally. I went by his room. There was no drinking going on."

"They are the toughest team in the country to run a man-to-man defense against," said Tarkanian. "Sonny Smith runs a great offense. I like what he does. I'm going to put some of that in myself next year."

After the UNLV loss, the Tigers were still one of three teams remaining in contention for the SEC title, along with Kentucky and Alabama. LSU, meanwhile, had utterly collapsed after beginning the season 14-0. A 4-5 SEC record after nine games pretty much eliminated them.

Next Auburn traveled to Rupp Arena—not the best place to go to shake off a lopsided loss. Indeed, the Tigers lost to Kentucky, 75-71. This Kentucky team was not quite the powerhouse of previous seasons. Under Eddie Sutton, they would go on to finish fourth in the conference, with storm clouds brewing on the horizon already.

Following the loss to UNLV on February 1, the Tigers dropped out of the AP Poll entirely, and wouldn't return again until a brief appearance the following January.

The Tigers went 3-3 to close out the final six games of the regular season, including losing a second time to now-12th ranked Alabama, this time at home. Probably the highlight of those final few games was a season-ending 100-62 demolishing of LSU in Auburn. The Tigers ended up in the middle of the pack of the SEC, as the fifth-place team—an unusual spot for them.

Van Allen Plexico:

It seemed like under Sonny we either finished second in the SEC, or near the bottom. Fifth place was just odd.

John Ringer:

The SEC was pretty good during those years. Alabama, Florida, Kentucky were all good. That mattered. If we finish fifth and those other teams are high up in the rankings, we're doing okay.

Indeed, beginning with Smith's arrival on the Plains, the Tigers had finished ninth, ninth, ninth, eighth, eighth, second, eighth, second, and fifth in the conference.

The SEC Tournament was held that year in Atlanta for the first time. The Tigers began play at the Omni against Kentucky, a surprisingly low 4-seed. Even more surprisingly, Auburn won, defeating the Wildcats, 79-72, to reach the semifinals.

Ragan Ingram, writing in the *Montgomery Advertiser*, said the "win keeps NCAA hopes alive" for 17-11 Auburn, too.

"Every single time we made a run, they hit us back with one of their own," said Kentucky's Ed Davender.

Auburn ran a box-and-one defense to slow down freshman Rex Chapman.

"We felt we had to gimmick the game," said Smith afterward. "I thought that was a big factor for us."

"We had a very good plan," said Gerald White. "We executed it well. We did the things we needed to do to win."

All of the starters scored in double figures, led by Jeff Moore with 23. Forward Mike Jones, beginning to emerge as a force for the Tigers inside, had 17.

"He's really stepped forward," Smith said of Jones. "He's been carrying the load scoring for us lately. Michael is beginning to become the man we can turn to."

Next up, the Tigers would meet 1-seed and nationally-ninth-ranked Alabama. And there the road would end for them, as Wimp's Tide swept them in all three matchups that season. The final from the Omni was 87-68. Alabama would go on to defeat LSU in the finals for the SEC title; that LSU team was an interesting story in itself. They were the 7-seed and had begun play as one of the bottom four teams on Thursday night, and were attempting to do what only 1985 Auburn had ever done, up until then: win the SEC Tournament by playing four games in four days. LSU made it all the way to Sunday and the title game. But there they ran into an Alabama team at the top of its game, and went down, 69-62.

Van Allen Plexico:
Dale Brown had vowed not to sleep until his LSU team lost, and they almost pulled it off. It was cool to watch, and obviously I didn't root for Alabama in the finals against them,

but I have to admit I was happy afterward that Auburn remained the only team to have managed that feat.

John Ringer:
An undermanned team that punched above their weight. Dale Brown was a kind of crazy coach that presented things the other teams weren't ready for. He was kind of manic. That's a good word to describe him. They were entertaining in that they were often undermanned but made good things happen on the basketball court.

Van Allen Plexico:
The only thing crazier than Dale Brown was a four-day sleep-deprived Dale Brown.

John Ringer:
He was a good recruiter, but not a great Xs and Os coach. He took a team that had Shaq (Shaquille O'Neal) and Chris Jackson and went to Duke and got destroyed because they got outcoached gigantically.

Following the semifinal exit from the SEC Tournament, the Tigers waited to find out where the NCAA Tournament would send them—if it chose them at all. Somehow, in those days, that never seemed like quite the done deal one might think.

Auburn was given the number 8 seed again, this time in the Midwest Regional, and was dispatched to Indianapolis to face 9-seed San Diego. Waiting in the wings just happened to be Robert Montgomery Knight and his home-state Indiana Hoosiers, who crushed Fairfield in the opening round.

Auburn defeated San Diego in a close contest, winning 62-61. They had trailed by 5 at the half, but made a strong second half run. Then they turned their attention to 1-seed Indiana. Surely no one knowledgeable about basketball gave the Tigers a chance to be competitive in that game.

The Tigers came very close to shocking the world, however.

Van Allen Plexico:

I remember the *Birmingham News* headline. Something like, "Tigers Top Toreros before 29,000." Apparently there were a lot of fans in the building—but I'd imagine they were mostly of the Hoosier variety. It was kind of ridiculous that teams could basically get home games in the tournament back then.

The Indiana game is one I still remember vividly. I was so mad at the referees for the way they called the game. It was probably the first basketball game in my life that I remember yelling at the refs the whole time.

We were pushing Indiana around early, and had the lead. Mike Jones in particular was going off on them—they couldn't stop him. He later said, "I had the hot hand, and they were giving it to me."

Then Bobby Knight started whining and complaining to the refs. He and the refs congregated near midcourt, while Sonny stood off a short distance to one side of them, just openly laughing at the display Knight was putting on. But then, somehow, magically, Auburn started getting called for all kinds of fouls. Amazing how that happened. Next thing you know, Jones is on the bench with foul trouble and Indiana is on a run. We never could catch back up after that.

I wanted to throw a chair at someone myself.

John Ringer:

Bobby Knight had a reputation for intimidating officials and he absolutely did so in this NCAA tournament game. Auburn was pushing Indiana around, making good shots and getting the rebounds and loose balls. That is, until Knight had a fit and the officials changed how they were calling the game in response.

And it also didn't help that it was basically a home game for them in the NCAA tournament.

That Indiana team went on to win the title. They were good, but at halftime Auburn was only down 5. Early in the first half, Auburn was up, and Knight threw his fit, got the refs' attention. They started calling everything his way, and everything went against Auburn. Chris Morris and Frank Ford both fouled out. I think that was the difference. Jeff Moore had 4 at the end, Terrance Howard had 4. Knight's fussing at the refs worked. It mattered. Indiana was good on defense, and we had a tough time shooting on them, but Mike Jones had 30 in that game.

I think Mike Jones is one of the big "What If?" stories in Auburn Hoops. He had as much talent as some of these other great players we've had. A ton of basketball ability. Great shooter, explosive, could make things happen. I was excited to see him develop and where he could take us and what the team would look like, built around him. He averaged 16 points and 7 rebounds as a sophomore this season. I was excited to see where he could go. We were losing some other players, so he could be the future. We needed someone to be The Guy, and I thought Jones could be that guy, but it didn't work out that way.

In the next season, before he was ruled ineligible, he was averaging 22 pts, 10 rebounds and 3 assists per game. He had been a *Parade* high school all-American.

Van Allen Plexico:
And we weren't getting a ton of those.

A very partisan crowd of 34,576—only about a hundred of them Auburn fans, according to reporters who were there—looked on in the Hoosier Dome as the Hoosiers battled the Tigers. What they saw early on must have shocked them.

Auburn roared out to a 22-10 lead, with Chris Morris throwing down a thunderous alley-oop dunk about six minutes in.

"If you want to get beat by fifty points, that's all right with me!" screamed Knight to his players during the timeout after that sequence. "His outburst was loaded with expletives," noted reporter Ragan Ingram, who could hear it all clearly from the sideline.

After Knight's outburst, Auburn was whistled for six personal fouls over the next three minutes. Frank Ford received his third foul and had to sit out the remainder of the first half. Meanwhile, the massively pro-Indiana crowd booed Auburn's players relentlessly.

"Squeaking wheels get the grease," Smith said after the game. "I don't know how hard he was working the officials. I know for sure I was trying hard. But he gets more response than Sonny Smith.

"I don't know if (Knight) gets calls on the road. I think the crowd had a lot more to do with that. I don't think the officials were crooks. I think they got intimidated by the crowd and all that red."

Then came the shoving.

Urged on by Knight's rage, the Indiana players appeared determined to prove they weren't as intimidated by Auburn as they were by their own coach. Dean Garrett got into a shoving match with Jeff Moore, followed by an exchange of words. A couple of minutes later, Garret fouled Mike Jones as he was shooting. Indiana's Steve Alford attempted to lean into the Auburn huddle before Jones's foul shots, only to be summarily ejected by Gerald White. More words were exchanged, and the players had to be separated.

At that point, Knight and Smith met at midcourt, only to have Knight begin screaming at Smith.

"I can't remember what was said," Smith told reporters later. "I couldn't pass a lie detector test right now either."

"Gerald White trying to intimidate Steve after he's been playing for me for four years is like a sparrow trying to rape an elephant," Knight said after the game.

"I shouldn't have (shoved Alford)," White said later, "but Alford shouldn't have done what he did, either."

That bit aside, apparently the two coaches did settle things down a bit at the half.

"He apologized," Smith said. "I did too. We were both a little concerned at what was going on."

By the half, Indiana had finally taken the lead, 53-48. Foul trouble kept Auburn's top weapons on the bench for long stretches. Lack of depth beyond them proved fatal. In the second half, the Hoosiers pulled away. The final score was 107-90.

"I thought Indiana did a better job of adjusting to the officiating than we did," said Smith. Indiana was called for 15 fouls in the game; Auburn was called for 25.

Mike Jones finished with 31 points for the Tigers, going 9-for-9 from the free throw line. "Michael was just outstanding," Smith said. "He's really come a long way for us."

Both Chris Morris and Jeff Moore fouled out.

"We were giving it all," said Morris later. "We weren't able to adjust to the way the officials were calling the game."

"Considering what all has been said about this team this year, this team has had a pretty good year. They went through a lot here today with the officiating and the crowd, but I'm proud of them and I love 'em."

"I knew there was no tomorrow for me," said Frank Ford, after playing in his final Auburn game. "I knew if we lost, it would be the last time I'd ever suit up for Auburn. It's been a great four years. I believe most definitely I'm going out with some respect. Even though we lost today, me and Gerald and Melvin (Haralson) have done a lot of things for Auburn basketball."

"When I was deciding where to go to school," senior Gerald White said, "there were three things I wanted to accomplish. First, I wanted to play where my mom could come and see me play. Second, I wanted to be happy and play basketball, and third, I wanted to graduate. I'm happy to accomplish those goals, and to have accomplished some things for Auburn."

Auburn's season ended with a record of 18-13. Indiana went on to beat Duke and LSU to win the Regional, and then UNLV and Syracuse to win the national championship.

But for a brief while there in Indianapolis, the Tigers had them on the ropes.

Van Allen Plexico:
We know about Barkley and Person and Chris Morris and all, but I'm curious if there was a player that's not as well known to folks that you feel like really contributed tremendously to the team's success that maybe the name is not a household name, like those are?

Sonny Smith:
Frank Ford. We got Frank Ford out of Florida. He was the player of the year in Florida, but he wasn't tremendously skilled. He was just a big-time winner, he just knew how to win. When we got Frank Ford, I think I thought to myself, "We can turn this program around - right here with this guy - because he's going to help us get other good guys. Guys like a Barkley, like a Person, like Chris Morris. And we can go from

there. And we can become a good-sized winner. But we needed that one guy.

Frank Ford was a guy with a bigtime reputation out of Florida. And he was one of those guys where these recruiting surveys would pick up as the top guy. He was not any better than the guys that I mentioned to you. But he had that big name that we could use as a recruiting tool.

And he became a four-year player for us and was really, really good. I think if I had to pick somebody out that made the biggest contribution towards it for years, it probably had to be Frank Ford.

Frank Ford became my assistant when I went to VCU, and he was just as good as an assistant coach. Of course, he died at a really young age.

Ford passed away in 2018 at the age of 53, after what was described as "a long illness." At that time, he was fourteenth on Auburn's all-time scoring list, with 1,389 points. He started a school-record 127 consecutive games and led the Tigers to the NCAA Tournament in all four of his seasons, before being drafted by the Los Angeles Lakers.

THE 1987-88 SEASON
19-11 (11-7, 2nd in the SEC)
NCAA Tournament: Round of 32

Jeff Moore (C)	Derrick Dennison (F)
Chris Morris (F)	John Caylor (F)
Mike Jones (F)	Matt Geiger (C)
Terrance Howard (G)	Keenan Carpenter (G)
Johnny Lynn (G)	Dustin Hester (G)

The Tigers started off the 1987-88 season well enough. They absolutely demolished South Alabama, 120-67, at the BJCC in Birmingham, on November 27. In that game, Auburn set a team record for most points ever scored in an opening half, at 64.

Mike Jones, emerging as a major star alongside Chris Morris and Jeff Moore, scored 29 points with 10 rebounds. "He looked phenomenal at times," said Smith.

The Tigers also got a glimpse of their near future during the game, as freshman center Matt Geiger and freshman guard Keenan Carpenter scored 9 points each.

Already there was talk of Morris stepping up into the dominant role once held by Barkley and Person.

"It's time for him to assume a role of leadership," Smith said.

No one at that moment could have predicted just how true Sonny's words would be, for soon, out of the "big three" of this team, Morris would be the only one left.

The rest of December was mostly very good for the Tigers—until it wasn't.

They ran off wins against VCU and San Jose St, lost a high-scoring affair at Illinois, 107-103, and then beat Grambling and Mercer at home. At that point their record stood at 6-1.

Things looked good for this Tigers team. Unfortunately, the last week of 1987 would prove disastrous for Auburn basketball.

On Monday, December 28, rising star forward Mike Jones was removed from the Auburn team over academic difficulties. Arguably the last of the truly great players recruited onto Sonny Smith's Eighties Auburn teams, his dismissal marked a turning point—as Kevin Scarbinsky had prophesied in 1986, the Tigers' roller coaster was now heading downhill.

"There's no question we have been dealt a major setback," Smith said. "Mike Jones had been doing it all."

Van Allen Plexico:
Doing it all, except going to class, apparently.

I was a freshman or sophomore that quarter and I had a class with Mike Jones. I remember he would sleep through it. He was not terribly interested. I also got the impression he was unhappy in general with his Auburn experience at that point.

After class one day, I happened to walk out of the room just behind him and a couple of his friends, and as we walked across the concourse, I heard him saying, "The only reason I came here was because it was close to home." That worried me a bit, to put it mildly.

Not long after that, he was out of the program.

"The news didn't catch any of us by surprise," Smith added. "Mike has been one of those guys who's struggled every quarter, and it always came down to the wire. I feel sorry for (him), because I know this isn't the way he wanted to end his college career.

"This team can respond to this challenge in one of two ways. Either we can pull together and make a run at our fifth straight NCAA bid or we can fold up the tents and write off the second half of the 1987-88 season. I know the senior class doesn't want to call it quits. Now is the time for guys like Jeff Moore, Chris Morris and Terrance Howard to take charge and lead this team. Everybody's going to have to reach down inside and give a little extra."

In 2020, Sonny Smith told Phillip Marshall, "Mike Jones would have been a (NBA) lottery pick. He beat Georgia by himself over at Georgia. He played hard. He was special in practice and at games. Once he left the arena, the world was a different place. He went overseas and made enough money to buy the team in Cyprus. He married a girl over there. When he decided he'd made enough money he decided to come over here. He's doing a lot for basketball in Columbus and is a good citizen."

John Ringer:
I think he was comparable to Chris Morris on the ceiling side, but he never got to get there.

On Tuesday, December 29, the Tigers traveled to Atlanta to take part in the Cotton States Kiwanis Classic tournament. Even without Jones, they beat Villanova, 65-64, on opening night, earning them the opportunity to face tourney hosts Georgia Tech in the finals at the Omni.

John Ringer:
We attended the Georgia Tech game in the Omni on December 30, and I had been looking forward to it all year. Many of my friends went to Georgia Tech and they had a really good team that year. (This was the Kenny Anderson,

Brian Oliver, Dennis Scott team that made the Final Four that year). But I knew that Auburn could beat them with a full-strength team. Unfortunately, Jones was off the team right before this game and then Jeff Moore got hurt. He broke his hand on the rim on a play where he was hit by multiple Georgia Tech players and no foul was called.

Without Moore, the Tigers were beaten by the Yellowjackets, 83-72. The Tigers were only down 3 points when he exited the game with nearly eight minutes remaining. After that, Tech pulled away for the win.

Despite his early exit from the final game due to his injury, Jeff Moore scored 25 points and grabbed 10 rebounds. He was named the tournament MVP.

Moore had broken a bone between his left thumb and first finger. He wasn't sure when the injury had occurred. He was taken to the Hughston Clinic in Columbus, Georgia that night.

Smith said in 2020: "Jeff Moore, if he hadn't broken his hand at Georgia Tech, I think he would have been a (NBA) lottery pick."

In 2022, in conversation with the authors, Smith elaborated:

Sonny Smith:
Jeff Moore breaks his hand in a freak accident in the Georgia Tech game. He's going in for a dunk—they had breakaway rims back in those days—the guy broke the rim down trying to block Jeff Moore's dunk.

He was as good as anybody. He was the best player in the state of Alabama that year, from Midfield.

The rim was broken down, (and it) snapped the rim back on his hand and that broke his hand. And we lost him for a year there. And Jeff Moore at the time had better stats coming in than Barkley or Person or Chris Morris, and he had a better upside because he could really shoot the ball. And that break right there, I thought it was the biggest thing that stopped us from going as far as we could go. And there might have been others. But that one right there kind of stood out to me—just a rim snapping back on your best players' hand. And that was the Georgia Tech game. Bobby Crimmins was the coach of that team.

John Ringer:
I was at that game, coach. I was mad that they didn't call a foul on that play.

Sonny Smith:
You know, as I look back on that thing—and I didn't think of it at the time—I realized that Jeff did get fouled on the play. But everybody was so concerned, because his hand was mangled, with that thing snapping back. I don't know, I don't guess any of us thought about it again, because we were so concerned about Jeff, but he did get fouled on the play. He really did.

With Mike Jones gone and Jeff Moore unavailable, the burden fell almost entirely on the shoulders of Chris Morris to carry the team the rest of the season.

"He (Chris Morris) should have his name on something or have his jersey retired," Smith told a reporter in 2020. "One season he almost carried us. We're playing at Illinois one year and it's down to the final shot. They come to the bench. Chris looks at me and says 'Sonny, run that play where you throw it up in the air and I dunk it.' It was called 5-up. He didn't know that. I ran the play and he almost tore the rim down. He was an easy guy to coach. He played hard, tried hard and didn't give you any trouble."

Smith had experimented with playing some of his players at different positions–including Morris at guard–after the dismissal of Jones. After the Tech loss, however, Smith said, "I learned (tonight) you can't play people out of position and expect to compete with a team of Georgia Tech's caliber. We've got to go back to Auburn and regroup for the conference schedule."

On January 6 the Tigers began SEC play, and the season went better than some might have expected. In fact, it started out shockingly well.

The Tigers scored a big win over 15th-ranked Florida that night at home, 72-67. It would be the first of two big wins against the Gators that season. Then they traveled to Rupp Arena to face mighty Kentucky.

Before the game, one of the Auburn players held up a match to Chris Morris and asked, "How are you like this match?" Morris responded, "I'm going to be the fire that burns Kentucky."

Indeed, Kentucky burned that evening.

The Tigers, playing a slow-tempo game, shot only 37 percent but managed to hold Kentucky to 34 percent shooting.

The game was tied, 50-50, in the closing seconds when John Caylor, the 6-7 sophomore charged with filling the void left by the dismissed Michael Jones, went to the line. Caylor missed the front end of the one-and-one, however, and Rex Chapman scored a pair of free throws at the other end, giving Kentucky the lead, 52-50.

Caylor redeemed himself on the next possession, nailing a 3-pointer to put Auburn ahead, 53-52.

"Everybody probably thinks we didn't have that set up, but we got in the huddle and told John we were going to give him a chance to win the game," said Smith. "Chris (Morris) went down for the rebound dunk if there was one."

Kentucky chose not to call timeout and instead inbounded the ball and raced to the other end of the court. There Chapman missed a jump shot with three seconds left, and Caylor secured the rebound to run out the clock.

It was Kentucky's first loss of the season. Auburn moved to 9-2 overall and 2-0 in the SEC. It would be an important win later, in determining the final standings in the conference.

"This is a dream, but it ain't no nightmare," Smith said. "The last one (their 1984 win in Rupp) may be the sweetest, but this one is the biggest. Oh my goodness, what a win!"

Matt Geiger and Derrick Dennison joined Caylor as players newly contributing in major ways to the Tigers' fortunes.

"We did this without Chris Morris having a big game, but John (Caylor) had a great game on the boards. I told him he's not here for me to talk to on the bench, he's here to play now. And Matt Geiger was a big key. He got on the offensive boards with four fouls. Derrick Dennison was super off the bench."

The rest of January didn't go nearly as well, with the Tigers posting a 2-5 record over the next seven games. They then swapped a win at Florida with a loss at home to Kentucky. As of February 10, their SEC record stood at 5-6, and their chances of competing for the conference title appeared slim.

Then they went on a tear. Beginning with a victory over Georgia on February 13, the Tigers won 6 of their remaining 7 games, including wins at 17th-ranked Vanderbilt and at LSU to close out the regular season. Their final conference record was now 11-7, good enough for second place overall in the SEC. Not bad for a team that had lost two of its top three players before the conference schedule had even begun.

Van Allen Plexico:
Auburn ended the season in second place in the SEC behind Kentucky, but we split the season games with them, 1-1—and this Kentucky team later had to forfeit their conference title over recruiting violations. When I heard that last thing on the news—and I was a sophomore at the time—I immediately telephoned the Auburn Athletics office and asked if we were going to claim the SEC title for this season and raise a banner in the Coliseum. The person who answered told me, no, the title would simply be vacated. I remember being intensely disappointed by that decision—and would be again, similarly, with the 2004 football team, after USC had to vacate their ill-won title that year, with Auburn undefeated and in second place.

The Tigers drew 7th place Georgia as their opening opponent in the SEC Tournament, being played that year in the Maravich Assembly Center in Baton Rouge. Auburn had split the season series with Georgia, but the Bulldogs got the better of the Tigers that night, sending them home with a 65-60 loss. Georgia would go on to beat Florida in the semifinals and make it to the tournament finals, where they would lose a close contest to champions Kentucky.

Phillip Marshall described the Tigers in this game as "lethargic" and said they "played much of the game as if in slow motion."

Georgia took the lead 56-54 on a layup by Alec Kessler, uncle of Auburn's Walker Kessler.

The game was still in reach in the final seconds. Georgia led, 62-60, and Toney Mack missed the front end of a one-and-one, giving the Tigers a chance to tie or win. Unfortunately, with 10 seconds remaining, Patrick Hamilton of UGA stripped the ball from Jeff

Moore, who had returned from his hand injury. The Bulldogs made three free throws in the final seconds to seal the win.

"I was trying to take a charge, but he just stuck the ball up in my face," said Hamilton after the game. "Fortunately, I was able to come up with it."

This marked the second time in three years that Auburn had finished second in the conference, only to lose their opening game in the SEC Tournament.

"Georgia deserved to win," said Smith. "They deserved to win because they wanted it more than we did. I still have utmost confidence in this team. I don't have confidence in the team that played tonight, but I have confidence in the team that played the season.

We won't play like this again. We can't play like this again. We'd have to schedule a junior high to make it an even game."

Jeff Moore, back from injury, led Auburn with 22 points, followed by Chris Morris with 14.

Six days after their unexpected exit from the SEC Tournament, the Tigers squared off against Bradley—and their star player, Hersey Hawkins—in the first round of the NCAA Tournament. Playing in the Omni in Atlanta in the Southeast Regional, the Tigers found themselves in as tough of a fight as they'd faced all season.

Just as they had been the two previous years, the Tigers were given an 8 seed, meaning for the third year in a row they'd be playing a very competitive game against the 9-seed in the first round, and then likely face the 1-seed in the second round. It had worked out for them in 1986, when they'd downed 1-seed St John's. It hadn't worked out against Indiana in 1987, and 1988 would be the latter situation all over again.

The Bradley game was an exciting affair; Phillip Marshall called it "a classic; a battle of wills, a test of physical stamina and heart."

Bradley led by as many as 14 points, and were up 53-45 at the half, prompting Smith to advise his players to choose their shots more carefully and focus more on rebounding.

In the second half, the Tigers came back to tie the game and then take the lead, as the pace marginally slowed.

Auburn led by two, 88-86, with 6 seconds left, but Bradley had possession of the ball, and everyone in the arena knew where it would be going. Bradley's Hawkins was the consensus National Player of the Year, a future NBA All-Star, and (at that time) the fourth-highest-scoring player in NCAA Division 1 history, averaging over 36 points per game. Yes, everyone knew where the ball was going.

But he couldn't score if he never got the ball.

When the ball came in to Hawkins, who was running off a single pick to get a clear shot, Auburn's Terrance Howard stepped in and knocked the ball away. As the final seconds ticked away, he gathered it in and raced down the court for a dunk, just as time expired.

The Tigers had prevailed, 90-86.

"It was a big play," said Howard later. "I guess I've never made one bigger than that."

"I don't know who the guy was, but he made a big play. It was a good, clean steal," said Hawkins.

Van Allen Plexico:

Terrance Howard had a few big moments for Auburn, as basically our starting point guard his senior year. But none really compared to what he did in that game against Bradley, preventing the National Player of the Year from even getting a shot off that could win the game—and instead getting his own dunk to seal the deal at the buzzer.

When we say Auburn has never lost in the Round of 64, Terrance Howard is a big part of that.

Another key in the outcome was free-throw shooting. The Tigers made 23 of 27, while the otherwise hot-shooting Bradley Braves managed only 10 of 21.

Hawkins, coming into the game with a 36 points-per-game average as the leading scorer in the country, went for 44 against the Tigers.

It wasn't enough.

Chris Morris of Auburn responded with 36 points of his own, along with 12 rebounds and 3 blocked shots. "This is about the best game I ever played," he said later. "I wouldn't say I was trying to compete with (Hawkins). You couldn't stop him. I had to work hard and play better defense."

"He's everything he was made up to be," said Jeff Moore of Hawkins. "You might control him to about 40 or 45, but you aren't going to stop him."

"With the style of play they use, they are the best basketball team we have ever played," Smith said afterward. "They take advantage of every part of their offense. That is an outstanding basketball team. When you see four guys running and three guys rebounding, you don't know what to do. And that's the way it looked out there a lot of times. I've never seen anybody run so fast. They were already out of bounds when they caught the ball. Nobody in our league can run that way on anybody."

"One of our primary concerns was that we felt like they could have the best front line we had played against all year," said Bradley coach Stan Albeck.

The Tigers held Bradley point guard Anthony Manuel to zero points scored. "They did a great job on him," Albeck said. He added, "There is no question Morris has to be the best forward we've played against all season. He was absolutely sensational. We couldn't stop him. I think the other thing that hurt us was their free-throw shooting. They were almost letter perfect."

Sonny Smith:

You can never say enough about Chris Morris. He was incredibly, incredibly talented. We're playing at Illinois. It's a game where both teams are scoring wildly. It's getting close to 100 points for each (team) and it comes down to a final basket. We took the time out, or the Illinois coach did, one of the two. They come (and) huddle up and Chris Morris says, "Sonny, run that play where you throw it up there and I dunk it!"

"Yeah, we will run that, Chris. What is that play?" I don't know the name of the play, I just run it. "Five up" was the name of the play. We would run Chris up towards the top of the key and go screen for him with a little guy, so they couldn't switch it. If they did, he's going to dunk it. So they switched it; a 5'11" (player is) guarding him. He liked to have torn the rim down. (Then) he looked over and winked like, "Sonny, see I can coach, too!"

Chris Morris was a great player. We played Bradley when they had Hersey Hawkins. Hawkins was one of the leading scorers in the country. And he and Chris Morris had a battle. It's in the NCAA Tournament. We won the game. I'm not sure the number of points, but I've never seen two players go at each other as hard as Hersey Hawkins and Chris Morris did, and that was in Atlanta. And that was Chris Morris' home and I wanted him to really shine.

John Ringer:
I was at that game too, coach.

Sonny Smith:
We won that one! With Chris Morris. He was a great kid. Everybody thought he might be hard to coach, but he was never hard to coach. He was something. His wife is in charge of AAU basketball for women in the city of Houston. And Chris, in all his pro days, he stayed healthy. But now he's having (leg problems) Anyone who can jump as high as he did is going to have bad knees. You know, landing is a tough thing. Getting up there is not too tough, but getting down is tough.

John Ringer:
My younger brother and I attended this game in the Omni. I had a note from my parents and checked us out of high school that day to attend the game. Hawkins was a great shooter and the nation's leading scorer that year. But Auburn did not give up when things were going poorly and the team stormed back to win the game. Seeing Auburn win a game in the NCAA tournament in person was one of the highlights of my time as an Auburn fan.

The other funny thing here was, we got on the MARTA train to ride to the game, and then we noticed a bunch of our teachers and our assistant principal on the same train. They were all doing what we were doing. We had to hide!

Van Allen Plexico:
It was a very exciting game.

John Ringer:
It was very high-scoring for a game of that time. Bradley led by 8 at the half.

Auburn outscored them by 12 after halftime.

Chris Morris had 36 points, 12 rebounds, 4 assists, 3 blocks and 2 steals. That's a game right there.

Hawkins had 44 of their 90 points.

Van Allen Plexico:
That's incredible about Morris's and Hawkins's stat lines. It did turn into a monster duel between the two of them for a while.

At the end, though, it was the Terrance Howard game. The steal and dunk at the buzzer. Amazing.

John Ringer:
He scored 4 total, so that was half his points for the game.

After the game, Auburn assistant coach Ned Fowler—who had been scouting the other game in their bracket—had to report to Smith that number 3 ranked Oklahoma, the Tigers' next opponent, "run a lot like Bradley, but they have better talent than Bradley." That news flash surely couldn't have gone over well with anyone in orange and blue. Not after what they'd just survived in their game.

Van Allen Plexico:
I had almost forgotten about Ned Fowler, but we have to say something about him here. He had been the head coach at Tulane, and their entire basketball program was disbanded following a serious game-fixing and points-shaving scandal that was uncovered there. Fowler was cleared of any involvement, but the scandal tainted his reputation and he couldn't get a basketball job for a couple of years, until Sonny brought him in as an assistant.

When Fowler joined the Auburn staff, he immediately encountered Sonny Smith's famed sense of humor. "Ned," Sonny told him, "I brought you in to fix our defense. But if you can't fix the defense, just go ahead and fix the games."

The problem at Tulane, Fowler maintained, was that the university had decided to simply drop the basketball program in the wake of the scandal.

"Dropping the program magnified the situation ten thousand-fold. If the program isn't dropped, people wouldn't remember anything happened at Tulane. We probably would've been put on probation for a year, maybe two... The decision nearly destroyed me."

Fowler was selling insurance in New Orleans when Smith hired him for Auburn's staff.

"He is more of a disciplined and patient coach than me," Smith explained at the time. "We finished last in the SEC in defense last year and I thought he could help in that area."

Two days later, the Tigers had to face the loud, brash, audacious Oklahoma Sooners, led by a coach the media loved to compare to actor Jack Nicholson, and with a roster of players with nicknames like "Sky" King and "Soul Man."

Win, and Auburn would be bound for their home-away-from-home, the Birmingham-Jefferson Civic Center, where the Southeast Regional's Sweet Sixteen would be played.

Unfortunately, a seriously loaded basketball team stood in their way. Oklahoma featured future NBA players Stacy "Sky" King at center, Harvey Grant at forward (twin brother of the Chicago Bulls' Horace Grant), and guards Ricky Grace and Mookie Blaylock, along with three-point artist Dave "Soul Man" Sieger.

The Sooners, 32-3, more or less had their way with the Tigers—who didn't do themselves many favors in the stats department. Auburn shot only 34.5 percent, committed 24 fouls and turned the ball over 25 times.

Morris and Caylor ran into foul trouble early on.

"When I wasn't scoring, I knew it was going to be a difficult night," said Morris. "Then I made some silly fouls."

"I was surprised (Morris) didn't come back in," said OU coach Billy Tubbs. "He got those quick fouls and turned the ball over and then he disappeared, but I loved it. I wondered where he was, but I wasn't going to send Sonny a note and ask."

"We've been doing it (that way) since I got here," said Smith, of sitting a player the rest of the first half after they picked up two fouls.

"They're the best team we've played," said Auburn's Johnny Lynn later. "I'm not just saying that because they killed us. They've got great forwards, great guards, and great coaching. I think they might win it. They can win it if they play hard."

"They're better than Kentucky," said Howard. "One thing they have that Kentucky doesn't have is the man in the middle." Howard was referring to OU's Stacey King, who led all scorers with 37.

"It wasn't supposed to be that easy for him to get the ball," said center Matt Geiger, who was unable to limit King. "He really shot well. He's just a great player."

"We've got to just let this game go and think about the good things we've done," Lynn concluded.

"When I left the locker room," Smith said, "I told them to forget about this game. I told them to remember what they had done up to this game."

It was the final game in an Auburn uniform for Chris Morris, Jeff Moore, Terrance Howard and Johnny Lynn. They'd lost Mike Jones to academic issues earlier in the year.

Speaking of Chris Morris in 2017, Sonny Smith said, "People had the impression he was a hard player to coach. He was very easy to coach. He was just an emotional player. He played extremely hard. He was one of the most gifted athletes we've ever had here. His vertical jump, his speed from one end of the court to the other, and he became an outstanding perimeter shooter. And to be able to play fourteen years in the pros ought to give you a pretty good idea of how good he was. And you can tell he has a genuine love for Auburn. It seems to have grown. I don't think he ever got the recognition for all he accomplished in basketball. He's one of the best players we ever recruited."

Van Allen Plexico:
Chris Morris was my all-time favorite Auburn player—until Bryce Brown came along! Now he has to settle for being second.

John Ringer:
That was a great Oklahoma team. The only problem they had was they were in the same conference with Kansas and Danny Manning. They played great defense and were a high-

scoring team. They were a really great team. They came out and jumped on us with both feet, and led 51-37 at the half.

Auburn played better in the second half, but it was too much to overcome.

Van Allen Plexico:
I thought that Oklahoma team would definitely go on and win the tournament. I was shocked that Larry Brown's Kansas, the "one-man team" starring Danny Manning and a bunch of unknowns, went on to beat them for the national championship. It was the one time we got eliminated by the national runners-up instead of by the champions.

John Ringer:
I thought the NCAA title game that year, with Kansas upsetting the Sooners, was one of the best performances by a single player I've ever seen. It was Manning and a bunch of players that couldn't have gotten playing time at Oklahoma.

He was so great, he made all the difference on that one night, and took it all the way for Kansas.

THE 1988-89 SEASON
9-19 (2-16, 10th in the SEC)

Derrick Dennison (F)	Robert McKie (C)
John Caylor (F)	Kirt Hankton (F)
Matt Geiger (C)	Kelvin Ardister (F)
Keenan Carpenter (G)	Johnny Benjamin (G)
Dustin Hester (G)	Chris Brandt (C)
Zane Arnold (C)	Champ Wrencher (G)

Van Allen Plexico:
Man, did the lineup ever change after the 1987-88 season! Just a whole bunch of new names appearing on the roster for this season. And a bunch of former bench players moving into the starting lineup.

John Ringer

It was a big step down, in terms of the talent on this team compared to previous years. We didn't score as much and we gave up more points. A big drop on the defensive end. Opponents shot well against them.

Van Allen Plexico:

This team lacked those big names. We remember some of these guys fondly, but they weren't future NBA stars

John Ringer:

Matt Geiger, the tall, skinny center, was the only one who went on to play in the NBA.

Van Allen Plexico:

And he transferred away, to Georgia Tech.

Zane Arnold was on that team. Now, that's not the most common name ever, but I have a story!

A number of years ago, after I moved to the metro St Louis area to take my current job teaching at Southwestern Illinois, I was speaking with our full-time Geography professor. His name is Jeff Arnold. At one point he mentioned his son, Zane. I nodded and kept talking with him for a minute, and then all of a sudden I put two and two together and it hit me. And I was like, "Hey–wait a minute! Your son's name is 'Zane Arnold'?!" And he nodded, perplexed. And I had to explain to him that Auburn had actually had a basketball player by that name when I was in school there. I'm not sure he believed it then, or believes it now! That kid probably thought he was the only "Zane Arnold" to ever walk the Earth!

The 1988-89 team would be Sonny Smith's last at Auburn.

The Tigers would face it without one of their more colorful players. Forward John Caylor would have been entering his junior season, but a problem with a blood clot in his arm sidelined him for the year.

Auburn started out the season 4-0 overall, and with a win over Central Florida on December 29, their record stood at 7-2.

But with the new year came the SEC schedule in full—whereupon they proceeded to lose 11 straight games. Ten were to SEC teams, the eleventh was to in-state rival UAB.

The Tigers finally found the win column on February 11, with a 70-68 victory over Mississippi State. The win came thanks to a Keenan Carpenter 3-pointer with eight seconds left, followed by a block by Robert McKie.

"I just happened to get it and looked up at the clock and let it go," Carpenter said after the game. "We got the monkey off our back."

The Tigers held the Bulldogs scoreless over the final three and a half minutes of play.

"Auburn did everything they had to do to win this ballgame," said MSU coach Richard Williams. "We did not lose this ballgame; Auburn won it. I'm extremely happy for Sonny. I know what he's going through, and I know how much this win means to them. We have been there before. So even though this loss hurts, I am happy for Auburn."

But then they dropped two more, before something truly remarkable: This Auburn team—this team that stood at 1-13 in the SEC, to that point—beat Kentucky.

With the game tied at 75 and six seconds to go, Derrick Dennison was fouled in the act of shooting.

Before going to the line, Dennison got up from the floor and raised both fists to the student section.

"I was saying I was going to make the free throws," he explained later. "I've always dreamed of being in that situation—hitting a shot at the end or making free throws. It's the first time I've ever done it."

Dennison knocked down both shots. Auburn led by two, 77-75.

Then Sean Sutton of Kentucky missed his final shot at the buzzer. Auburn had held on for just their second SEC win of the year.

Dennison ran over and hugged Sonny Smith.

"Derrick Dennison was one of the biggest keys for us to win the game," Smith said. "I told him to take it to the hole, and he did just that."

Kentucky, to be fair, wasn't playing well either. This marked their sixth straight loss, dropping their record to 6-8 in the SEC.

After the Kentucky win, the Tigers lost their final three games of the regular season, then went off to Knoxville for the SEC

Tournament in the still-pretty-new Thompson-Boling Arena, and exited quickly and quietly after an 80-68 loss to Ole Miss.

"We could have won eight SEC games," said Smith that evening. "That's unbelievable for this outfit. They only quit in two games. To go out and fight every time is a credit to these people."

The season was done, just like that. A run of five straight NCAA Tournament bids was over, as well. They wouldn't return for a decade; not until Cliff Ellis's 1999 team made it back.

As for Sonny Smith, the *Montgomery Advertiser* reported as the Tigers were exiting the SEC Tournament, "Smith has been the subject of job talk lately. Virginia Commonwealth University officials have been courting Smith for the coaching job there. Smith has hedged on every statement about his future."

"People tell me, 'Sonny, you always leave a doubt,'" he told reporters at the time. "I'm 52 years old. Somebody wants to make me rich, I've got to leave a doubt. I love Auburn University. They gave me a chance to coach at this level. I don't owe Auburn anything because I think I've paid them back. I really want to stay at Auburn. I think I'll be back next year. But if the guy can stick cotton in his mouth and talk like the Godfather (an offer you can't refuse), I'll listen."

Speaking to Phillip Marshall in 2020, Smith elaborated: "There were rumors about the NCAA coming in. There were some accusations. The Eric Ramsey situation (involving improprieties in the football program) was going on. My feeling was – and I was totally wrong – that if it came down to the NCAA investigating football and basketball, they would throw me to the wolves. I ended up being cleared. I didn't want to go to VCU. I didn't even go into the meeting in the room when I went to VCU. I took an agent with me, he went in and talked, came out, shook my hand and said "Congratulations."

On Sunday, March 19, 1989, Sonny Smith announced he had been hired as the new head coach at VCU.

As Phillip Marshall described the scene at Smith's home that day, "there was no celebration. And that's sad." Smith, he said, is going to VCU "not because he wants to, but because he feels he must."

"I've gone about as far as I can go," Smith said, "and it's a long climb back to where we've been. I'd still be here if we'd recruited worth a nickel. We've said finances is the reason, but that's not really true. I told the staff to get four players or I was leaving. We didn't get them."

"When Smith arrived in 1978," Marshall noted, "Auburn was about to go on probation. It had never played a basketball game on national television or been to a postseason tournament." Under Smith, it achieved all of those things and more.

"We ought to all be sitting around here excited," Smith said after the VCU announcement, "but I just don't feel it. I haven't felt it all along.

"I hope people don't remember me just for last season," he added. "I would like for people to remember me as an Auburn man. And that's what I was."

In 2022, Smith elaborated on this decision in a discussion with the authors:

Sonny Smith:

I should have been kicked in the rear end for even thinking like (this).

The NCAA was coming in to (investigate) the football program, (because) the young man named Ramsey turned the football program in. And his best friend was one of my players. And they were best friends. So I figured with the NCAA coming in, that he was going to join forces with this friend of his (and implicate the basketball program as well) and it scared me. It really scared me, and at that time I wasn't looking to move. I wasn't looking to move.

Somebody came up with a really big offer. I went to talk to him. I won't get into too much. I went to talk to him. I didn't even go in the room with the people that decided who was getting the job. And the guy that I sent in—which is like an agent—he came out and grabbed my hand. He said, "You're the new coach of VCU." He had robbed those people. And I had to take it, you know, because of that. And it's the first job I ever got that they didn't even talk to me about.

Leaving Auburn was not one of my choices that I wanted to make. I was scared into that. And I was wrong the whole time. I probably could have finished my career at Auburn if I'd had good sense.

And so Sonny Smith departed the Plains for VCU, where he would go on to coach for nine seasons–three seasons longer than any other coach in VCU history.

Meanwhile, the Sonny Smith Era at Auburn had come to an end–at least, for the moment. But it wouldn't be the last Auburn people saw of Sonny. Oh, heavens no. After nearly a decade at VCU, among other activities, he would return to the Plains as part of the Auburn broadcast team, tossing out his homespun witticisms along with his incisive basketball analysis–to the delight of fans old and new.

Van Allen Plexico (to Sonny Smith, 2022):
Is there a game where you wish you had a do-over?

Sonny Smith:
I lost a game against Florida one time down there. Because I really hated the coach at the time, I won't mention his name.

I called the wrong play. I wanted to beat him with a spectacular play, so it would look bad on his resume. So I called the wrong play. I should have run the play for Barkley. And I didn't do that. And I lost a game. I never, ever mentioned that before. But that was one time that it really bothered me what I called. Because Norm Sloan and I were bitter enemies, by the way, and I wanted to make him look real bad.

We were at mid court and we were about to hit each other. Neither one of us could knock out a fly. Norm Sloan was the worst guy to deal with that I ever dealt with. Off the court he was one of the best. He was everyone's friend. When he got onto the court he turned into evil at its highest level. I'm not saying anything about him that I haven't already told him.

John Ringer:
You've always been known as a very funny, genuinely funny person, both when you were a coach and as a broadcaster. But I think sometimes that reputation hides how much you care about basketball and about winning, and the competitive side of you. Do you feel like that's true?

Sonny Smith:
That is true. It's not "feel like," it's absolutely true. But I was unwilling to change. I was unwilling to do what you needed to do to look more professional, more into it, smarter. Because I knew how smart I was, you know, but I just didn't think I was willing to give that up so people would think different of me.

I was always kind of a funny kind of guy, you know, joked around a lot. But there's one other thing behind it. I probably have never said openly before, but I was making so much money being funny that it was more so than coaching. I would get (invited to give) speeches that (otherwise) I would never have gotten, because of that. And I remember I was speaking in Boston, one time, and the crowd was going crazy, because I was kind of on a roll. And (afterward) I was walking around, and they had about a twenty-minute wait between people, and a guy said, "That must have been Hubie Brown, because I've never heard that other guy, whoever he was." And that was me—I was killing them in Boston.

And the thing about it, I was never able to give that up, so that I would look more professional, so that I would act more professional, because I knew what I knew. And I hoped I was going to try to use it. You had to make up your mind about what I knew. And I would say to some extent that hurt me, more so than it ever helped me. But it made a lot of money for me, at one time. Not so much now.

Van Allen Plexico:
In my research for this book I found where John Feinstein, the basketball writer, had written that Dean Smith had really complimentary things to say about you. He said that Dean Smith said, "I'd always thought of Sonny as just kind of funny and easygoing," but he said something had happened and Dean Smith realized just how intense and competitive you were. And I thought, "Man—when Dean Smith is saying that about you? That's pretty good."

John Ringer:
That was probably after that (NCAA Tournament) game (with North Carolina) that we were talking about earlier.

Sonny Smith:
I've heard it from other people. I was unwilling to give in to that type of thing. You know, act like something that you weren't.

And I look back on it. I think I could have gotten higher or better (in the coaching ranks) if I'd been more professional than I was. (I had that) "Ol' Sonny, he's crazy" type of attitude. But I was unwilling to give up on that. And I'm now not sorry, because that's carried over for me into other things that I've been able to be successful at.

And I used to think I wasn't acting enough like a coach... If I were to ask you, "What's the first thing you heard about Sonny?" (It would probably be) "Oh, Sonny, he's funny." You know, that kind of carries over to now. But I thought back then that it might probably hurt me a little bit.

I wouldn't take it back, though.

Van Allen Plexico:
Is there anything that you wish people now understood better about your time as Auburn coach? Is there a misperception out there that you think maybe people have that you would like to correct?

Sonny Smith:
I don't know. Auburn people appear to have, like, adopted me or something, you know what I mean? I'm an Auburn guy to everybody. I don't know that I was always that way. I don't know. I didn't pay attention to that type of thing. So that's really a hard question for me to answer, I don't know.

(Auburn) had never been to an NCAA (Tournament), then we went five straight years. We almost won it all. We were there all the time. I was SEC Coach of the Year three or four times, I don't know how many times, two times at least in this league, and in every league I was ever in, I was the Coach of the Year. So I didn't feel like I ever had to justify to anybody how good I was or how bad it was because I think I had this stuff (awards) on the wall. It's not that I'm bragging. I mean, I knew what I could do. And I didn't feel like I had to "act the part."

Van Allen Plexico:
How much do you enjoy being on the broadcast team (now), and how do you enjoy doing the analysis of basketball?

Sonny Smith:
That is a very good question. The reason I do this is to get front row seats. If I had to sit about halfway up, I couldn't hold the interest I have for basketball.

And fortunately I have been able to do it with such great people, with Rod and with Andy. You don't have to be critical to do it. You just tell people what you think is happening. You might not make a ton of friends but you don't lose many at all. It has been an easy job for me. I enjoy it. It has kept me close to the game. And at my age, something needs to keep me close to the game.

Sometimes I'm afraid of what I might say. When I did it with Rod Bramblett, he was one of the all-time greats. They have a button where you can turn your partner off. So I would get on one of these rants and I could see Rod's hand creeping towards the button. He was going to shut me off. I have learned. I haven't seen Andy reach for the button this year. I'm doing pretty good. I'm staying off the officials better than normal, I think. People think I'm making that up (fussing about the referees) but I'm actually mad.

But officials are so much better today than they have ever been in my life because they are so organized. They send the best ones to big games. The officiating is so much better. It is keeping up with basketball, for sure.

Van Allen Plexico (to John Ringer):
Is Sonny underrated historically?

John Ringer:
I think so. He won 339, lost 304. At Auburn, he went 173-154. In the SEC, he was under .500, especially because of those early years and the last year.

I think he took over a program that hadn't done much, and made it competitive with the NCAA powers. He deserves a lot of credit. He had us competitive with the top of the SEC for about a five-year window, but those were a really fun five years.

This 1989 team shows the recruiting was trending downward.

Van Allen Plexico:
Would you have retained him after this season?

John Ringer:
It was one bad year after several good years. I would've kept him. But I would've wanted to know, "How are we going to change that trajectory? What are we going to do about recruiting and so forth?"

He earned more time based on what he accomplished in other seasons.

In 2007, Sonny Smith was inducted into the Alabama Sports Hall of Fame. As of 2022, he remains the color analyst for the Auburn Network basketball broadcasts.

- 2 -

THE TOMMY JOE EAGLES ERA
1989 - 1994

THE HIRE

On Monday, April 3, 1989, Athletic Director Pat Dye called a news conference to introduce Tommy Joe Eagles as the new Auburn head basketball coach. That day also just happened to be Eagles' fortieth birthday.

Eagles had a record of 87-40 in four years at Louisiana Tech, with two NCAA Tournament and two NIT appearances.

"If a school wanted to take a chance on a guy who is not a big name, it couldn't get a better one than Eagles," said Louisiana Tech's sports information director, Keith Prince. "He has all the qualities you look for. He is a good community person and a church-goer and the kids like him. I think Auburn made a wise decision. We hate to lose him."

Auburn's search was conducted by Associate AD Hindman Wall. Wall settled on two names—Eagles and West Virginia's Gale Catlett—but Catlett withdrew his name from consideration. That could mean he got a better offer to stay, or it could mean Auburn gave him the opportunity to withdraw rather than not being chosen.

Eagles had been the Louisiana State Player of the Year in high school basketball, leading Doyline High to the 1967 state title. He chose Louisiana Tech for college despite having many scholarship offers to other schools mainly because his future wife had decided to go there. "I think because I came here, that's the reason he came," she said in a 2017 interview.

Once at La Tech, Eagles exhibited leadership traits immediately.

"His fierce competitiveness, leadership and his ethics and morals went way above the rest of us," said George Corley, co-captain of the team with Eagles. "If we were doing something wrong, Tommy Joe was the one that got us back in line.

"He was the guy at halftime, if he felt like you weren't doing your job, he knew how to come and talk to you. He didn't sit in the corner. (The coach) leaned on him if we had a problem on the team. He was the kind of guy that would get it done in the dressing room and on the court."

Eagles' mantra would become, "Do as I say. Exactly as I say. Do not deviate and we will be successful."

"The three things I remember about him most were how intense he was, how competitive he was and then how much of a leader he was," said SID Prince. "He had that fire. He wanted to win. He would not accept losing. You could see it in him as a young guy, as a player."

After he joined the La Tech staff as an assistant, he hit the road recruiting.

"He and Steve Welch were very good recruiters," said Dave Nitz, longtime broadcaster for the Bulldogs. "They went out and found them. Tommy Joe was great at that. His personality lent to it. He had that knack for making you feel comfortable when you were around him. His personality was just infectious."

Eagles brought in "Big Willie" Simmons from New Orleans and future Dream Teamer Karl Malone from Summerfield, Louisiana.

Eagles served for six years as an assistant at Louisiana Tech before becoming the head coach in 1985. Just as he got the Auburn job on his 40th birthday, he got the Louisiana Tech job on his 36th.

"Everything I have done since playing here has been directed at someday becoming the head basketball coach at Louisiana Tech," he said at the introductory press conference in Ruston. "It is the job I had always hoped for, and it is every bit as exciting as I felt it would be. I don't think it is any secret how much I love Louisiana Tech. This is one of the happiest days of my life."

"I don't think our fans realize that in the Eighties, we were the Gonzaga of today," said Dwayne Woodard, a Tech graduate and longtime fan. "We were a perennial Top 35 team. Tommy Joe was a huge reason for that."

The fact that Eagles' entire life seemed to have been leading him to being the head coach of Louisiana Tech made it hard for some to understand why he would leave, just four years later, to go to Auburn.

Van Allen Plexico:

One thing I want to mention before we get into the Tommy Joe Eagles era: Everyone said Tommy Joe was the nicest guy ever, and that seemed to be the case. But he had a hard, tough streak to him, too–and he played it up.

For example, we had a pretty decent-sized pep band in the bottom of the student section in those days, complete with a guy on electric guitar and a guy on a full drum set. The team would come out first, along with the assistant coaches. And then, a moment later, and very dramatically, Tommy Joe would come stalking out of the tunnel and onto the side of the court, and the pep band would kick into "Bad to the Bone," by George Thoroughgood and the Delaware Destroyers. And they'd play that as Eagles walked around the court and took his place on the side. It was always very entertaining. I never did find out whether they did that at his request or simply decided to do it on their own.

I've always had a bad feeling about dragging him away from his dream job at Louisiana Tech to put him through five years of SEC torment and then fire him.

John Ringer:

He had success at Louisiana Tech. He seemed like a guy who could make things happen. But apparently his style worked best at that level.

That said, in his first season at Auburn, he immediately made us more competitive than the previous team had been. But we went 13-18 overall.

Van Allen Plexico:
He had his moments, but he never seemed able to get it over the hump.

John Ringer:
I think the SEC as a whole was pretty good, pretty solid, during his time. I think he couldn't recruit the top-shelf players to make a difference in this league. He'd brought Karl Malone to Louisiana Tech, but he was a local down there. He got Wesley Person to Auburn, but he was a legacy.

THE 1989-90 SEASON
13-18 (8-10, 7th in the SEC)

Ronnie Battle (G)	Zane Arnold (C)
Reggie Gallon (G)	Robert McKie (C)
Derrick Dennison (F)	Chris Brandt (C)
John Caylor (F)	Champ Wrencher (G)
Dustin Hester (G)	Larry Patrick (G)

Two important names that arrived on the Plains at the same time as Tommy Joe Eagles were Reggie Gallon and Ronnie Battle. Gallon was an extremely solid and dependable point guard who played for four years for the Tigers. Battle, a highly-sought prospect coming out of Chavala High in Russell County, would go on to pass Chris Morris and move into fifth place on Auburn's all-time scoring list. (He would later be passed on that list by Wesley Person, who arrived on campus a year later.)

Despite these two exciting freshmen recruits coming in and playing immediately, Tommy Joe Eagles' tenure at Auburn did not start out in promising fashion. His 1989-90 team dropped its opening five games without a win. By the time the SEC schedule began on January 3 at Knoxville, the Tigers' record was just 3-7.

His first win in conference came against Mississippi State on January 10. He managed a big win over Kentucky on January 24, along with a four-game win streak in mid-February. But then the season ended with three straight losses, including a sweep by

Alabama. They wound up with an SEC record of 8-10, good for seventh place in the conference.

The Tigers may have entered the 1990 SEC Tournament in Orlando on a losing streak, but they took advantage of Kentucky's absence (due to probation) to skip the opening round and begin play on Friday instead of Thursday night. There they defeated 16th ranked LSU, 78-76, to move on to the semifinals. This was an LSU squad with future NBA all-stars Shaquille O'Neal and Chris Jackson among its ranks, as well as big man Stanley Roberts and Vernel Singleton.

Auburn trailed, 76-75, in the final seconds, but they had control of the ball.

"I was wanting Ronnie (Battle) to shoot it," said John Caylor after the win. Instead, the ball came to him, and he knocked down the shot with eight seconds left to lift the Tigers to the win.

"We have no one who took charge of a young team," complained LSU's Dale Brown afterward. "I went into the locker room right after the game (and) asked if anybody had anything to say. Nobody spoke up."

Chris Jackson, the LSU point guard, said, "When things aren't going well, nobody wants to speak up."

Auburn point guard Reggie Gallon said Eagles, on the other hand, was quite vocal.

He told us we were right where we wanted to be and we were playing good ball. So evidently he knew something we didn't know. (But) when someone's been telling you something all year and it keeps happening, you have to believe him."

"I think if it had ever once crossed their minds that they didn't have a chance to win, you'd be talking to LSU right now," Eagles said after the game. "It all comes back to our willingness to never quit. We could have quit, but we didn't."

Derrick Dennison led all scorers with 34 points, outdueling Shaq and Roberts.

After the game, Auburn's John Caylor spoke with reporters about his health issues. He had missed the 1988-89 season due to a blood clot in his arm, and was granted a medical redshirt. Now he was a fourth-year junior, and was considering ending his basketball career with the end of the season.

"It's something I've got to work out. I'm going to take a few days off after the season and think about it. I've got to decide if I want to play basketball and take a chance on being injured or live a normal life."

He said he'd been affected by the death of Hank Gathers of Loyola-Marymount, who collapsed during a game. Additionally, the arm had given him problems recently.

"Late in the season, it has been hurting a lot. I try not to play with fear, but it sticks in my mind."

Caylor would come back for one last season as an Auburn Tiger.

The day after defeating LSU, Auburn faced archrival Alabama in the semifinals. They brought in a record of only 13-17 overall, but had proven against LSU that they could compete.

Unfortunately, they ran into an extremely hot Alabama team and were beaten soundly, 87-71. It probably didn't help that several Tide players said they got extra motivation from Caylor's speculation before the game that Alabama couldn't beat Auburn three times in the same season. As it turned out, they could. They held Derrick Dennison to only 8 points, 26 below his output in the previous game.

The Tide would go on to defeat Ole Miss in the Finals, winning Wimp Sanderson his third SEC Tournament championship.

Eagles praised his team as they wrapped up his first season on the Plains, noting that they'd been predicted to finish last in the SEC, but had finished sixth, at 8-10. They'd also made it to the Tournament semifinals.

Not the worst of starts for a new coach in his first season and with a depleted roster. The question was, could he improve from there?

The next four years would tell the tale.

THE 1990-91 SEASON
13-16 (5-13, 8th in the SEC)

Wesley Person (G)
Ronnie Battle (G)
Reggie Gallon (G)
Derrick Dennison (F)
John Caylor (F)
Zane Arnold (C)

Robert McKie (C)
Chris Brandt (C)
Champ Wrencher (G)
Larry Patrick (G)
Cameron Boozer (C)

During the offseason, Auburn picked up one very important new addition to the Tigers' lineup: Wesley Person, the younger brother of Chuck, Auburn's all-time scoring leader. Wesley, nicknamed "Stick" because of his slender build, would go on to have a spectacular career as a Tiger before being chosen by Phoenix in the first round of the NBA Draft.

The 1990-91 season seemed to get off to a much better start than Eagles' rookie season had begun, with the Tigers carrying a 7-2 record out of their pre-SEC play. Their only two losses were away from home, coming to Villanova (in the Sugar Bowl Tournament in New Orleans) and UAB (in new Bartow Arena)–nothing to be too ashamed of.

But then came January, and the SEC schedule kicked in, and things took a downward turn rather quickly.

They started 1-4 after losses to Alabama, Florida, LSU and Vandy, and by February 6 they were 3-8. Their only wins had come against Ole Miss, Tennessee and Georgia. From there they went on to complete sweeps of Ole Miss and Tennessee—but that would be the extent of their wins. After January 23 they went 2-9 the rest of the way. The season ended with a 114-93 crushing by 13th-ranked Kentucky.

With a conference record of 5-13, ranking them eighth in the SEC, they limped into the conference tournament in Nashville.

When it came to Auburn, fans watching the 1991 SEC Tournament on television could be forgiven for suspecting they'd accidentally hit play on an old VHS tape from the previous year's tournament.

For the Tigers, the event played out like a rerun of the previous year.

Again, Auburn was able to skip to the second day of the event, thanks to Kentucky still being on probation. (Only the 9th and 10th place teams had to play on opening night.)

Again, the Tigers faced a strong LSU team in the quarterfinals–a team that had swept them in the regular season, as they had the year before–and won.

And again, they ran into an Alabama buzzsaw in the semifinals, and lost.

The win against LSU featured a 52-point turnaround from their previous matchup on February 13 in Baton Rouge. Part of that had to do with who was missing from the LSU lineup: Shaq.

"I thought we looked like lost sheep out there," said LSU's Dale Brown.

A hairline fracture had been discovered in O'Neal's left leg earlier in the week, causing him to miss the tournament.

"If they looked like lost sheep, then maybe it was because Auburn was the wolves," responded Tommy Joe Eagles.

The wolves ran into a wolf trap the following day, as 24th-ranked Alabama crushed them in the semifinals, 77-59. Auburn led throughout the first half and actually out rebounded Alabama for the game—and badly in the second half. But after halftime the Tide found its offense, took the lead and then pulled away.

"We were a little excited, and missed a lot of easy shots," said Eagles afterward. "Our team has worked hard all year long, and I hate to see the season end because I feel our team had moved to a new level this week."

Alabama would go on to win its third straight SEC Tournament, defeating Tennessee in the finals, propelled by future NBA stars Robert Horry and Latrell Sprewell.

Van Allen Plexico:

I saw Robert Horry play—and lose—in the state high school playoffs his senior year.

He played for Andalusia, and coming into the playoffs he was considered a great player and a prized recruit of Alabama. But he had to play his final high school games in Auburn, because the state tournament was being held in Memorial Coliseum.

I happened to be taking a football-coaching class in the Coliseum that quarter, and after class one day I decided to wander around the corridors a bit, curious what all was inside there. Before that quarter, I'd never even known there were classrooms in that building! As it turns out, there are all kinds of rooms under there. As well as a hallway that leads straight out onto the arena floor.

I turned a couple of corners and, lo and behold, I walked out onto the perimeter of the basketball court, which was surprising enough to me–but then I saw there was an actual game going on. So I went and sat down in the lower bleachers nearby, whereupon I realized two things. One: it was the state high school tournament, and two, I was sitting right next to Sonny Smith and several of the Auburn players!

So I hung out there and watched with them.

The two teams playing were the Iron Men of Holt and Andalusia. I recognized Horry, who was bound for Tuscaloosa, so I immediately started to root for Holt. But I didn't think they had a chance. For one thing, Andalusia had future seven-time NBA champion Horry. For another, the Holt guys all looked to be about five-foot-two each. They seemed very short, compared to the Andalusia guys.

And, would you believe, the Iron Men of Holt won? They did.

It was one of the more entertaining basketball games I've ever watched. And I got in for free, without even knowing it was going on before I sat down to see it.

So Horry might have won a bunch of NBA titles with the Lakers and Spurs, but he couldn't handle the Iron Men!

Ronnie Battle finished the 1990-91 season as Auburn's high scorer, with 17 points per game, putting him just ahead of freshman sensation Wesley Person. Person, however, would gain the upper hand in that contest the following two seasons, relegating the great Battle to second place both years, prior to his graduation.

THE 1991-92 SEASON
12-15 (5-11, 5th in the SEC West)

Wesley Person (G)
Ronnie Battle (G)
Aaron Swinson (F)
Reggie Gallon (G)
Aubrey Wiley (F)

Rod Joyce (F)
Willie Jones (C)
Chris Brandt (C)
Champ Wrencher (G)
Cameron Boozer (C)

On November 18, 1991, the NCAA placed Auburn's Men's Basketball and Tennis programs on two years' probation, stemming from recruiting and "extra benefit" infractions.

Coach Eagles and one of his assistants, Ralph Radford, were found to have "ignored NCAA rules both intentionally and inadvertently." Eagles was banned from off-campus recruiting for the five weeks prior to the April 15 national signing date, and "Radford was reassigned to an athletic department job in which he has no contact with athletes and recruits."

"I did not come to Auburn University to jeopardize the school, the program, my staff or myself," Eagles stated after the announcement of penalties. "I am embarrassed over the very existence of this situation."

The NCAA's penalties were considered "relatively light" due to Auburn's cooperation with the investigation and self-reporting of infractions. The investigation was considered as happening concurrently with the investigation into the Eric Ramsey affair in the football program, which would lead to probation and penalties during the 1993-94 seasons. Because of that, neither the football nor the basketball programs were in danger of receiving the "death penalty" for repeat violations.

In addition to the NCAA's postseason ban, the SEC rules did not permit Auburn to compete in the SEC Tournament in the spring of 1992. So, no sooner had Kentucky returned to the tournament than it was back to nine participants again, due to Auburn's absence.

As of 1992, the SEC welcomed two new members to the conference: Arkansas and South Carolina. For basketball as well as for football, the conference was divided into two 6-team divisions, East and West. Auburn would finish next-to-last in the West, at 5-11 (12-15 overall), and third from the bottom counting all teams.

The Tigers started off the year with another loss to UAB in Bartow Arena in Birmingham, this time by a score of 88-74. They finished the non-conference schedule with an away loss to Chattanooga, 87-75.

Conference play was disappointing, though Auburn did win three straight in January, beating Ole Miss, Alabama and South Carolina in consecutive games. The 81-63 home win over Alabama came when the Tide was a nationally-ranked top ten team, sitting at 9 in the AP Poll. It also ended a streak of nine straight games in the series won by the Crimson Tide. The Tigers led from start to finish and dominated the Tide the entire way.

"We needed this for our team and for Auburn," Eagles said afterward. "It was a real good performance—our team played with a lot of composure and played to win down the stretch. It was a very deserved win."

"They beat us in all phases of the game," said Alabama's Wimp Sanderson.

"(Pat Dye) told us something good was going to happen to us this season," said Tigers point guard Reggie Gallon, referring to a meeting with the Auburn AD prior to the season, when the NCAA sanctions had been announced. "The Auburn fans can get out their Auburn stuff and wear it with pride. We've finally got something to be proud of."

"This is the biggest win of my career—of my life," said guard Ronnie Battle, "because of that (losing) streak. It's over and I don't have to hear about it again."

From there, however, the Tigers would win only two more SEC games the rest of the season, beating Georgia and conference cellar-dweller Ole Miss in February. A loss to Alabama in Coleman Coliseum brought the season to an ignominious ending.

Fortunately, the Tigers were losing only center Chris Brandt and guard Champ Wrencher to graduation; the core of the team—Person, Battle, Gallon, and Aaron Swinson would be back. So too would be forward Aubrey Wiley. Wiley was a solid player for the Tigers, but is today perhaps better known as the husband of Women's Basketball three-time All-American Vickie Orr and father of 2019 Final Four team member Austin Wiley.

"They've got guts and courage in bucketfulls," Eagles said of his players after the season-ending loss in Tuscaloosa. "I've never had a team that's gone through so much adversity. And they never quit. I'm so proud of them."

Speaking of the players the Tigers had coming back the next season, Alabama's Wimp Sanderson said, "Auburn is going to be something to behold (next season). We ain't going down there."

THE 1992-93 SEASON
15-12 (8-8, 3rd in the SEC West)
NIT: First Round

Wesley Person (G)
Ronnie Battle (G)
Aaron Swinson (F)
Reggie Gallon (G)
Aubrey Wiley (F)

Rod Joyce (F)
Cameron Boozer (C)
Lance Weems (G)
Mark Hutton (F)

Of the five seasons Tommy Joe Eagles coached the Tigers, the 1992-93 season produced the best results. The fact that the Tigers finished that season only 8-8 in the SEC that year, however, and made the NIT rather than the NCAA Tournament, speaks volumes for why Eagles would only be Auburn's coach for one more season. Under Eagles, Auburn never posted a winning record in the SEC, never made the NCAAs and never won a postseason game other than in the SEC Tournament.

The Tigers began conference play with three straight losses, but followed that skid with three straight wins, capping it off with a 100-89 road win over number 8 Arkansas, to stand at 3-3 on January 23.

In the win over the Hogs, Auburn shot a blistering 67% from the field, never trailed and led by as much as 24 points.

"This is something all Auburn fans across the country should be proud of," Eagles said after the huge win.

"Coach Eagles said 'Don't play not to lose, play to win.' We played to win," said Ronnie Battle.

"That had to be one of Auburn's finest games," said Nolan Richardson, the legendary coach of Arkansas. "That doesn't surprise me. Sometimes we were in their face and they still made (the shot). There's not much you can do about that."

Throughout the rest of January and into February the Tigers mostly alternated wins and losses, including a welcome 86-74 win over UAB in Birmingham on February 9. But on the 17th of that month they began a run that closed out their regular season with five wins and only one loss. Unsurprisingly, that lone loss was to second-ranked Kentucky at Rupp–but the way that game ended was both exhilarating and excruciating for the Tigers.

With less than 2 seconds remaining against the Wildcats, Kentucky scored to go up by two, 80-78. Auburn's Mark Hutton inbounded the ball using a long, overhanded, football-type pass that was partially deflected on the way but still somehow found the hands of Wesley Person, who squared up and released a potentially-game-winning three-point attempt just before the buzzer sounded. The ball hit the rim and bounced off.

"Oh yes," Person said afterward, when asked if he'd thought his shot was going in. "I thought I had put my best stuff on it."

"I thought the shot was dead middle," said Kentucky Coach Rick Pitino. "They did what they had to do to execute down the stretch and we got lucky."

"I'm tired of being the Senior Day opponent for Kentucky," Eagles half-joked. "I want that on the record."

After the Kentucky loss, they beat Alabama at home, 78-70, before completing the season sweep of now-13th-ranked Arkansas, 81-80.

Van Allen Plexico:

I had just moved back to Auburn a few days before that home game against Arkansas in 1993. My roommate, Dennis, and I went to the game and yelled our heads off for the Tigers. When it was over, we dutifully headed up to Toomer's Corner to be a part of the inevitable celebration.

The problem was, nobody else was there. I have no idea why, but apparently nobody else felt it was worth rolling the trees over. But this was a highly-ranked Arkansas team—a team that would win the national championship the next year, with mostly the same players—and a really big win. We had every intention of rolling the Corner.

Now, I've been to plenty of Toomer's Corner celebrations in my life, but I'd never been one to bring a roll of toilet paper myself. Up until that point, I'd never had to. Usually there would be plenty already on hand, and you just grab one off the ground and toss it back up there. But, this time, my buddy and I were there, but there was no TP!

So we looked around and thought for a minute, and then turned our attention to Toomer's Drugs, right across the intersection.

"Do you think they have toilet paper?" I asked.

"Maybe?" he replied.

Now, in retrospect—of course they did. But I'd never thought about it before.

So we strolled over there, asked for TP, and they took a pack of it out of a cabinet and sold it to us for a couple of bucks.

As we were leaving the store, I was wondering, "Do they know what we plan to do with it?"

Well, again, in retrospect, of course they did. It was Toomer's Drugs, for crying out loud.

"Roll it good!" called out the guy behind the counter as we left. So, yeah, they definitely knew.

So Dennis and I rolled Toomer's Corner by ourselves that day. It was kind of a surreal experience, being the only ones out there.

But we did indeed "roll it good."

Auburn's final regular-season record of 8-8 in the conference meant they had to open play in the SEC Tournament in Rupp Arena against the worst team in the Eastern Division, Tennessee, on Thursday night. The game did not go as Auburn fans would have hoped; the Vols won, 78-76, and Eagles' only team with a non-losing record in the SEC was sent home immediately.

All was not lost, however. The Tigers had at last qualified for postseason play beyond the SEC variety. Being invited to the 1993 NIT marked Auburn's first appearance in any such event since the 1988 team had fallen to Oklahoma in the second round of the NCAAs.

Auburn faced their future head coach Cliff Ellis's Clemson Tigers, whose record in the ACC was not terribly different from Auburn's that season in the SEC.

The Tigers from South Carolina prevailed over the Tigers from Alabama, 84-72, and Auburn's season was done. (Ellis's Clemson would go on to lose to UAB in the second round; just over a year later, he would become the new Auburn head coach.)

THE 1993-94 SEASON
11-17 (3-13, 6th in the SEC West)

Wesley Person (G)	Lance Weems (G)
Aaron Swinson (F)	Mark Hutton (F)
Aubrey Wiley (F)	Leonard Smith (G)
Rod Joyce (F)	Pat Burke (C)
Wes Flanigan (G)	Shawn Stuart (G)
Cameron Boozer (C)	

The 1993-94 season would be Tommy Joe Eagles' final campaign with the Auburn Tigers. What lay ahead for him, however, no one could have imagined.

The season would see Auburn back at the bottom of the SEC West, with only three conference wins all year long. Throw in another loss to UAB and a three-game sweep by Alabama, and it was clear by the end that a change was coming.

The SEC gauntlet began on January 5 with a home loss to Georgia in overtime. The Tigers would not taste victory in the conference until a win over LSU on February 12–a run of ten straight SEC losses. Three of those defeats came in overtime, and one of them in double-overtime.

By the time Auburn faced LSU at home on February 12, they had lost ten straight SEC games. But then something strange happened: The Tigers in orange and blue went off.

Senior forward Aaron Swinson scored 30 points and grabbed 8 rebounds as the Tigers overall shot 62 percent and hung 111 on the Bayou Bengals, who only managed 83 points themselves.

"They could have beaten anyone today," said LSU's Dale Brown. "It was their destiny."

The 28-point thrashing of LSU unleashed a mini-run of victories that eventually extended to four straight, before the Tigers dropped their final three—one of which was to national number 1 team Arkansas, on their way to the national championship.

In the SEC Tournament at the Pyramid in Memphis, the Tigers faced Vanderbilt, a team that had hammered them 84-60 in Nashville on February 9. This time, the tables were turned, and the Tigers crushed the Commodores, 81-56, to advance to the second round for the first time since Eagles' first season.

Unfortunately, there the Tigers met old nemesis Alabama, and fell to the Tide, 83-55. It was Alabama's biggest win in program history over Auburn.

Apparently, it was also the last straw.

On March 15, the Tuesday after the SEC Tournament ended, and after five seasons at the helm of the program, Auburn fired Tommy Joe Eagles.

The coach reportedly accepted a $140,000 settlement from Auburn after a get-together with university president Dr. William Muse.

"After meeting with the president, it is clear to me that Auburn basketball needs a new direction," Eagles said in a statement after the meeting. "I bear no ill will toward Dr. Muse or toward Auburn."

Eagles had seemed at first like the right man for the job, and he was well-liked by nearly everyone. But he was never able to get the Tigers over the hump in terms of recruiting, post-season play, or wins. After half a decade of effort, the university had decided to move on.

In the four SEC Tournaments in which the Tigers participated during Eagles' five seasons with the Tigers, Auburn was eliminated by Alabama three times and by Tennessee once. They advanced beyond the first game three times, beating LSU twice and Vanderbilt once. They never won a second game in an SEC Tournament. And they participated in only one other postseason tournament, losing to Clemson in the first round of the 1993 NIT.

Just having Wesley Person on the team was probably the high point of the Eagles era for Auburn. He was drafted 23rd overall by the Phoenix Suns in the 1994 NBA Draft, where he briefly played alongside Charles Barkley, and was named to the NBA All-Rookie Second Team. He went on to an 11-year career in the NBA, also playing in Cleveland, Memphis, Portland, Atlanta, Miami and

Denver. Reports suggest he earned over $40 million during his pro career. Auburn later retired his jersey, number 11.

Van Allen Plexico:
Wesley Person was a great player for us. I only wish he could've been a part of some more successful teams. Certainly he did everything he could as a part of those teams.

And then came a very shocking event, just a short time after Auburn terminated the coach.

John Ringer:
It was very sad, what happened to Tommy Joe Eagles after Auburn fired him.

But we were justified in letting him go. We hadn't made the tournament in several years and it was time for a change.

THE TRAGEDY

Not long after separating from Auburn, Tommy Joe Eagles was hired as the new head coach at the University of New Orleans. By all reports, he was thrilled; it wasn't his beloved Louisiana Tech, but it was a good job in his home state, close to home and at a level where he'd proven to be competitive before.

Just after being hired, he went on a recruiting trip that included a stop in Salt Lake City on July 30 to visit some former players and assistant coaches. He was shooting basketball with former Auburn player Aaron Swinson when he "made an easy pass to Swinson and kneeled over." Then he collapsed to the floor. Shortly afterward, he was pronounced dead. He was 45 years old.

The AP reported on August 1, 1994 that an autopsy had shown Eagles had an enlarged heart, "probably from a virus," according to K.D. Kilpatrick of Kilpatrick Funeral Home in Ruston, Louisiana.

"He was the type of guy who you thought would live to be 120," said former Louisiana Tech teammate George Corley. "It shocked me to the end. It was devastating, one of the biggest blows for me. Tommy Joe and I were really close. My wife and his wife were extremely close. It was a big loss for us all."

"I just think God has his hand on Tommy Joe," his widow, Connie Eagles, said in 2017. "He would go on basketball trips and he would get in late on a Saturday night and he'd be teaching a Sunday school class on Sunday morning. He was a really good father as well. My children were blessed. When you are in that position, you are away from your kids a lot.

"I got a lot of letters from his players after he passed away. One was even from a kid I never laid eyes on who was an athlete from Alabama. We were at a conference meeting and the kid got an award. He wrote that when he was being presented the award, he could see Tommy Joe really paying attention. Tommy Joe went up to him afterwards and congratulated him. He wanted me to know how much that meant to him."

In 2017, Eagles was inducted into the Louisiana Tech Athletics Hall of Fame.

Van Allen Plexico:
I try to look on whatever little bit of "bright side" there might be here. Tommy Joe was on his way back to Louisiana to coach, which was his home state and where he was happiest, I think. I'd like to believe he would've been successful at New Orleans. I'd also like to think he was at peace with his tenure at Auburn and the way things ended there, and was looking forward to the new challenge, when he passed away. I hope that was the case. He was by all accounts a really good guy and I always enjoyed seeing him on our sideline, even when the team wasn't playing at its best.

I will always think of him coming out on the floor of the Coliseum when I hear, "Bad to the Bone."

- 3 -
THE CLIFF ELLIS ERA
1994 - 2004

The coach who would soon be hired to replace Tommy Joe Eagles was one with a somewhat familiar face to Auburn fans. He'd coached against the Tigers at both South Alabama and Clemson in recent years.

Van Allen Plexico:
When we talk about the Cliff Ellis era at Auburn, I think we first have to mention the "Cliff Dwellers."

Upon his arrival, and in order to fire up the students and get them more involved in the program and louder at games, Ellis instituted a name for the student section of the coliseum. He had the cheerleaders give out free t-shirts with that name on them to any student at the games who wanted one. The shirts varied from season to season, but were always bright orange, with big and bold white letters that read, CLIFF DWELLERS. I was in graduate school and was going to all the games back then, and I was able to get one. I know quite a few other folks who had them, and some have told me they still do.

It was cool to have a nickname for the student section, well before the days of "The Jungle," and we enjoyed it a great deal. It helped, of course, when we started winning consistently, after the first few years under Ellis.

John Ringer:

He had taken Clemson to the NCAA three times in eight years. One year they won the ACC, when it was really good. So that was an impressive accomplishment. He was a solid coach, and *solid* was a long way up from where Auburn was at that point.

I was okay with the hire. It made sense to me. It wasn't the flashiest national hire, but Auburn wasn't going to get that kind of coach at that time. We needed someone who could build a firm foundation, and he struck me as a coach who could do that. Plus he had connections to the state, from his time at South Alabama.

Van Allen Plexico:

My first reaction was, "Wait–the guy who said he was 'burned out' coaching at Clemson? Suddenly he's not burned out anymore?"

I always wondered if that was some kind of ploy to get him out of a deal at Clemson, so Auburn could hire him. I think he liked the idea of not having to coach against UNC and Duke and that whole ACC murderer's row of teams every night. Getting to coach at Starkville and Oxford and being hailed as a mighty conqueror if you win at Tuscaloosa probably sounded pretty attractive to him, after a decade of what he'd faced at Clemson.

We joke about the relatively easy schedule Clemson's *football* team usually has to overcome, but the flip side of that coin is what their *basketball* program has to deal with, being in the same conference as Duke, North Carolina, NC State, Virginia, Wake Forest, and on and on. It's pretty brutal.

THE HIRE

On April 5, 1994, the *Montgomery Advertiser* ran a story by Paul Newberry of the Associated Press, with the headline, "AU Search Drags into Third Week." The first line was, "Does anyone want this job?"

"Mack McCarthy of Tennessee-Chattanooga was reportedly the front-runner for the job," Newberry reported. "Then he said he didn't want the post when it appeared set to go to Duke assistant Mike Brey. Then Brey said he didn't want it, either."

> **Van Allen Plexico:**
> I do remember some talk that we could land Brey, a hot, up-and-coming assistant to Coach K at Duke. That seemed exciting—if someone like that couldn't build us a solid program, who could? But then he appeared to back out, for reasons that were never disclosed—though we can certainly speculate about them. Probably some of the same reasons that caused Sonny to consider leaving, a few years earlier.

Auburn trustee Jack Venable noted that the financial package Auburn was offering, which came to around $200,000 a year, was not competitive compared to what other schools could offer. "Yes, it could be a problem in getting a coach to come from a successful program."

Venable also noted a reluctance on the part of Auburn to hire another coach from a smaller program. "We tried that with Coach Eagles," he said. "There was not a nicer fellow in the world."

Just after that story went to press on April 5, Athletic Director David Housel broke the word that the Tigers had indeed found their man: Cliff Ellis, 48, the former coach at Clemson and South Alabama.

"I'm not a miracle worker. I can't walk on water. But I'm going to try to walk on water," Ellis said at his introductory press conference. "In the ACC, I had to deal with seven Kentuckys. In the SEC, I think there are more like-situations. If they can do it in Fayetteville, Arkansas, we can do it in Auburn."

"It's what I thrive on," Ellis replied when asked about the need for rebuilding at Auburn. "That's why Auburn was perfect for me. I had other opportunities. I had to make a decision, but this is the one that needs revitalizing. (That) is where Cliff Ellis gets his satisfaction. That's what I do best."

Ellis had resigned as Clemson's coach on January 7, though he finished out the remainder of the season, including leading the team to the NIT. At the time, rumors had it that he had "burned out" and didn't want to coach basketball any longer.

"I'm in the prime of my career," Ellis responded. "I feel like I had taken Clemson's basketball program as far as I could possibly take it."

"We're committed to having a competitive basketball program and supporting it at the level it needs to be competitive," said Auburn President William Muse. "We've done comparative analysis of basketball budgets for all the SEC schools. We know the areas we need to provide support."

Ellis's financial package at Auburn included a $100,000 base salary and other incentives that were expected to push the total deal to around $200,000, as expected.

When asked about Brey and other candidates that declined or were not selected for the job, Housel replied, "I will simply say this. You don't always marry the first person you date. And when you come to the altar, you don't talk about some of the ladies and gentlemen you have dated."

What challenges would Ellis face on the Plains? One national reporter (unnamed in the wire service report used here) put it this way: "When Cliff Ellis resigned after a decade as Clemson's basketball coach, he said he was looking for new challenges. Tuesday, he found a big one, taking over an Auburn team that has had only one winning season in six years. (Tommy Joe) Eagles, who resigned under pressure on March 15, left behind a program in shambles."

Ellis's team the day he arrived consisted of just six remaining players: Pat Burke, Jim Costner, Leroy Davis, Lance Weems, Franklin Williams and Wes Flanigan. He emphasized the need to get out on the road and start recruiting immediately, though he conceded he was "behind the eight ball when it comes to recruiting. All you can do now is salvage. What we have to do now is beg for mercy. It's a long shot."

THE 1994-95 SEASON
16-13 (7-9, 4th in the SEC West)
NIT: First Round

Moochie Norris (G)
Chris Davis (F)
Wes Flanigan (G)
Lance Weems (G)
Franklin Williams (F)

Pat Burke (C)
Ray Donald (G)
Jim Costner (C)
Leroy Davis (F)

Cliff Ellis's first season on the Plains resulted in an improved win/loss record—only 1 win away from breaking even in the SEC—and victories over UAB and a ranked Florida team, as well as a two-game sweep of ranked Mississippi State.

The Tigers' biggest win, however, was a stomping of fifth-ranked Arkansas in Beard-Eaves Coliseum on January 14. On the front page of the *Montgomery Advertiser*, the headline in the left-side column read, "Tigers Roast Hogs: Auburn uses long-range shooting to defeat number 5 Arkansas 104-90, handing the Razorbacks their worst SEC loss ever." The Sports section headlines were even better. Playing off Hogs coach Nolan Richardson's famed "Forty minutes of Hell" motto, the top banner read, "Forty Minutes of Heaven: Sizzling Auburn Stuns Razorbacks." Sports Editor Jim Johnston added his own opinion column headline to the side: "Ellis Gets a Win to Build Off Of."

"Auburn shot 70 percent from the field against college basketball's best defensive team," Johnston noted. "A team that lost a 22-point decision (in an exhibition game) to Marathon Oil less than two months ago held a 24-point lead over the defending national champions with 17:40 to play Saturday." They also made 13 of 21 three-point shots, and outrebounded Arkansas.

"I can't believe this happened. I never dreamed SEC basketball could be this good," said Auburn point guard Moochie Norris. "Right now, this is the best I've ever felt in my life."

"We've come a long way," said Ellis. "A further distance than I thought we would. You don't get the chance to have the defending national champions in your place very often. You have to capitalize on it."

"Guys that can't shoot, shoot out the lights against us. Guys that can't jump, jump out of the gym against us," said Richardson. "We bring out the best in everyone we play."

Arkansas made a late run to pull within single digits, but the Tigers responded by making their free throws down the stretch to preserve the win.

Wes Flanigan summed it up. About to shoot a free throw with only a couple of minutes remaining in the game and Auburn well ahead, an Arkansas player told him, "The pressure's on you." Flanigan scoffed at that. "There's no pressure on me. I'm going to beat you tonight."

Johnston summed it up with a prediction: "You can't count on seeing another college basketball game like Saturday's in your lifetime."

There might have been hope after crushing Arkansas that the Tigers were about to go on an unexpected run of wins and finish off the season strong. Alas, that did not occur. Other big wins that season were few and far between. They were swept by Alabama and LSU, and ended up 7-9 in the conference.

With the fourth seed in the SEC West, they met South Carolina on Thursday night and won big, 81-66.

That victory brought with it a matchup with now-third-ranked Kentucky, who had pounded them mercilessly at Rupp, 98-64, on January 4. This time the Tigers gave a slightly better accounting of themselves, but still fell to the Wildcats, 93-81. (Kentucky would go on to win the tournament finals with an overtime victory over Arkansas, who clearly recovered nicely from their mugging on the Plains.)

The season wasn't over, though. At 16-12 overall, Tigers made the field of the NIT, where they would meet Marquette—and do so in Beard-Eaves Coliseum. It marked only the second non-SEC postseason game for Auburn in seven years.

As they had the last time they played in the NIT, they lost.

In his book, *Cliff Ellis: The Winning Edge*, written with Phillip Marshall, Ellis talked about the significance of Auburn hosting that NIT game: "I knew we weren't going to the NCAA Tournament, but I believed that this team deserved to play in the postseason. I knew the people at the NIT, so I flew to meet with them in New York and took David (Housel) with me. Auburn had never hosted a national tournament game. I felt that in the first year this would be a great reward. I asked (the NIT folks) 'If we get in, please consider that we are a program that has won some big games but never has had a home NIT game.'

"We received a bid and hosted Marquette... (they were) a national program. It was an event; the fans really got into it. It was a great game. We built a big lead, but we couldn't hold it and lost. Marquette went on to the finals in New York. It was disappointing to lose, but it was a great event. It had gotten the people excited.

"We had started the season with 1,000 people at our game. By the end of the year, there were thousands. The Coliseum was full for the NIT game. It was loud. It was a great atmosphere. We had won the fans over, and (hosting that game) was really a significant win for the program."

Following that season, Ellis bought a house at Lake Martin and happily settled into the Auburn community.

"I felt really good after the first year," he said in his book. "I had won some coach of the year awards. I thought we were headed in the right direction. We had overachieved as a team and had nearly everyone back for the upcoming year."

Indeed, the Tigers landed one of their more impressive signing classes in the offseason of 1995, in what Ellis described as "a Top 15 class." Astonishingly, they snagged the "Mr. Basketball" winners from both Alabama and Kentucky, in guards Doc Robinson and Daymeon Fishback. Fishback's dad had played for Ellis at Cumberland, so there was an existing connection there; Robinson appreciated Auburn's style of basketball and liked the assistant coaches.

In addition to those two guards, this class included Chris Porter and Mamadou N'Diaye. Porter was, in Ellis's words, "not heavily recruited," though he would have a major impact on the Plains after a brief stint at Chipola Junior College. N'Diaye was a seven-foot-tall center from Senegal. Those four players would form the core of the squad that would dominate the SEC just a few years later.

THE 1995-96 SEASON
19-13 (6-10, 5th in the SEC West)
NIT: First Round

Wes Flanigan (G)
Lance Weems (G)
Franklin Williams (F)
Pat Burke (C)
Ray Donald (G)

Derek Caldwell (G)
Alvin Jefferson (F)
Bryant Smith (G)
Adirian Chilliest (F)

Unfortunately, just prior to the start of the 1995-96 season, two mainstays from the previous season were lost to the Tigers. Starting point guard Moochie Norris and power forward Chris Davis ran into issues with their junior college credits. In an era before the "clearinghouse" that makes such rulings early, Auburn's administration decided to play things safe and not allow the two to play. Both transferred, with Norris eventually ending up in the NBA. The Tigers, meanwhile, had to forge ahead without two starters they'd prepared all offseason to have available.

They opened the season playing in a tournament in Puerto Rico, and won the first two games to reach the finals on the strength of Lance Weems and Wes Flanigan at guard. In the title game, they met a 13th-ranked Louisville team that threatened to run them out of the gym in the first half. Ellis remarked later that he had to light into the Tigers at halftime and encourage them to "show we are better than this." Amazingly, Auburn came back to win the game and the tournament. "It took sheer will, guts and determination to pull off that upset," Ellis said in his book. "It was a win I'll never forget and one I don't think Auburn fans will ever forget. It marks one of the great comebacks in Auburn basketball history."

Somehow this team then won a second tournament, this one over Baylor in Waco, Texas. They went into the SEC schedule with a record of 12-1. A couple of games into it, they rang up the Razorbacks for another huge upset, 101-76, behind a barrage of three-pointers from Lance Weems. The *Montgomery Advertiser's* Johnston had been proven wrong; Forty Minutes of Hell had frozen over again, and only a year later.

After the second upset of mighty Arkansas in back-to-back years, the season took a downward turn for Auburn; Ellis attributed it in part to their unexpected lack of depth taking its toll over time. Briefly ranked in the Top 25, they ended up 19-13 overall, 6-10 in the SEC, and with the 5 seed in the West in the SEC Tournament in New Orleans. They did manage a first-round win over Vanderbilt, 68-65, but lost to a very strong Mississippi State team in the quarterfinals, 69-58. Those Bulldogs would go on to beat Kentucky by double-digits to win the tournament.

Auburn ended the season by hosting an NIT game for the second-straight season. (It's remarkable to consider that a team that finished with only 6 wins in the conference, and finished fifth in its division, not only made a postseason tournament but hosted its first-round game.) Again they lost, though, falling to Tulane in overtime, 87-73.

The season hadn't turned out quite the way Auburn fans might have hoped, but in two years with the Tigers, Cliff Ellis had led them to opening-round wins in the SEC Tournament and back-to-back postseason tournament appearances–easily Auburn's best showing since the heyday of Sonny Smith's great teams.

THE 1996-1997 SEASON
16-15 (6-10, 3rd in the SEC West)

Wes Flanigan (G)	Pat Burke (C)
Doc Robinson (G)	Derek Caldwell (G)
Daymeon Fishback (G)	Alvin Jefferson (F)
Mamadou N'Diaye (C)	Bryant Smith (G)
Franklin Williams (F)	Adirian Chilliest (F)

After losing to UAB and then losing two out of three games in the Big Island Invitational Tournament to begin the season, the Tigers looked to struggle even worse in 1996-97 than they had at the end of the previous year.

Fortunately, the schedule improved for them immediately after that. They had five straight home games, and won four of them, losing only to Baylor. They closed out the pre-SEC portion of the schedule with three more wins and went into league play at 9-4.

The SEC portion of the season was another mixed bag, with more losses than wins, and never more than two wins in a row. They closed out the regular season by dropping four of their last five.

One of their six SEC wins had been over Tennessee, and the Tigers faced the Vols again in the first round of the tournament at the Pyramid in Memphis. Auburn won handily, 67-54, to advance to the quarterfinals. There, however, they ran into Kentucky—never a welcome sight before the final game of the tournament. Rick Pitino's Wildcats pounded Auburn mercilessly, winning 92-50. They outrebounded the Tigers by an eye-popping 30 boards, 56-26. The newspaper headline the next day read, "A Heavy Dose of Reality."

"We really had no answer for them," said guard Wes Flanigan, who was hit with a technical foul after a brief altercation with Kentucky's star, Ron Mercer. Mercer had elbowed Flanigan in the head; Flanigan didn't retaliate, but he did stand up to Mercer. Notorious referee John Clougherty signaled the technical on Flanigan anyway.

"It always seems like when Clougherty is refereeing, I'm always the guilty person," Flanigan observed.

Ellis stated after the game that he felt the Tigers deserved to make the NIT field, and hoped they would.

They did not.

There would be no more postseason action; just like that, the 1996-97 season had come and gone.

THE 1997-98 SEASON
16-14 (7-9, 3rd in the SEC West)
NIT: Second Round

Doc Robinson (G)
Daymeon Fishback (G)
Scott Pohlman (G)
Mamadou N'Diaye (C)
Franklin Williams (F)

Bryant Smith (G)
Adirian Chilliest (F)
Randy Hughes (F)
Clifton Robinson (G)

While still not achieving a winning record in the conference, the Tigers did finish with another winning record overall, and missed .500 in the SEC by just one game. The rookies of that great recruiting class were maturing into solid players, and better days were coming.

After a home overtime win over Mississippi State on February 7, the Tigers stood at 6-4 in the conference and the future looked very bright. But then things turned sour; they lost five of their last six regular-season games and ended up 7-9.

In the SEC Tournament in the Georgia Dome, they drew Florida, the team that had started that losing streak, and again the Gators' star, Kenyan Weaks, was too much for them. Weaks went for a career-high 31 points and 10 rebounds as Florida beat Auburn again, 68-64.

The Tigers left Atlanta wondering if they would even make the NIT field.

They needn't have worried. Ellis did put the Tigers in the NIT for the third time in his four seasons, and this time they won a game, defeating the Southern Miss Golden Eagles at home on March 11, by a score of 77-62. That win broke their five-game losing streak and sent them to the Bradley Center in Milwaukee to play another bunch of Golden Eagles. This time they faced Marquette, the team that had eliminated them in the first round a couple of years earlier. Again the Tigers couldn't overcome the team from Wisconsin, and the season had come to an end with just one win in their final seven games.

Based on the previous several seasons under Cliff Ellis, no one could have predicted what this Auburn team would accomplish just a few short months later.

THE 1998-99 SEASON
29-4 (14-2, 1st in the SEC West)
NCAA Tournament: Sweet 16

Chris Porter (F)
Doc Robinson (G)
Daymeon Fishback (G)
Scott Pohlman (G)
Mamadou N'Diaye (C)
Franklin Williams (F)

Bryant Smith (G)
Adirian Chilliest (F)
Jay Heard (G)
Mac McGadney (F)
Reggie Sharp (G)

The Tigers began the 1998-99 season with a lineup that included Chris Porter, Scott Pohlman, Doc Robinson, Daymeon Fishback, Mamadou N'Diaye and Bryant Smith.

They won the SEC regular season title outright, and won it by two games over Kentucky. They wouldn't lose a game until January 20, a winning streak of 17 games, not counting exhibitions; and after that, they began a new streak and didn't lose again until February 24. Those two losses were their only missteps in the entire regular season. Their other two losses would be at the ends of their runs in the SEC and NCAA tournaments. Both of those losses came to the team ranked at that time as 14th in the country. And half their losses the entire season came at the hands of Tubby Smith's Kentucky.

After an undefeated nonconference run in November and December, the Tigers opened SEC play with a win over Tennessee. The next game up, the Tigers pounded 19th-ranked Arkansas, 83-66, on January 6.

The winning continued until January 20, when the Tigers had to travel to Rupp Arena to meet the defending SEC and National Champions, the Kentucky Wildcats.

"One would think Auburn could not do any better than (starting the season 17-0)," said *Montgomery Advertiser* Sports Editor J.C. Clemons. "But in the SEC, you can't get to the top without conquering Mt. Kentucky."

"If anybody still doubts this (Auburn) team, they've been living in a tunnel for a long time. Facts are facts, and it's Auburn—not Duke, not Kentucky—it's Auburn (that's 17-0). We did it. You can't take it away. Usually they'd be yawning (at Rupp Arena) when Auburn came to town. They won't be yawning (this time)."

"The thing I like so much about Auburn is they are so unselfish. They are a great role team," said Florida coach Billy Donovan. "They have great chemistry."

Much good was said of the leadership of Doc Robinson at point guard after the Florida win. "He knew what it was like to win," Ellis said of Robinson, who had led his high school team to the state title. "He brought that to the table when he came here."

"It'll be fun. We know (Kentucky) will be a war," Ellis noted, "but it's the kind of game you look forward to."

The number 6 Tigers did their best, but it simply wasn't enough against the number 7 Wildcats in Rupp. Auburn fell, 72-62. Three of the Tigers' players, including Robinson, were mostly ineffective due to illness–the ubiquitous "flu" sports teams always use to describe any respiratory illness.

"When you take a guy like (Robinson) and he can't play, it's tough," Ellis said. "But I don't want to use that as an excuse. Kentucky played a good game and hit the shots when they needed to."

Fortunately for the Tigers, even as they were losing in Lexington, Ole Miss–one of the teams challenging them for the division title–lost to Miss State, preserving Auburn's two-game lead in the West.

"We must now look at our mistakes and go from there," said star forward Chris Porter after the game. "We will make ourselves better as a team from this loss."

Three days later, the Tigers got themselves back on the winning track with a 73-58 win over Alabama in Tuscaloosa. They finished out the regular season with just one more loss–a 104-88 defeat at Arkansas. With a win at Miss State on February 27, the Tigers locked up the SEC Championship. Cliff Ellis was voted the SEC Coach of the Year, and Chris Porter and Doc Robinson were both named to the first-team All-SEC team. The Tigers wouldn't land two players on the first team again until 2022.

When Auburn began play in the SEC Tournament in the Georgia Dome in the quarterfinals–as the winners of the West, they were able to skip the opening round–they were ranked 4th in the country and faced old nemesis Alabama. What they did to the Tide that day was not for the faint of heart to witness: they annihilated the Tide by 32 points, winning 93-61, and completing the three-game season sweep. It was the first time since 1960 that Auburn beat Alabama three times in the same season.

Auburn's game plan was to run Alabama ragged—to use the Tigers' depth to tire out the Tide players. "We worked their defense so hard by running the floor and substituting that it was actually *our* best defense—getting them tired from chasing us," said Auburn assistant coach Shannon Weaver. "When teams get tired, they tend to turn the ball over."

"Until we beat Kentucky, it's not totally complete," said Fishback, a native of Kentucky himself. "But we're playing well right now and we got a lot of confidence with this win. I think we're hungry for this one."

Said Kevin Sims of the *Montgomery Advertiser*, "Ellis has already converted Auburn (fans)... The Auburn RVs—the ones normally gassed up only during football season—were muscling in on what has been Kentucky and Arkansas parking spaces at the Georgia Dome."

A Tennessee team that finished 12-4 actually won the East over Kentucky, and so they entered the SEC Tournament with the 1-seed in the East. The Vols promptly fell in their opening game to Miss State, 62-58. This turned out to be unfortunate for Auburn, because it meant Kentucky, as the number 2 seed in the East, was sent to the other side of the bracket, and would face the Tigers in the semis.

Once again, the Wildcats prevailed. This time, they won by 12 points, 69-57. Auburn was out of the SEC Tournament before the final game again.

None of that really mattered, though, because the Tigers had captured a number 1 seed in the NCAA Tournament–the first time they'd ever achieved that position. Sitting atop the South Regional, they opened play in the RCA Dome in Indianapolis against Winthrop, and promptly strangled the Eagles, 80-41.

Next up was Oklahoma State, coached by former Kentucky boss Eddie Sutton. The Cowboys had finished fourth in the Big 12. They couldn't hang with Auburn in the Round of 32, and fell, 81-74.

"It feels great to be going to the Sweet 16," said Bryant Smith, a senior on this team, after the win over the Cowboys. "It's something we set as a goal but I didn't know if I would ever get there."

That game had very quickly become the Scott Pohlman show. At one point he scored 13 points in 5 minutes of game action.

"I don't understand what (Oklahoma State) was doing. They were paying too much attention to Chris Porter, I guess," said Adrian Chilliest. "They forgot about Scotty and you can't do that. Well, you can, but now you see what happens."

"When you have a guy hot like that and feeling the rhythm, you just give him the ball," said Doc Robinson. "We saw he was in the zone or whatever, so we ran plays that set up shots for him. That makes things kind of easy for me."

"He ran me to death today," Oklahoma State's point guard, Doug Gottlieb, said of Pohlman. "He played a tremendous game today. He hit big shots and, every time he got open, it seemed like he hit."

"I don't know what it was," Pohlman said. "I was just getting good looks (at the basket). I don't know how to explain it. I don't know how to explain the feeling I have right now. This is just a dream come true. This is a special win because we won a tough game and we're in the Sweet 16. I don't think it gets any better than this feeling right now."

Pohlman finished with 28 points, leading all scorers in the game.

Now the Tigers got to travel to the NCAA Regional hub city of Knoxville, Tennessee, to play 4-seed Ohio State in the Sweet Sixteen in Thompson-Bolling Arena. This time the competition was too much for the Tigers–particularly the guard play–and they fell to Scoonie Penn, Michael Redd and the rest of the Buckeyes, 72-64.

"Down the stretch, we boxed out really well," said Ohio State's Redd. "That was our plan tonight—to keep them off the boards."

Penn had given the Tigers fits for 30 minutes, but was pulled with his fourth foul midway through the second half. Auburn responded with a 9-2 run to seemingly take control of the game. Ohio State coach Jim O'Brien felt he had no choice but to put Penn back into the game, and it made all the difference. The Buckeyes surged ahead again, on the strength of 13 points from Penn in the final 10 minutes.

"When Scoonie was on the bench, I was trying to buy as much time as I could," O'Brien said. "We got behind and I didn't want to lose the game with our best player on the bench. Putting him back in wasn't that big of a deal."

"I didn't know when (Coach O'Brien) would put me back in the game," Penn said, "but when it started to get bad, he put me in and told me not to have any dumb fouls. I've played like that before, and I just concentrated on what I needed to do."

"They won eight games last year and look at them now with Penn," Ellis said of the Buckeyes' point guard, who had transferred in from Boston College. "He's a turnaround player. He's not a good player, he's a great player."

Van Allen Plexico:

I remember being so disappointed when they lost in the SEC Tournament and then in the NCAAs. This was the best Auburn team I'd ever seen—it looked to be even better than the 1986 team. I don't think I ever imagined they would actually win the national championship, but I thought they could go at least as far as the 1986 team did—to the Elite Eight—and maybe make the Final Four.

It really does show how important guard play can be in the big show. When your guards get hot—like with Jared and

Bryce in 2019–you can go a long way. Scoonie Penn got super-hot and took the Buckeyes all the way to the Final Four. They ran over us along the way.

Auburn became the first number 1 seed to exit the tournament. Ohio State continued on, defeating St John's and reaching the Final Four, before losing to UConn.

Ellis was named the SEC and National Coach of the Year.

John Ringer:
It was an incredibly fun team, and it was great to have a team that was competitive and won.

Chris Porter is the one you think of immediately, but there were so many other good, well-coached players. It was a fun team to watch.

They played a certain style. It was not a great shooting team, but they would turn you over, and when the defense was playing well, they could beat anybody.

Van Allen Plexico:
We had a good "big man" center in Mamadou N'Diaye—a rarity for us. Doc was great at the point. Daymeon Fishback had been Mr. Kentucky Basketball; it still amazes me we were able to get someone with that accolade to his name, even with the family connections he had to Ellis. And Chris Porter was amazing, obviously. Plus guys like Scott Pohlman and Bryant Smith and Adrian Chilliest and more. Just a great lineup.

John Ringer:
This team was similar to Bruce's team in 2021-22. They lost at Rupp Arena and lost at Arkansas. They won a lot of games early that weren't quite as tough. A lot of it was athletic ability and good defense. When they played a team with as much or more talent, that was a problem for them.

Van Allen Plexico:
I was super-disappointed when they lost to Ohio State in the Sweet 16. As the number 1 seed in the region, I thought that was a game we'd be able to win.

John Ringer:
I thought we could make the Final Four that year. Penn and Redd carved us up. We did not have a great game. The Buckeyes held us to 26 points in the first half. It ended up 72-64. That was probably the lowest point total we scored in a half all year.

THE 1999-2000 SEASON
24-10 (9-7, 2nd in the SEC West)
NCAA Tournament: Round of 32

Chris Porter (F)	Mac McGadney (F)
Doc Robinson (G)	Reggie Sharp (G)
Daymeon Fishback (G)	Marquis Daniels (G)
Scott Pohlman (G)	Jamison Brewer (G)
Mamadou N'Diaye (C)	David Hamilton (F)
Jay Heard (G)	

The following season started off with the Tigers as blazing hot as they'd been the previous year. They defeated UAB, 65-59, hosting them in Auburn for the first time since 1995. They dropped a neutral-site game to Stanford, but then went on a tear, not losing again until January 22. The run included a home win over Kentucky, 66-63, on January 11. By that point, their record stood at 16-1.

A 79-77 overtime loss at Ole Miss ended their streak, followed by a loss three days later at 11th-ranked Tennessee in Knoxville. The Tigers turned things around, winning a three-game stretch of home games, including beating Alabama and Arkansas. From that point on, though, they'd go 2-5 to finish out the regular season. Meanwhile, a crisis was brewing inside the team; a crisis that would deprive them of their best player.

After a stellar first season with the Tigers, in which he earned SEC Rookie of the Year and Player of the Year honors, junior college transfer forward Chris Porter had returned to Auburn in the hopes of helping his team make the Final Four, as well as graduating with his degree in Criminal Justice.

Instead, Porter found himself on the other end of the NCAA's justice system.

It happened three games from the end of the regular season. As the Tigers were on a road trip to Gainesville to play Florida, Porter, an AP preseason All-American, admitted to Ellis that he had accepted $2500 from someone—a person Porter did not believe to be a sports agent at the time. Porter was suspended and sent back to Auburn while the team went on play the Gators without him and get blown out, 88-59.

Porter had appeared on the cover of *Sports Illustrated* coming into the season, with SI choosing Auburn as the nation's number 1 team. "And Chris Porter is the reason why," the cover noted in big letters, over Porter dunking the basketball.

The dreaded cover jinx had struck again.

Porter admitted to school and SEC officials that he had accepted the money. He said he had done so to prevent his mother from being evicted from her home in Abbeville. He didn't realize at the time that taking the money would harm his eligibility, he said.

"Chris has admitted to a mistake," Ellis told reporters afterward. "He has been honest and forthcoming. I'm now hoping honesty prevails and Chris will be allowed back on the court."

"I know that Chris had been distraught over what seemingly had been a family matter," Ellis added. "And last Thursday he was allowed to go home to Abbeville to attend to a family concern."

Ellis said team officials repeatedly had to chase away "suspicious people" from hotel lobbies, presumably referring to unscrupulous sports agents wishing to sign star athletes to contracts before anyone else could. Ellis said the team had taken to registering Porter, Mamadou N'diaye and Doc Robinson under false names to throw off the agents. "I am sick of people who prey on young people and hit them at a weak moment. If you are put in a situation, you can't turn to a coach, you can't turn to a booster, so sometimes in a weak moment you fall prey," said Ellis.

Auburn coaches were hoping Porter would be quickly reinstated by the SEC, before senior day on March 1.

"He has done too much for this game and for Auburn University not to be a part of (senior day)," Ellis said. "I just hope he is allowed to come back to this game that he loves so much."

Unfortunately, he was not. And word of that came down just as the Tigers were finishing off the same team that had beaten them so mercilessly just two weeks earlier.

Auburn may have limped into the SEC Tournament on a four-game losing streak, but they turned things around quickly when they got to the Georgia Dome, even without Porter. They beat number 11 Florida in the quarterfinals, 78-70, on Friday.

The day they'd played Florida the previous time had been the same day they'd gotten the news that Chris Porter was suspended. This time, after the second game with the Gators, word came down that Porter's appeal had failed. He was off the team for good.

"I am very sorry for what I did," Porter said in a prepared statement. "I think the verdict was a little too harsh, I admit I was wrong. I am still supporting the team a hundred percent. I love my teammates, coaches and fans."

"He said he didn't have any idea the money came from an agent," said Auburn AD David Housel, noting that Porter had said he thought it came from "a friend of a friend."

Meanwhile, the rest of the team proceeded to go out and take care of Florida in surprising fashion.

"We underestimated them," said Gators forward Mike Miller.

"We put everything we had into this game," Ellis said.

"I came in with the mindset that we have precious little time left together," said senior Daymeon Fishback, who scored 21 points, grabbed 14 rebounds and went 6-6 from the free throw line. Despite playing with a painful cyst in one knee, Fishback decided to pick up the slack left behind by Porter and carry his team to victory.

"He really stepped it up tonight," said Scott Pohlman. "He's a big boost to us. He always has been."

On Saturday they followed up their remarkable win over Florida with a 77-72 win over a surprising South Carolina team that had already knocked Alabama and a top-ten-ranked Tennessee out.

Just like that, and without their preseason All-American forward, Auburn was in the finals of the SEC Tournament, where they would face the Arkansas Razorbacks.

Van Allen Plexico:
The only thing I remember thinking when the Chris Porter news broke was, "Of course." It just seemed like such an

"Auburn thing" for our best player to suddenly be in trouble and kicked off the team. Something similar would happen a few years later with Cam Newton and the football team, of course. So I wasn't surprised then, either. I probably would've been much more surprised if the team had held together all the way through the season and actually made it to the Final Four.

John Ringer:
(In regard to the zero-tolerance attitude of the NCAA and the penalty on Porter.) It was such a different time.

And so disappointing. He was the star. That was the derailing of the momentum of that team. They weren't the same after losing him.

But give Ellis credit here. We lost Porter, we lost the last two regular-season games, and then turned around and had this run in the SEC Tournament. Ellis changed how the team played, and adjusted to Porter not being there.

It seems odd to describe any Arkansas basketball team from this era as "Cinderella," but this bunch of Hogs had finished the regular season third in the West, one spot behind Auburn, and had split the home-and-home series with the Tigers. While never winning more than two consecutive games in the regular season, they had gotten things together when it counted. They had rallied and beaten a bad Georgia team in the first round and then upset 16th-ranked Kentucky to advance to the semis, where they then upset the top-seeded SEC West team, LSU. The finals therefore pitted West 2 vs West 3, with Auburn having the added challenge of preventing Arkansas from duplicating their own miraculous feat: winning it all after starting on the first day of the tournament.

It was a tight contest and the Tigers hung in there for a while, but ultimately Nolan Richardson's Hogs pulled it out, 75-67. This despite Auburn winning the rebounding battle, 41-20, while allowing Arkansas only 3 offensive rebounds the entire game. The Tigers, however, committed 17 turnovers, leading to 26 Razorback points. Auburn also had to play with freshman Marquis Daniels replacing the missing Chris Porter.

What Arkansas lacked in height, they more than made up for in quickness, stealing the ball on multiple occasions and getting quick transition scores.

"Their press got us off-kilter a little bit," Ellis said afterward.

This Arkansas team became the first to win the SEC Tournament after starting on the opening night and winning four straight games since Sonny Smith's Auburn team accomplished the feat in 1985. It marked Nolan Richardson's first SEC title with Arkansas in nine tries to that point.

Van Allen Plexico:
This was my first ever chance to see the SEC Tournament in person. I was living in the Atlanta area and working at the hospital in Lawrenceville, doing graphic design and public relations work. Somehow I managed to buy a ticket book for the entire tournament. There was a medical conference happening at the World Congress Center that week, so I convinced my boss that it would be a great idea to send me down there on Friday afternoon to check out the medical whatever. I have no idea what it was all about; I walked briefly through the exhibit, then headed straight across the lawn to the Georgia Dome, arriving just in time to witness Auburn taking down an 11th-ranked Florida team, coached by Billy Donovan. It was so great.

I went back for the win over South Carolina on Saturday and I was there for the final game on Sunday. When that one was over, I was so disappointed, I sat there in the middle ring of the Dome and watched Arkansas receive the trophy and celebrate, and I didn't feel like moving. The Georgia Dome workers eventually had to come up and order me to leave. I just wanted to sit there and sulk.

The Tigers found themselves back in the NCAA Tournament once again, this time sent to Minneapolis as part of the Midwest Regional. A 7-seed, they opened play against 10-seed Creighton, and won, 72-69. Mack McGadney sealed the deal for the Tigers with a 3-point shot in the final 2 minutes.

"It's been said that big-time players make big-time shots," McGadney said afterward. "I guess that means I'm becoming a big-time player, right?"

There was a bit of drama before the game was over, however.

Mamadou N'diaye hit two free throws to give the Tigers a 72-63 lead, but then Creighton hit a three-pointer, stole the inbounds and hit another three. With less than four seconds left, the score was suddenly 72-69. Fishback inbounded the ball in a long pass that sailed past N'diaye without being touched. Now Creighton had 3.8 seconds to score and send a game that should have been over with to overtime.

They got the ball in bounds on Auburn's end of the court. Creighton's Ben Walker launched a long three-point shot. N'diaye blocked it.

Game over.

"It never should have happened," Ellis said afterward. "The game should've been over."

Fortunately for the Tigers, it was.

From there they continued to the Round of 32, where they met the 2-seed in the Midwest Region, Iowa State. The Cyclones handled the Tigers relatively easily, winning 79-60. The crowd in the Metrodome in Minneapolis was described as overwhelmingly pro-Cyclone. Only a few hundred Auburn fans sat in the rows behind the Auburn bench. "What a disadvantage it must have been for Auburn," noted Iowa State coach Larry Eustachy.

Auburn double-teamed and triple-teamed Iowa State's star player, Marcus Fizer, but that just opened up his teammates for long shots.

"The plan worked. For a while," said Jay Tate in the *Montgomery Advertiser*. "But as Fizer's teammates began to hit shots from the outside, Auburn couldn't stay with the 6-foot-8 forward full-time. Shortly after, the Cyclones slammed the Tigers from all sides."

The season was at an end, as were the Auburn careers of several major contributors over the past few years–seniors from the winningest class in Auburn history.

"I didn't want to think about it at first," said N'diaye, "but really, I have no regrets. Yes, I wish we went to the Final Four and won a championship, but I'm thankful for everything."

"Of course I'm sad. There was a lot of emotion but we learned a lot from each other and from (Coach Ellis)," said Doc Robinson. "I'll take all the experiences I've had at Auburn and move on in my life."

"I thought how much we've been blessed over these four years," said Daymeon Fishback.

THE 2000-2001 SEASON
18-14 (7-9, 5th in the SEC West)
NIT: Second Round

Scott Pohlman (G)	David Hamilton (F)
Mack McGadney (F)	Adam Harrington (G)
Reggie Sharp (G)	Lincoln Glass (G)
Marquis Daniels (G)	Abdou Diame (F)
Jamison Brewer (G)	Kyle Davis (C)

The big names from the last several seasons were mostly gone by 2000-01. This would be Marquis Daniels' team, along with Scott Pohlman and Adam Harrington and Jamison Brewer and Mack McGadney.

Pohlman and Reggie Sharp were the only seniors on the team. Inexperience showed; the Tigers lost to Mercer, Toledo and South Alabama before the holidays, and then dropped three of their first four SEC games. By the time the regular season was over, they'd managed to win just 7 conference games, good for 5th in the West.

They lost in overtime to Tennessee in the first game of the SEC Tournament, 73-66. Tennessee would go on to lose in the next round to Ole Miss, who actually won the West that year and made it to the title game.

Despite their early exit from the league tourney, the Tigers received an invitation to the NIT where they would host another first round game.

Van Allen Plexico:
One thing about Cliff Ellis: I don't know how he did it, but he was consistently able to get Auburn into the NIT, if we didn't make the big show—even in years that we had a pretty shaky W/L record. And he was able to get us at least one home

game in it, a lot of the time. I mean, we would have preferred to be in the NCAA Tournament every year, but if that wasn't going to happen, the NIT certainly beat staying home with no more basketball to play for the season.

The Tigers beat Miami, 60-58, at home, but then had to travel to Indiana to face Purdue. The Boilermakers took them down, 79-61, in Mackey Arena.

After the game, excited Purdue players spoke of planning to go on and win the tournament. Instead, they fell to Alabama in the very next game.

Kyle Davis led Auburn against Purdue with 19 points and 9 rebounds. Reporters remarked afterward on the youth of this Auburn team: the Tigers played nine freshmen and sophomores in the last few games of the season. That would be of great help in the future—just not the immediate future.

THE 2001-2002 SEASON
12-16 (4-12, 6th in the SEC West)

Mack McGadney (F)	Derrick Bird (G)
Marquis Daniels (G)	Brandon Robinson (G)
Adam Harrington (G)	Marco Killingsworth (F)
Lincoln Glass (G)	Dwayne Mitchell (G)
Abdou Diame (F)	Lewis Monroe (G)
Kyle Davis (C)	

The 6-8 sophomore center, Kyle Davis, played a bigger role in scoring this season, along with 6-8 freshman forward Marco Killingsworth. Mack McGadney and Lincoln Glass were the only seniors to contribute much at all this year. The roster was young but promising, but results would not be immediately forthcoming.

The Tigers made it out of the non-conference portion of the schedule with a record of 8-3, but things took a quick turn south when the new year rolled around. Auburn lost six SEC games in a row, and that streak would've been three games longer, except for an unexpected upset of 14th-ranked Alabama, 59-56, at home on January 12.

Davis had undergone surgery on his elbow just five days earlier. Ellis held him out for most of the game. With fifteen minutes remaining, however, Davis was begging the coach to put him in, and Ellis finally relented.

"Every block that I made, every rebound that I grabbed, I could just feel pain shoot all the way up my arm. It was killing me the whole week that I was watching practice. I made the decision (that I wanted to play) right before the game. I said, 'Coach, this is Alabama. I have to be out there.'"

Davis's presence helped the Tigers at first, but then the Tide went on a 13-0 run to take the lead with less than two minutes to go. Marquis Daniels finally stopped the bleeding with a three-pointer to tie the game at 56-56, and then Davis forced an Alabama turnover. Auburn pulled the game out with free throws, along with another tough Davis rebound.

"Kyle is the blocked shot man," said forward Brandon Robinson. "Kyle is the type of guy that when he's hurt, he tries to play through it. Nobody knew what he was going to do. He dressed up and came out, out of his own heart, which we thank him for."

The Tigers won only three more games the rest of the season, and then fell to 11th-ranked Florida in the first round of the SEC Tournament.

Given their overall record of 12-16, there would be no additional postseason play. But the young men of this team would soon become the seasoned veterans necessary to reach the NCAA Tournament again—and to advance surprisingly far into it.

THE 2002-2003 SEASON
22-12 (8-8, 2nd in the SEC West)
NCAA Tournament Sweet 16

Marquis Daniels (G)
Kyle Davis (C)
Derrick Bird (G)
Brandon Robinson (G)
Marco Killingsworth (F)

Lewis Monroe (G)
Nathan Watson (G)
Troy Gaines (G)
Chris Lollar (G)

In Marquis Daniels' senior season, the Tigers put it all together for a very good run.

They lost one game between December 2 and January 22, a 13-1 run that ended in grand fashion, with a 77-68 win over Alabama in Beard-Eaves. After dropping a couple of road games against ranked Kentucky and Georgia, as well as a home game to Tennessee, the Tigers finished out the regular season with a 4-5 run. They ended up 8-8 in the SEC and entered the conference tournament in New Orleans as the 2-seed in the West.

In round 1 of the SEC Tournament, the Tigers got a rematch against Tennessee. This time they prevailed, 66-53. Unfortunately, and as happened so many times over the years, they ran into Kentucky in the next round and fell to the Wildcats, 78-58.

A .500 record in the conference and a win in the SEC Tournament was enough to get them their final NCAA invitation of the Cliff Ellis era. They were dispatched to the East Regional, as the 10 seed. They would go on to surprise everyone, push the eventual champions to the brink, and come tantalizingly close to making the Elite Eight.

On March 21 they faced St Joseph's in St Petersburg and pulled out an overtime win, 65-63. That put them up against the 2-seed in the Regional two days later: the Wake Forest Demon Deacons. Few gave the Tigers a chance in that game, but they fought their way to a 68-62 victory.

As Jay Tate put it in the *Montgomery Advertiser*, the Tigers, "outduel(ed) one of the nation's most physical teams, in nearly every category, again silencing critics who insisted before the tournament that the Tigers simply didn't belong."

"We're not worried about what anyone else says," said point guard Lewis Monroe. "We know we can play. We've already gone farther than anyone thought we would."

Monroe, along with sophomores Marco Killingsworth, Brandon Robinson and Nathan Watson, carried the team during a long stretch when star Marquis Daniels was on the bench with foul trouble. By the time Daniels was able to come back in, the Tigers had gone from trailing Wake Forest to leading by 6.

"As soon as (Daniels) went out of the game, I looked at the rest of the players out on the floor and said, 'Hey, we have got to pick it up. We have to do what he would do,'" said Monroe. "We started hitting big shots and getting steals and the tempo turned our way."

AUBURN BASKETBALL

The win over Wake Forest put Auburn in the Sweet Sixteen for the first time since 1999. Their opponent would be the 3-seed Syracuse Orangemen of Jim Boeheim, featuring future NBA Top 75 player Carmelo Anthony.

The Tigers gave Syracuse all they could've wanted and more in that game, played in Albany, New York, before falling, 79-78.

Trailing by double digits for much of the game, and by 17 at one point, Auburn used a triangle-and-two defense to limit the Orangemen's star players—including holding superstar Anthony scoreless in the first half. Then Auburn went on a run of 3-point shots, making four in a row, and pulled the game within single digits. For a moment it appeared the Tigers might pull it out.

But then Syracuse started visiting the charity stripe, and they didn't miss. Particularly their lone senior, Kueth Duany. After the Orange missed the front ends of three straight one-and-ones, keeping Auburn in the game, Duany made four free throws in a row to provide the winning margin.

"We made a heck of a run in the second half," said Ellis afterward. "It just wasn't enough. It's a tough deal."

"At the end," said Syracuse coach Jim Boeheim, referring to his players' free-throws in the final minutes, "they hit everything. If it hadn't been for our free-throw shooting, we'd be going home right now."

Marquis Daniels, in his final game in an Auburn uniform, scored 27.

"We played with heart and soul. The Sweet Sixteen is sweet but the farther you go, the harder you fall," said Ellis. "It's been a great season."

Syracuse would go on to win the Regional and then defeat Texas in the Final Four, before completing a remarkable run to win the national championship. Yet they barely, barely beat Auburn—in yet *another* instance of the Tigers being knocked out of an NCAA Tournament by the eventual champions.

In 2022, Carmelo Anthony ended up on the NBA 75 all-time team. But for much of a game in 2003 in Albany, he was outplayed by Marquis Daniels.

John Ringer:
That was a good team. Ellis had built them back up. They were good on defense. They had a good run, losing to a very good Kentucky team in the SEC Tournament.

In their last NCAA Tournament game, they were down by 10 at the half to Carmelo Anthony's national champion Syracuse team, and came back and only lost by 1.

Van Allen Plexico:
I don't remember much about Marquis Daniels until the end of that season.

John Ringer:
He was smooth; a very good shooter.

That's true–he was one of the more underrated Auburn players, because we really don't remember much about him until the end of this season.

It's funny–in his last three years, he scored a lot. He averaged 18 points per game his last year. He was solid; a guy who was an All-SEC player at the end of his career. A difference-maker, a team leader, despite perhaps not possessing the ceiling of a Morris or a Barkley.

In August 2018, Marquis Daniels became a graduate assistant for the Auburn basketball team. Up to that point, he'd played in the NBA for ten years, up through 2013. In his first season back on the Plains, he got to participate in a Final Four run for the ages.

Said head coach Bruce Pearl in March of 2019, as the Tigers were preparing for their Sweet 16 matchup with North Carolina, "When you've got an assistant coach that used to play in the NBA that believes in what you do and how you do it, and is able to convey that to the players with the good, the bad and the ugly or times of adversity and challenges, it's incredibly stabilizing for us. Marquis has been a tremendously stabilizing influence on our team."

"He was all in as a player," said Daniels' former head coach at Auburn, Cliff Ellis. "He was all in to the system. He just was dedicated and committed to being a champion. He's been that way. He was that way throughout his career at Auburn. He was that way in the NBA. ... In my mind, he's just one of those guys that's a champion, not only in basketball, but in life. I love him like a son."

"Being around college students, being around the college game, being around coaches, the players, they look up to me," said Daniels in 2019. "It's good for them to see the road that it's gonna take to get there. The hard work, the early mornings, the late nights. Understanding that nothing's given."

As of 2022, Daniels is Director of Player Development for Auburn Basketball.

THE 2003-2004 SEASON
14-14 (5-11, 4th in the SEC West)

Kyle Davis (C)
Brandon Robinson (G)
Marco Killingsworth (F)
Lewis Monroe (G)
Nathan Watson (G)
Troy Gaines (G)

Chris Lollar (G)
Ian Young (G)
Quinnel Brown (F)
Ronny LeMelle (G)
Dwayne Curtis (C)

The 2003-04 season would be the final one for Cliff Ellis as Auburn's coach. While the Tigers finished with a .500 record of 14-14 overall, their SEC record of 5-11 was only good enough for fourth place in the West. Added to that, they failed to advance in the SEC Tournament, losing to Georgia–a team they'd beaten at home earlier in the season–73-59, on the opening night in the Georgia Dome.

Following the season, Cliff Ellis was dismissed by Auburn University.

Van Allen Plexico:
It always seemed like Cliff Ellis would build up to a really good team, during the year he had a bunch of talented seniors, and then go like 2-3 years with mediocrity or no success at all, and then we'd build up to another team that could get to the postseason and win a couple of games. There just wasn't much "reloading." It felt more like nearly-perpetual "rebuilding."

Ellis was quoted by WLTX-TV as saying his firing represented "a very emotional time" for him, and he pointed out that during his tenure his Auburn teams had experienced enough success to "put us near the top of the SEC in terms of games won and trips to the NCAA tournament. That is why this decision by the Auburn administration is so disappointing."

The Tigers under Ellis won their first SEC regular-season title in decades, as well as making the NCAA and NIT tournaments in 7 of his 10 seasons, and posting only 1 losing season. But the 2003-04 season had been disappointing, and possible NCAA sanctions loomed—the same threat that had partially caused Sonny Smith to head to VCU more than a decade earlier.

"This shocked everybody," said junior forward Marco Killingsworth. "I didn't ever think it was going to happen. We met with the coaches after the season and he was talking about next year. We didn't think this was going to happen at all."

Auburn's interim president, Ed Richardson, reportedly told Ellis, "A change in the leadership of our program is needed. My evaluation of the program indicates to me that we need to move in a different direction." He went on to add, "I am aware of the many accomplishments of coach Ellis in his tenure here. I appreciate what he has done with the program. It is simply time for a change."

Athletic Director David Housel noted the program "has not consistently met our competitive goals," having finished league play with a winning record only twice during Ellis's decade in charge.

Auburn had to pay Ellis $750,000 at termination, as his contract had been extended for two more years automatically at the end of the previous season, due to their run in the NCAA Tournament.

Associate Head Coach Shannon Weaver described Ellis' meeting with his players after the firing as "very emotional and very personal between him and his players. Those are his kids. He reiterated the things that he's always said to them about what's important in life and what's important to be successful. He got a chance to tell them once again how he feels about them and he told them this is not where it ends, that they will always be part of his family."

In an interview with reporter Sam Blum in 2019, Ellis argued that Auburn made a mistake in firing him.

"We had all those great players, but you know, there just was a poor, I don't know, (the firing) was just a panic attack, I guess, so to speak. It was a dumb move for the players and the program. And it would have kept going on and on.

"My shock was how bad it went south (after the firing) until Bruce got there. From 2004, alright, what was last year, 2017? So, for 13 years, or whatever it was, it was awful. It was awful. It was sad. It was sad.

"I'm appreciative (of Auburn), and I follow Auburn, I love Auburn. I pull for Auburn. Some of my best friends come from Auburn.

"All those people that had built that (success in basketball) up, it was just taken away. And then it went back to (being a) football school because it wasn't nothing for basketball. It wasn't.

"We had 6,000 Cliff Dwellers in that Marquis Daniels, Scottie Pohlman, all that era. We had 6,000 Cliff Dwellers at one time. Think about that. At a time when Auburn basketball was nothing. So they love it. They love it, they love it, they love it. And when I see a game now—I don't get to watch much because I got my own team—but as you watch them now, those students are into it. They want it, they love it, they love it.

"It's just sad they built that, how many million-dollar facility? (Auburn Arena, after Ellis was fired) We played at Beard-Eaves. How many million-dollar facility? They built that... they paid these coaches (after Ellis) these exorbitant prices, and lost. I mean, how many millions of dollars did Auburn invest before it turned around? If it was a business, if (Auburn's administrative) people had been running a business, they'd have gone bankrupt."

Auburn Arena cost $86 million, and was ready for the 2010-2011 season. Jeff Lebo signed a 2005 contract that paid him $750,000 annually for seven years, along with incentives he never touched. The next head coach, Tony Barbee, was paid $1.5 million annually.

Ellis remains the second-winningest coach in Auburn history, with 186 wins, behind only Joel Eaves with 213, and just ahead of Sonny Smith, with 173. He is the winningest coach in Clemson history and South Alabama history.

John Ringer:

It's tough to say "fire him" at this point, because we'd just made the sweet 16! For me, that was, "What are you thinking?" It was not a good year that next year; it was disappointing, and there was not a lot of strong talent on the team, kind of like the last Sonny Smith team. Kyle Davis blocked some shots, but the rest of those guys?

Van Allen Plexico:
I have a hard time evaluating the last years of the Ellis Era. We had experienced some success–more than Auburn was used to at any time other than that great five-year run with Sonny–but we also had drop-offs in there.

John Ringer:
I think there was a big red flag there in terms of recruiting and the team getting worse. But we're spoiled now in the Bruce Pearl era. Ellis was making the NCAA Tournament as often as not, and that was good enough for me at the time. But there was a noticeable drop-off in talent, and I get why we fired him, even though I might not have done so myself.

Van Allen Plexico:
I don't think he was ever a coach the Auburn fan base would have fought for. We all liked him okay, and appreciated the success we had under him, but his personality was kind of flat and he never got the fans super-excited. Even the year we won so much (1998-99) and got the number 1 seed in the NCAA Tournament, there was still a kind of "low roar" about it, rather than crackling energy like we have these days. With Ellis, it was mostly just "okay."

John Ringer:
We were excited in 1999 but, by the time we fired him, that seemed a long time ago.

- 4 -

THE JEFF LEBO / TONY BARBEE INTERREGNUM 2004 - 2014

LEBO TO AUBURN

When the powers-that-be at Auburn decided to move on from Cliff Ellis after a decade of relative success, they looked to make a splashy hire. After all, the perceived "problem" with Ellis wasn't that he didn't win (second-most wins in Auburn history), or that he didn't get Auburn into the postseason more often than not (5 NCAA Tournament appearances and 2 NIT bids in 10 seasons, including two trips to the Sweet 16). The perceived "problem" was that he hadn't won enough for everyone. Auburn wanted to go deeper in the SEC Tournament and more consistently make the NCAA Tournament, and get back to the Elite Eight (as Sonny Smith had done once)—or better.

After a three-week search, Auburn decided to hire Jeff Lebo, who was at that time the coach at UT-Chattanooga and who had been a stalwart player for Dean Smith at North Carolina, as the 19th coach of Auburn Basketball. Lebo's salary would be $750,000 per year.

Among others reportedly interviewed were UAB's Mike Anderson and Jeff Capel of VCU. Capel had replaced Mack McCarthy, Sonny Smith's assistant that Smith had turned the program over to in his final season.

"I am excited about the opportunity to coach basketball at Auburn," Lebo said at the announcement. "I have been at Auburn a number of times as an opposing coach and I found it a difficult place to play. Since that time, I am convinced Auburn is a place that can have competitive success in basketball on a consistent basis. I was impressed with the commitment that the administration demonstrated towards having a successful program on the court and in the classroom. I look forward to getting started and building a program that will succeed in both areas."

Prior to coming to Auburn, Lebo had coached Tennessee Tech for four years, as well as two at UTC. At those two stops, he had compiled a record of 115-63. With his years as an assistant added in, he had been a part of five NCAA Tournament appearances, two NIT appearances, and six conference championships. At UTC he was 40-20 in his two seasons.

"I am pleased to welcome Jeff Lebo to the University and the Auburn community," said interim Auburn president Ed Richardson. "In our discussions during the search process, Coach Lebo indicated he clearly understands the balance between athletics and academics. As a matter of fact, Jeff was an Academic All-ACC selection as a student. His commitment to the ideal of student-athletes makes him the right person for our program. I anticipate a long and productive tenure for Jeff at Auburn University."

"(Lebo) brings a wealth of experience and success as a player at North Carolina under the winningest basketball coach in NCAA history and followed that with successful coaching tenures at two SEC schools as an assistant," added Hal Baird, Athletic Assistant to the President. "As a head coach, he resurrected two programs at Tennessee Tech and Tennessee-Chattanooga. He is widely recognized as one of the young rising coaching stars in NCAA basketball."

Van Allen Plexico:
I was like, "Who?"

But I was definitely ready to be impressed. I wanted us to look like geniuses for finding him and hiring him away from Chattanooga.

John Ringer:
I was happy when Lebo was hired. I thought he was a solid coach.

My overall perception of him was, we played a bunch of weak non-conference teams early in the season under him, and it padded the stats and made us look better than we were. But then we couldn't get into the NCAA Tournament because we'd played a bunch of cupcakes in the non-conference schedule, so our overall quality wins ranking was too low.

On February 23, 2004, Auburn interim president Ed Richardson and lawyers representing the university met with the NCAA Committee on Infractions to discuss a two-year investigation into the recruitment of Jackie Butler and Chadd Moore by Coach Cliff Ellis's staff. Allegations included the offering of cash and cars to the players.

If Auburn failed to sway the committee, the men's basketball program could have been hit with a postseason ban, scholarship reductions or a probationary period requiring increased monitoring.

"Any time you have a sanction against the university it reflects on the leadership, reflects on the reputation, it causes concerns about recruiting," said Richardson, just before the hearing with the NCAA. "It just has a very negative view. But it's just like any other time you go to court, you don't know how it will come out."

Auburn surprised the NCAA infractions committee by disputing every major infraction they had been charged with. In most cases, universities admit to at least one major violation by the time the case reaches the hearing stage, hoping for lighter punishment as a result.

The university had already self-imposed the loss of a scholarship, as punishment for the non-major violations it found in its own investigation.

The allegations against Auburn were originally made by Mike Walker, a Mississippi sports agent, in March of 2001. Moore and

Butler played summer basketball for AAU basketball coach Mark Komara, whom the NCAA alleged was a representative of Auburn and was involved in improper recruitment.

The ruling by the committee came on April 27, 2004.

Assistant coach Shannon Weaver had been implicated in the violations, but was cleared by the NCAA.

Cliff Ellis had been fired on March 18 and was no longer with the Auburn program. He was not implicated in the charges by the NCAA.

The NCAA placed Auburn's basketball program on two years of probation, taking away one scholarship but otherwise exonerating Auburn of major rules violations.

THE 2004-2005 SEASON
14-17 (4-12, 6th in the SEC West)

Toney Douglas (G)	Daniel Hayles (G)
Ian Young (G)	Brett Howell (G)
Quinnel Brown (F)	Ronny LeMelle (G)
Nathan Watson (G)	Troy Gaines (G)
Frank Tolbert (G)	Kyle Derozan (F)

With the probation situation resolved, for better or worse, and a fresh start on the horizon, Auburn fans hoped their new coach would get things rolling right away and put the storm clouds of NCAA investigations in the rear-view mirror by winning some basketball games.

Unfortunately, the Lebo Era at Auburn would not go the way Auburn or Lebo would have hoped.

The 2004-05 SEC season started with a 5-game losing streak, and it ended with a 5-game losing streak, save for a home win in the final game, against Arkansas. In between, the Tigers alternated wins and losses from late January through early February.

Auburn finished last in the West and had to face 3-seed Vanderbilt in the first round of the SEC Tournament in Atlanta. There they prevailed, 77-73, over the Commodores. This outcome was particularly surprising in that, in the two teams' previous game in Nashville on February 16, Auburn had made *only 3 baskets in the entire second half.*

The second-half bug nearly bit them again, as they watched a 21-point lead evaporate in the final minutes. At one point, Vandy scored 14 unanswered points. Somehow the Tigers held on to win by 4.

"The last eight minutes of the game, it's one of those deals where you just want it over with," said Lebo after seeing Vandy make a late charge. "It was nice to finally hear the buzzer go off. If we'd played one more minute, we'd have lost by 12."

The next night, the Tigers went up against LSU and their 310-pound center, Glen Davis. Auburn had no answer for him and the Tigers fell, 89-58.

There would be no more games in 2005 for this Auburn team. They finished up 14-17 overall–the same number of wins as the previous year's team–and 4-12 in the SEC, dead last in the West. They had at least managed one tournament game win.

THE BALLAD OF TONEY DOUGLAS

Prior to the 2004-05 season, four-star recruit and *Parade/McDonald's* All-American Toney Douglas signed with Auburn as a shooting guard—the position he'd been listed at as a recruit.

Douglas, playing for Lebo at shooting guard, led the Tigers in scoring that season as a freshman, with an almost 17 points per game average. With the second-highest scoring average in the country among freshmen, Douglas was named to the Freshman All-SEC Team and was a third-team Freshman All-American.

After his first season at Auburn, Douglas requested to move to point guard, the position he felt he was more likely to play in the NBA. Lebo denied the request, prompting Douglas to transfer to Florida State. (Lebo had granted the transfer with the condition that he not move to another SEC school.)

After sitting out a year, Douglas played point guard for FSU, where in his senior season he would earn First Team All-ACC honors.

He would go on to be drafted by the Los Angeles Lakers, and would play for six other NBA teams in his time before moving to the overseas leagues.

John Ringer:
I think Douglas was clearly the big player that got away in the Lebo era. He could have made a difference in the trajectory of the program, if he had remained at Auburn.

Lebo had been a guard in college at UNC and I think he had expectations about what a point guard would or should do. That's my theory. They wanted him to be focused on scoring, not on distributing the ball.

THE 2005-06 SEASON
12-16 (4-12, 5th in the SEC West)

Rasheem Barrett (G)	Quantez Robertson (G)
Korvotney Barber (F)	Josh Dollard (F)
Frank Tolbert (G)	Michael Woodard (G)
Daniel Hayles (G)	Joey Cameron (F)
Brett Howell (G)	Emmanuel Willis (F)
Ronny LeMelle (G)	

This was a team that featured Frank Tolbert, Ronny LeMelle, Rasheem Barrett, Quantez Robertson, Josh Dollard and McDonald's All-American Korvotney Barber–several of them stalwarts for the Tigers throughout much of Lebo's tenure.

The Tigers would finish 4-12 in the league again in 2006, though a 4-12 Ole Miss finished below them in last place, due to a two-game sweep of the Rebels by the Tigers. Their overall record included two fewer wins than the year before.

Again they opened SEC Tournament play against Vanderbilt. This time, however, playing in Nashville, the Commodores were able to win, 76-71.

As Ryan Sterritt of the *College and Magnolia* blog put it, "This season was during the forgotten years of Auburn basketball, and was Jeff Lebo's second season. On probation and after losing a great coach in Cliff Ellis, the Tigers had competed with essentially a group of nobodies in Lebo's first season.

"However, there was actually some optimism going into the year. Lebo had surprisingly pulled in a respectable recruiting class, highlighted by only the second McDonald's All-American to ever come to Auburn, Korvotney Barber (RIP). [Barber was found dead in the waters off Panama City Beach in 2013, an apparent drowning victim.]

"The team would show some promise of talent, but... most of the talent was freshman and Lebo would be unable to capitalize with recruiting falling off in subsequent years."

Overall, this was a season to forget.

THE 2006-2007 SEASON
17-15 (7-9, 4th in the SEC West)

Rasheem Barrett (G)	Quan Prowell (F)
Frank Tolbert (G)	DeWayne Reed (G)
Korvotney Barber (F)	Archie Miaway (G)
Quantez Robertson (G)	Kelvin Lucas (G)
Josh Dollard (F)	Lucas Hargrove (F)

In Lebo's third season, the team took a slight uptick toward semi-respectability.

They improved their conference win total by 3, from 4-12 to 7-9– just missing out on a .500 record by one game. Overall, they finally returned to having a winning season, at 17-15.

The 83-80 win at home against 22nd-ranked Tennessee on January 17 was Lebo's first win at Auburn over a ranked team. Six days later they beat 12th-ranked Alabama in Beard-Eaves by a staggering 24 points, 81-57.

"We took a step into the pond with the win over Tennessee. We wanted to get up to our chin," Lebo said after beating the Tide. "We decided to dive in with a second win... That's as good as we can play, in the second half. It's fun to watch if you're an Auburn fan."

Prior to the game, Auburn's coaches had noticed when watching video of Alabama games that the Tide players tended to allow their perimeter passes to be tipped. The Tigers attacked this vulnerability in a big way, turning the ball over and then making 68 percent of their second-half shots.

"We played good defense tonight," said Auburn's Korvotney Barber, who scored 18. "We ran the court well, but we won because of our defense."

For Alabama's side of the report, the *Montgomery Advertiser* headline read, "UA Searching for Answers," and "Alabama has another meltdown."

Sadly, the Tigers didn't win back-to-back SEC games until almost the end of the season, when they ran off three straight victories between February 21 and 28. In the middle of that stretch, they knocked off now-25th-ranked Alabama a second time, 86-77, in Tuscaloosa. Junior transfer Quan Prowell scored 15 in the second half for the Tigers. As hard as it is to imagine, this was only the second win for Auburn inside Coleman Coliseum in 23 years, and it was their first sweep of Alabama since 1999.

After an 80-65 loss to Georgia in the first round of the SEC Tournament, however, the season came to an end. There would be no NCAA or even NIT for the Tigers again in 2007.

THE 2007-2008 SEASON
14-16 (4-12, 6th in the SEC West)

Rasheem Barrett (G)	Korvotney Barber (F)
Frank Tolbert (G)	Quantez Robertson (G)
Quan Prowell (F)	Matt Heramb (F)
DeWayne Reed (G)	Larry Williams (G)
Lucas Hargrove (F)	Boubacar Sylla (C)

Following an encouraging 2006-07, the Tigers returned to their recent bad form in 2007-08, winning only four SEC games (again) and finishing last in the West (again). It was like a rerun of two years earlier, right down to losing the first game in the SEC Tournament (again) to Vanderbilt (again). They won 2 of their final 13 games. The highlight of the season was probably a January 19 win over 18th-ranked Ole Miss at home, 80-77.

When a narrow win over Ole Miss at home is your big accomplishment, you know it hasn't been the greatest season ever.

Van Allen Plexico:
We'll be saving some trees by not going on for pages about some of the teams from this particular era.

THE 2008-2009 SEASON
24-12 (10-6, 2nd in the SEC West)
NIT: Third Round

Rasheem Barrett (G)	Quantez Robertson (G)
Korvotney Barber (F)	Larry Williams (G)
DeWayne Reed (G)	Frankie Sullivan (G)
Lucas Hargrove (F)	Brendon Knox (C)
Tay Waller (G)	Johnnie Lett (F)

The high point of Jeff Lebo's six-year tenure on the Plains would have to be 2008-09.

That season, the Tigers won 24 games and finished second in the West, with a league record of 10-6.

The season did not begin in promising fashion, with Auburn losing to Mercer, Dayton and Northern Iowa in three of their first six games. Those early losses would later prove to be critical. After that, however, they reversed course and reeled off seven straight wins to finish out the non-conference portion of the schedule.

League play didn't begin much better than the overall season had, with the Tigers dropping three of their first four games. When February rolled around, however, they got their act together and only lost one of their final nine regular-season games–that one at 23rd-ranked LSU.

They entered the SEC Tournament in St Petersburg as the 2-seed in the West. They were seeded behind only LSU on their side of the conference and came in on a four-game winning streak, which had included another sweep of Alabama. There they met Florida in the first round and won, 61-58, behind Korvotney Barber's 12 points, 10 rebounds and an emphatic dunk in the final 30 seconds of the game.

The Florida game was seen by many as essentially a play-in game for an NCAA Tournament bid. Two SEC teams were considered locks—LSU and Tennessee—while South Carolina was seen by many as having played their way out of the NCAAs. Once-mighty

Kentucky had only managed fourth place in the East at 8-8 in the conference, and their second-round loss to LSU was seen by some as disqualifying. On top of all that, no major conference had received fewer than three NCAA bids in over twenty years. If the SEC received three, it was believed by many that Auburn had made a case to be the third team, regardless of how the rest of the SEC Tournament unfolded.

"Auburn has made a strong case (for getting into the NCAAs) down the stretch," commented Mark Long of the AP, "entering the (SEC) Tournament as the league's hottest team and then beating Florida in what was practically a home game for the Gators."

Alas, the Tigers lost in the next round, 94-85, to Tennessee. With that loss went their chances of making the big show. They were not invited to the NCAAs for the sixth consecutive season. Instead, they would have to settle for the NIT.

"Auburn finished 22-11—the third-best mark in school history—and won 10 SEC games for the first time in a decade," noted Jay Tate in the *Montgomery Advertiser*. (But) "Losses to Mercer and Northern Iowa critically damaged the Tigers' standing in the (RPI)." Had the Tigers avoided those two inexplicable losses, they'd have been 24-9 and almost-sure-things for the NCAA Tournament.

"Our RPI was still (not what we needed it to be) and a couple more wins would've made a big difference," said Lebo.

One would think the SEC having fewer teams as clear-cut qualifiers would have helped Auburn get in. Unfortunately, the opposite turned out to be the case. The fact that the SEC was down overall that season—only two at-large bids out of twelve teams—meant that Auburn's wins against conference opponents counted less than normal, which hurt the Tigers' position with the NCAAs.

"Our team is disappointed. Our kids are disappointed," said Lebo when the news broke. "There's not a whole lot you can say to them. I don't want to diminish the year that they had. We're hurt. They made a heck of a run at the end and put themselves in position to get in."

The Tigers instead received a number 1 seed in the NIT, starting with a game against UT-Martin. Meanwhile, Mississippi State upset LSU to win the SEC Tournament and get the automatic bid, giving the SEC three teams in the NCAA Tournament after all.

"I believe we should have (gotten into the NCAAs), said Auburn senior Rasheem Barrett. "We still get postseason play. We still get to play another basketball game."

The Tigers didn't just get another game–they got three more games, and all of them in the somewhat warm confines of Beard-Eaves Memorial Coliseum. They made their deepest run in the NIT ever, and their deepest tournament run overall since Marquis Daniels took them to the Sweet 16 in 2003.

They defeated 8-seed UT-Martin, 87-82, on March 18. Two days later, they took down 4-seed Tulsa, 74-55. To win the bracket and advance to New York, they would have to make it three in a row and defeat 3-seed Baylor. This they failed to do. The season came to an end on March 24 with a home loss to the Bears, 74-72.

Trailing by 7 in the final minute, the Tigers managed to trim Baylor's lead to 1 with nine seconds left to play. Unfortunately, Auburn's DeWayne Reed missed two free throws that would've given the Tigers the lead, and then a desperation 3-point shot at the buzzer by Rasheem Barrett hit the back of the rim.

"To tell you the truth, it looked good," Barret said of his final shot. "I had a wide-open look. I thought it was good."

"We battled awfully hard and had a couple of chances there at the end," Lebo said after the game, "but we just couldn't finish it off. Free throw shooting has cost us before. It cost us tonight at the end."

"It hurts bad," said Reed of his misses. "To miss two free throws like that, with the game on the line, that hurts. I had confidence in my shot, I just missed."

THE 2009-2010 SEASON
15-17 (6-10, 5th in the SEC West)

DeWayne Reed (G)	Andre Malone (G)
Lucas Hargrove (F)	Brendon Knox (C)
Tay Waller (G)	Johnnie Lett (F)
Larry Williams (G)	Ty Armstrong (F)
Frankie Sullivan (G)	Josh Wallace (G)
Kenny Gabriel (F)	Rob Chubb (C)
Earnest Ross (G)	Jake Drum (F)

The losing ways returned with the 2009-10 season.

Once again, Lebo's Tigers started slow, dropping their first three SEC games and five of their first six.

They did manage to rally and win their last five home games, starting with a 58-57 win over Alabama on January 30. During that same stretch, however, they failed to win a single road game, and finished up with only one conference victory away from home—84-80 over LSU, back on January 20.

The 89-80 win over Mississippi State on March 3 was important, however. It would be Auburn's final basketball game in Beard-Eaves Memorial Coliseum. After 41 years in the big gray cake box, the Tigers were moving to a new home.

"I was dreading this game and I was sick to my stomach for most of the game," said Lebo afterward. "The anticipation made me want to win it even more. We had six seniors that you want to honor and send this place out in the right way."

The Bulldogs were seen as on the bubble of the NCAA Tournament and needed the win. They outclassed Auburn at most positions. Yet somehow, understanding the importance of the occasion, the Tigers found a way to get it done.

"In the first half, it was obvious that we didn't have the edge and Auburn did," said Miss State coach Rick Stansbury. "We tied it up on a couple of occasions, but every time, Auburn hit big shots. They had a bunch of big shots to keep the momentum going and win the game."

Meanwhile, the season continued in other venues. Following a regular-season-ending loss on the road at Alabama, Auburn held the 5th seed in the West. They met Florida on the first day of the SEC Tournament in Bridgestone Arena in Nashville. The Gators came out on top, 78-69.

There would be no more postseason for the Tigers. They returned home to the Loveliest Village with a final record of 15-17.

There was, however, one thing for the Tigers and their coach to look forward to: a brand-new place to play, coming later in 2010.

A NEW HOME

During the second half of Jeff Lebo's tenure on the Plains, talk began in earnest of building a modern new arena for Auburn Basketball.

In 2006, Jay Jacobs, then-AD at Auburn, met with Lebo and women's coach Nell Fortner, along with some of the Auburn trustees, to discuss building a new practice facility for basketball. Over time, that idea morphed into the much grander concept of constructing an entirely new arena on campus.

At the 2022 renaming ceremony, in which the facility was officially dubbed "Neville Arena," longtime Athletic Department employee Tim Jackson recounted the story of how then-AD Jay Jacobs put together a plan to (once again) renovate Beard-Eaves Memorial Coliseum, at a cost of $35 million. He took that plan to money man and former university trustee Bobby Lowder, who looked it over and then asked Jacobs, "Why not just build a new arena?"

"We can't afford to," Jacobs allegedly responded.

"We can't afford *not* to," came back Lowder's reply.

On August 29, 2008, ground was broken on that facility.

Ultimately, what was then called Auburn Arena cost $86 million to build. Able to seat 9,121 fans for basketball games, it would go on to replace Beard-Eaves Memorial Coliseum beginning with the 2010-11 season.

Auburn offers the following facts about the arena:

"The furthest seat in Auburn Arena is just 43 feet away from the court. A full two-thirds of the seats in the facility are less than 27 feet in elevation from courtside. Auburn students have their own entrance, lobby and concessions area at the Arena to service 1,500 floor-level seats.

"The Arena features a team store, six concession stands, three elevators, 94 HD televisions plus family restrooms and customer service kiosks on all seating levels. For special events, 12,000 square feet of banquet space, including tailgate and super suites, is available.

"For the teams, Auburn Arena offers an office suite for the coaches, locker rooms and a 13,970-square foot practice facility and weight room.

"Auburn's Jonathan B. Lovelace Museum & Hall of Honor is located on the concourse at the main entrance. Fans who visit the Lovelace Hall of Honor at Auburn Arena take an interactive walk through Auburn athletics history."

How the arena came to find its final form is a fascinating story in itself.

DESIGNING AUBURN ARENA

In March of 2022, Bennett Durango of the *Montgomery Advertiser* looked at how the arena came to be designed the way it was.

He noted that the height of the roof became one of the primary points of consideration. The goal was to include the more expensive seating options such as boxes and sweets while maintaining an intimate atmosphere for the games. Striking such a compromise was not easy. The architects met with Auburn donors in Auburn, Birmingham and Atlanta to get a sense of what was desired and what would work best.

Ultimately, the decision was made to forgo a level of luxury suites in order to bring the roof level down, decrease heating and cooling costs and increase the noise level.

"By not having those elevated suites or elevated second concourse," said architect Tom Waggoner, "it creates an intimacy of bringing that roof down.

"That's one of the reasons that the arena is so crazy," he added.

What the Arena ended up with is described as a "bunker suite" arrangement combining Duke's Cameron Indoor Stadium and Kansas's Allen Fieldhouse. As Durando describes it, "Premium seat-holders have options including a courtside lounge accessible via the scholarship entrance. The payoff was a blueprint for one of college basketball's great home-court advantages of the modern era."

"The home run of that building — or I shouldn't say home run — the half-court shot at the buzzer of that building, is the fact that you have this open concourse," said Waggoner. "It changes the game from a fan's perspective because you're always connected. It creates a standing-room-only intimidation factor."

Another unusual direction Auburn decided to go with the design was to have the student section fill much of the lower area on three sides. This came at the expense of losing even more premium seating space. With the goal being to create a home court advantage, though, it was necessary. And having the students filling that area prompted Auburn officials to go a step further—and a step more unorthodox—and put the TV camera location on the opposite side, so the students could all be visible on the broadcasts.

"We caught hell from ESPN and CBS," said Auburn's director of facility planning, Randy Byers. "They hate that setup." The television broadcasters prefer to have the two teams' benches visible across from the camera. "But it's best for us. It provides the perfect background for TV: students going nuts."

It was all worth it. "(We wanted to) create a home-court advantage," said Don Loudermilk, Auburn's liaison with the Kansas City-based firm 360 that designed the building. "Best way to do that is to keep the volume rather small.

"The whole idea of the project from the beginning was to try to bring the basketball program up to the level of the football program," he added. "Sort of exceeded expectations, I guess."

Auburn Arena–now Neville Arena–is today widely recognized as one of the best basketball facilities in the country. Sadly for Jeff Lebo, acknowledged as instrumental in getting the place built, he never got to coach a game in it.

On March 12, 2010, the day after the Tigers made an early exit from the SEC Tournament, Auburn AD Jay Jacobs fired Lebo.

In his six seasons, Lebo had taken the Tigers to postseason play only once: the 2009 NIT. With a senior-laden team in 2010, the Tigers regressed, finishing 6-10 in the conference in 15-17 overall. Only one starter would be returning for the next season.

"I want to thank Coach Lebo for all that he has done for Auburn University over the past six years," said Jacobs. "Coach Lebo has worked hard and has always represented Auburn with character, class and integrity. However, we feel like the time has come for Auburn basketball to move in a new direction.

"There's nothing about this decision that was easy," Jacobs added, sounding remarkably like his predecessor while dismissing

Tommy Joe Eagles from the same job. "I felt strongly that we needed to make a change.

"I can't say any finer things about the guy and the way he's represented Auburn throughout his six years here."

Auburn paid Lebo $1.5 million to buy out the three remaining years on his contract.

"We're going to look at everybody that has an interest in this job," Jacobs said. "We're going to find the right fit, the right guy that gives us the best chance to compete."

In fact, they did not.

John Ringer:

It was a big turning point for the program overall to get the Arena built. Beard-Eaves Coliseum is a cavernous building in the old style. We needed something better to move forward and be competitive. I think it was smart of them to build it the size they did.

Van Allen Plexico:

I know Beard-Eaves Memorial Coliseum very well. I went to tons of basketball games there—both Auburn games and high school playoff games. I had multiple classes in the classrooms underneath the stands—and people might be surprised to learn there are a lot of rooms under there. In fact, that's where the entire Athletic Department used to be housed, all together, before the football building was built in the late 1980s. And of course that was the building where you and I graduated from Auburn. (And I did that twice!) So I knew its strengths and its weaknesses as well as any layperson could, and I knew Auburn needed to do something.

They had updated it just a bit back in the 1990s, adding paint here and there and affixing the big tiger eyes graphics to the front of the building where the main entrance is located. But it was still what it was—big and dark and not very exciting.

I have to admit I was a little nervous, though, when they announced plans to entirely replace it. We were spending $90 million on a basketball arena, and those have a notoriously short shelf life before they become obsolete. I knew we needed something better, I just didn't want us to find ourselves in the same predicament just a few years later, after spending all that money. They needed to do it right, and they did.

John Ringer:
Auburn needed a facility with flexibility for the future. And they have that. They did a great job with the design and the location. They thought about a lot of stuff in terms of making it better for the students and for the fans; making the students a central part of the basketball experience. Other schools gave those prime lower seats to alumni, and now they regret it. You can't move them out. They paid a bunch of money.

Van Allen Plexico:
It's so weird that our basketball and football facilities are modeled on Old Dominion and Rice! Not two programs I would have guessed we would have looked to for inspiration in that way, but there you go.

(Yes, part of Jordan-Hare Stadium is modeled on Rice's stadium in Texas. The inner concourse ring in particular, I think. We talk about it in detail in our earlier book, *Decades of Dominance*.)

TONY BARBEE ARRIVES

The twentieth head basketball coach in Auburn history and its first African-American head coach in a major-revenue sport, Tony Barbee was 38 years old when he accepted the Auburn job, coming over from UTEP. His hiring was announced at a press conference on March 25, 2010.

"We have challenges in front of us, but we also have great opportunities with everything Auburn has to offer—a great university, outstanding community, tremendous fan support, and a terrific new arena and practice facility," Barbee said. "The time is now to take Auburn basketball to new heights."

The coaching search took less than two weeks and included other prospects such as Sam Houston State's Bob Marlin, North Texas coach Johnny Jones, Morehead State coach Donnie Tyndall, and Wright State coach Brad Brownell.

Said Jay Jacobs of the hire, "Coach Barbee has a vision of competing for championships at Auburn, and the passion to get us there. He is a phenomenal coach, an outstanding recruiter and a fierce competitor. ... We could not be happier to have him as the new face of Auburn basketball as we prepare to open a new era in a new arena next season."

Unspoken at the press conference but talked about by nearly everyone was the close association between Barbee and his former coach at UMass and coaching mentor, John Calipari—a man known both for his winning ways and his infamous skirting of rules.

The hire made for quite the bump in Barbee's finances. He'd earned roughly $300,000/year art UTEP, while Auburn agreed to pay him double what they'd paid Lebo: upwards of $1.5 million—a figure approximately ten times what Auburn had been offering for that position only a few years earlier.

John Ringer:
When Tony Barbee arrived on campus–when he walked in the door at Auburn–the first thing he said to the TipOff Club leadership was (paraphrasing), "Our expectation is that you will take the coaches out to a nice place for dinner after every game. You will buy the food for the coaches–the coaches you are already paying all this money for. We won't be paying for that."

Van Allen Plexico:
It seems like Barbee's main concerns were not having to pay for dinner—or for furniture. (That story is coming up shortly.)

John Ringer:
And fussing about Under Armour (being the official supplier of shoes and gear to Auburn). His position was basically, We'd be fine if we were a Nike school.

Van Allen Plexico:
How did you react to his hiring?

John Ringer:
I got it–he was supposed to be this ace recruiter that got great players for Kentucky. But it quickly became apparent that wasn't going to happen at Auburn–and that he wasn't a great game coach. He was hired to be a recruiter who delivered talent but he could not deliver. He blamed that lack of delivery on the Under Armor contract.

THE 2010-2011 SEASON
11-20 (4-12, 5th in the SEC West)

Earnest Ross (G)	Andre Malone (G)
Kenny Gabriel (F)	Chris Denson (G)
Rob Chubb (C)	Adrian Forbes (F)
Frankie Sullivan (G)	Ty Armstrong (F)
Josh Wallace (G)	Jake Drum (F)
Allen Payne (F)	Tony Neysmith (G)
Josh Langford (G)	

Barbee's first team at Auburn, led by Kenny Gabriel and Frankie Sullivan, lacked a single senior player. Its top seven scorers consisted of three sophomores, two juniors and two freshmen.

In the summer prior to that season, the Tigers suffered two devastating blows.

Frankie Sullivan, the leading scorer, and Ty Armstrong both suffered what were described as "major knee injuries" only days apart. Sullivan had surgery in July and wasn't sure if he would be able to play at all in the upcoming season.

"They are keeping me away from (any percentage on odds for a return) because they don't want to get my expectations up," Sullivan said after the operation. "I don't want to do that to the fans, either, because I don't know when or if I will play this season."

"When you look at the type of injury he's had and you look at the recovery process, it would lead you to believe he's out for the year," noted Barbee. "But the way he's working you never know how guys are going to respond to that type of injury."

Barbee's Tigers lost their first-ever game played in Auburn Arena. They fell in overtime to UNC-Asheville on November 12, by a score of 70-69. In fact, they wouldn't win in their new home for the first time until their fourth game, when they beat Middle Tennessee, 68-66.

Their record stood at 3-7 after their home loss to Presbyterian College, a week before Christmas.

Van Allen Plexico:
Hey—Presbyterian is where my grandfather graduated, and where my dad started out before he transferred to Auburn. The fighting Blue Hose!

This is not a program you want to see Auburn University lose to in any sport. Good gosh.

After the ignominious loss to Presbyterian, Barbee's team rallied and finished out the non-conference portion of the schedule with four straight wins, culminating in a 65-60 victory over Florida State on January 3.

Then the SEC portion of the schedule began, and the results took a very distinct turn for the worse.

Perhaps the low point came on January 8, when the Tigers scored 6 points total–*6 points!*—in the first half against LSU–an LSU team that had lost four of its previous five games. Though Auburn came back stronger in the second half with an 18-5 run, the damage was done and LSU won, 62-55.

By the time the regular season was over, the Tigers had won just four conference games. Their first SEC win under Barbee didn't come until January 29, with a 79-64 victory on the road at South Carolina.

Nathan Deal (writing in the Bleacher Report):
(Barbee) had a winning record (as a coach, coming in), but everything was set up for failure in his first season on the Plains. It became a harsh reality.

Auburn doesn't have a full roster, is devoid of true talent and the best players have been injured (i.e. Frankie Sullivan).

Before the season, you knew it would be bad. Auburn actually exceeded those expectations. They have been even worse.

Auburn plays for Barbee, but plays like Barbie.

No blame goes to Tony Barbee, because these are completely unfair conditions for a basketball coach. The players are trying, too. They're working their rears off. They just aren't good. Everything that can go wrong, does.

Barbee won only two home SEC games that season, beating Mississippi State and Ole Miss, before ending the regular season with a road win at LSU.

With the 5 seed in the West, Auburn faced Georgia in the first round of the SEC Tournament in Atlanta, and fell to the Bulldogs, 69-51.

Barbee's inaugural season was mercifully over.

THE 2011-2012 SEASON
15-16 (5-11, 10th in the SEC)

Kenny Gabriel (F)
Rob Chubb (C)
Frankie Sullivan (G)
Josh Wallace (G)
Allen Payne (F)
Josh Langford (G)
Jake Drum (F)

Chris Denson (G)
Adrian Forbes (F)
Tony Neysmith (G)
Varez Ward (G)
Willy Kouassi (C)
Noel Johnson (F)

As of Tony Barbee's second season on the Plains, the SEC abandoned the conference divisions format. There would be no more "East" and "West," just twelve teams playing one another.

The Tigers did a bit better this time around, winning five conference games and missing a winning record overall by just one game.

Again the late-season gauntlet wore them down, though. They lost 12 of their last 17 games, including all SEC road games for the year.

Kenny Gabriel was the only senior in the starting lineup, and averaged 12 points and 7 rebounds over the course of the season.

The Tigers lost in the first round of the SEC Tournament again, this time to Ole Miss, by a score of 68-54.

Following the season, point guard Varez Ward–a player Barbee had fought to get for years, going back to his early recruitment when Barbee was at UTEP–was arrested on charges of point shaving.

"It is obviously an extremely serious situation any time allegations of point shaving are made," said AD Jay Jacobs after word got out about the arrest. "When this matter was brought to our attention in 2012, Auburn immediately reported what we knew to the FBI, the NCAA and the SEC."

Eventually the case was dismissed when Ward agreed to go into a pre-trial diversion program and fully cooperate with the FBI. Neither he nor Auburn were found guilty of any wrongdoing.

THE 2012-2013 SEASON
9-23 (3-15, 14th in the SEC)

Rob Chubb (C)
Frankie Sullivan (G)
Allen Payne (F)
Chris Denson (G)
Noel Johnson (F)
Shaquille Johnson (G)
Jordan Price (G)

Josh Wallace (G)
Asauhn Dixon-Tatum (C)
Brian Greene (G)
Jordon Granger (F)
Shareif Adamu (F)
Nick Pellar (F)

Perhaps the most notable thing about the Tigers' 2012-13 campaign was that they played three overtime games–two of which went to double-overtime–and lost all three.

They went on to lose 15 of their final 16 games, the only exception being a 49-37 win over Alabama at home on February 6, when Cam Newton showed up at the Arena to root the Tigers on. It was the worst single-season stretch in Auburn history and the longest losing streak since 1989.

With a 3-15 conference record, they finished dead last in the newly-expanded, 14-team league, and faced 11-seed Texas A&M in the first game of the SEC Tournament in Nashville. They proceeded to lose that game, too, 71-62.

After three seasons as the Tigers' head coach, Tony Barbee's record stood at 35-59.

The less said about this season, the better.

THE 2013-2014 SEASON
14-16 (6-12, 12th in the SEC)

Allen Payne (F)
K.T. Harrell (G)
Chris Denson (G)
Asauhn Dixon-Tatum (C)
Tahj Shamsid-Deen (G)
Jordon Granger (F)

Dion Wade (G)
Malcolm Canada (G)
Chris Griffin (F)
Matthew Atewe (C)
Benas Griciunas (C)

The season that turned out to be Tony Barbee's final one on the Plains saw a doubling of SEC wins, but the basement had been so low already, a doubling only amounted to 6 wins, good for 12th place out of 14.

Van Allen Plexico:
The turnover of the roster during Tony Barbee's years as Auburn's coach was truly remarkable. It seems like, every season, more than half the players from the roster disappeared and new ones appeared–and then, the next year, most of them would be gone, too. It's almost like they didn't find playing for Barbee as appealing as he made it sound during the recruiting process.

In fact, ESPN notes that, of the 21 players Barbee signed while at Auburn, only nine remained on the roster as of his fourth season, due to player dismissals and transfers.

It's interesting to note that this season we picked up a seven-foot-tall center from Lithuania, by way of Findlay Prep School: Benas Griciunas. You'd think a seven-foot center could be dominant, but he only averaged 2 points and 1.8 rebounds per game all season.

Barbee's Tigers failed to win a conference game until January 30 against Alabama in Auburn Arena, 74-55. They actually managed to go 6-6 the rest of the way, beginning with that win.

They entered the SEC Tournament in Atlanta with the 12-seed and faced South Carolina. The Gamecocks handled them easily, winning 74-56.

Less than two hours after that game ended, Auburn AD Jay Jacobs tweeted the news that Barbee had been terminated. He had informed Barbee of that fact at the team hotel in Atlanta immediately after the game.

"After careful evaluation of the last four years, I feel this is best for the program," Jacobs said. "I believe we should compete for championships in men's basketball. It's time for somebody else to have a turn. We need to find somebody to come in here and take what we have here now and put some more in and compete for SEC titles."

And just like that, the Barbee Era was over.

Tony Barbee's final record at Auburn was 48-75, a number that looked remarkably similar to many of his game score totals as Auburn's coach. Perhaps worst of all, in his four seasons at Auburn, Barbee's teams never made the postseason and never won a single SEC Tournament game.

Phillip Marshall wrote about his earliest misgivings in regards to Barbee:

Phillip Marshall (in an Auburn Undercover article in 2015):
...What really got my attention was my first one-on-one interview with Barbee... Once in (his) office, I shook his hand and sat down. The very first words from Barbee to me were "Can you believe this office furniture?" I did not know what to say. My unspoken thought was that if I made $1.5 million a year and didn't like the office furniture, I'd buy my own.

John Ringer:
That's a perfect example of Barbee's priorities. It was about him. Not about going out and getting some good players, and so forth. That goes back to what I said about him wanting dinners bought for him and his staff. His mindset was, "My money is mine; Auburn is going to take care of everything else for me."

Phillip Marshall:

It quickly became obvious that Barbee and Auburn (did not make for) an ideal match. He signed a big-time prospect who had no chance to get into school at Auburn or anywhere else in the SEC and was angry that no one could make it happen. After that, it was one thing after another.

But, really, that wasn't the biggest problem. The biggest problem was that Barbee couldn't keep guys on his team. He lost players and games at an alarming rate. ...

In short, Barbee left a huge mess for Bruce Pearl to clean up.

Brian Stultz (writing in USA Today's AuburnWire):

You won't find many people connected to Auburn that (have) nice words to say about Tony Barbee. I include myself in that. I once wrote that he was "unearned arrogance wrapped in expensive suits."

Well, I say we should all let bygones be bygones because without Barbee, Auburn basketball wouldn't be where it is today. We should appreciate him for that.

It has worked out beautifully for Auburn. (Bruce) Pearl came in and immediately went to work on getting the interest of students and alumni alike back in the Tigers. Barbee wouldn't dare mingle with the fans.

Things have obviously worked out for Barbee as well. He's back under the guidance of John Calipari (and)...if I know him, has a golf club membership written into his contract.

Auburn would have never reached that point (of feeling like they had a chance to win every time they played a game) with you. So thanks, Tony Barbee. You reluctantly helped Auburn reach a point once unthinkable. You burnt it down so someone else could totally rebuild it.

In retrospect, Barbee's main accomplishment for Auburn was to occupy the head coach's position just long enough for Bruce Pearl to become available. And that he did. And what happened next would change everything for Auburn Basketball.

John Ringer:
That's exactly right. And to put Auburn back on the market for a head coach when Bruce Pearl was available.

I'm not a fan of Tony Barbee. There's not a coach in any sport we've hired that I have more hard feelings for than him. I don't think he cared about Auburn a bit, and I don't think he was a nice person to the people he worked with and that worked for him. He didn't have success and didn't do the things he said he would do.

Van Allen Plexico:
You may have noticed that when Auburn fired Tommy Joe Eagles and Cliff Ellis and Jeff Lebo, in each case the University's announcement praised them as people—talked about how much we still loved them and wished them well, and how we were just going in a different direction.

With Barbee, you didn't really see that. It was more like, "Don't let the door to Auburn Arena hit you on the backside on the way out." That speaks volumes.

Tony Barbee finished his stint as Auburn's head basketball coach with a cumulative record of 49–75 (.395), giving him the lowest winning percentage of any Auburn head coach with more than a two-season tenure in program history.

But all things basketball-related were about to get a whole lot better on the Plains. As soon as Jay Jacobs figured out how to convince a certain coach that his true destiny lay on the Plains…

- 5 -

THE BRUCE PEARL ERA
2014 - LIFE

On March 18, 2014, after six days of what Joel Erickson of AL.com described as a "whirlwind search," Jay Jacobs announced the hiring of former Tennessee head coach Bruce Pearl as Auburn's new coach.

Jacobs led the search alone. He immediately identified Pearl as his target and pursued him despite the former UT coach still being under a show-cause.

"From the moment I met Coach Pearl and heard his vision for our basketball program, it was clear he's the right man at the right time for Auburn," Jacobs said. "Coach Pearl is a proven winner who will bring energy and excitement to our program. We have raised the bar for Auburn basketball, and I could not be more excited for our student-athletes and our future under Coach Pearl's leadership. I know he agrees with me—it's time to win."

Pearl's resume sparkled: He owned a 231-99 record in ten seasons of Division I basketball, amassing eight NCAA Tournament appearances, three Sweet Sixteen finishes and one Elite Eight.

There was only one reason why a coach of Pearl's caliber would be available for Jacobs and Auburn to swoop in and hire: He was at that time in the final months of a three-year show-cause penalty imposed by the NCAA, meaning an institution that wished to hire him would essentially inherit the penalties originally levied on the coach, and the new school would have to "show cause" to the NCAA why it should be allowed to hire the coach without penalty. It also banned him from recruiting until August 23 of that year.

Auburn felt relatively confident in making the move in part because their assistant athletic director of compliance, Dave Didion, had been the lead investigator in the Pearl case originally, giving Auburn the sense that it could help Pearl navigate the tricky NCAA waters until the penalty expired. Reportedly, Didion agreed with Auburn's decision to pursue Pearl.

In truth, Auburn had little choice but to make the move when it did, because a coach of Pearl's caliber would not have been unemployed for long, once the penalties and the show-cause expired. Jacobs merely got the jump on everyone else by going after Pearl when he did. And in return, Pearl reportedly felt a sense of appreciation that Auburn wanted him badly enough to make the move so early.

As Joel Erickson put it, writing for *AL dot com*, "Popular with fans and media, Pearl has a big personality that makes him a good fit for building support for the school across the state. In addition to his lengthy history of winning, Pearl knows the SEC, and he understands what it's like to revitalize basketball at a school with a high-profile football program."

"I'm humbled and blessed to be back in the game that I love," Pearl said upon being announced as Auburn's twentieth head basketball coach. "I don't know how long it will take, but it's time to rebuild the Auburn basketball program, and bring it to a level of excellence so many of the other teams on campus enjoy.

"We will play for championships. We're fixing to get Auburn into that position where we'll be going to the NCAA tournament. ...Jay talked about raising the bar in men's basketball. Have you seen the contract I signed yet? When you see the number... He raised the bar in men's basketball. I'm just keeping it real, okay? ...I would not have gone (back to coaching) this year had I not felt this was the right opportunity. I was prepared to not coach this year."

Charles Barkley was pleased with the hire, stating, "Coach Pearl has a proven track record and he's a great fit for our program. WDE."

THE HIRE

Going into the Alabama game on January 30, 2014, in what would be the final year of the Barbee regime, both teams were below .500, with Auburn yet to have won a game in the SEC. That week, according to reporting by Tom Green for *AL dot com*, Jay Jacobs made the decision to look for a new coach at the end of the season. And Jacobs already knew whom he wanted that new coach to be.

"Bruce was the guy that was the coach I had on my mind for several weeks," Jacobs told Green in 2022. "We had a history of hiring coaches that maybe weren't at the same level. I didn't want to do that this time. I wanted to hire somebody that had a proven background of winning at different levels and could compete in the SEC."

Jacobs knew of Pearl's controversial history. He spoke with Dave Didion, who had served for five years as the NCAA's director of enforcement and had overseen the NCAA's investigation of Pearl at Tennessee. Now working as Auburn's assistant athletics director, Didion was in prime position to render judgment on Pearl to Jacobs.

Didion did not hesitate with his response: If it was up to him, he would hire Pearl.

"(Didion's response) shocked me a little bit," Jacobs said later, "because Dave is a black-and-white guy when it comes to the rules."

Jacobs asked Didion why he felt so strongly that way. According to Jacobs, Didion replied, "Because Jay, he made a mistake. He was remorseful for it immediately. I just believe people like that — he's a good person — once they make a mistake, I don't think they'll ever make the same one again."

Jacobs then asked SEC Commissioner Mike Slive his opinion. Slive was unequivocal as well. "It is time for Bruce Pearl to be back in the SEC."

With those endorsements in his pocket, Jacobs had little trouble convincing Auburn president Jay Gogue, who gave his blessing to the AD to pursue Pearl.

Green tells the story of the meetings (plural!) between Jacobs and Pearl in full detail in an article published on *AL dot com* in March of 2022, and it is worth a read. A brief summary goes like this:

Jacobs met with Pearl in a hotel room in Bristol, Connecticut, the home of ESPN, where Pearl was working as a TV analyst. They talked deep into the evening, and Jacobs came away surprised with how reluctant Pearl was to even consider returning to basketball coaching at that time.

"Bruce was struggling to consider himself a viable candidate," Jacobs said later. "He had a lot of remorse and embarrassment for his family because of what went on at Tennessee. He was really more or less talking to himself about how could he do this? How could he get through the show-cause? Quite frankly, it wasn't the interview that you have with the guy who was trying to become your next head coach."

The two met again the next morning to continue the conversation. Before they met for the second time in two days, Pearl spoke with his wife, Brandy. She advised him that, before the meeting, he should fully imagine himself as Auburn's coach; to put on an imaginary Auburn jacket and see how it felt. He took her advice.

"It felt good," Pearl said later. "It felt like the jacket fit."

Pearl discussed the job with his family and with a former Tennessee player, Jordan Howell, who knew the Auburn situation fairly well. Howell extolled the virtues and the potential of the Auburn program, describing its success under Sonny Smith and Cliff Ellis.

Green quotes Pearl's son, Steven: "It would mean way more (to be successful at Auburn) than doing it at another place that already had a bunch of history and a bunch of success. I think BP wanted to take on that challenge of doing it here, because I think it makes it more special when you do it at a place that doesn't have a ton of history."

Green quotes an important statement by Pearl: "Getting fired at Tennessee was very painful. Still is. I didn't know if I ever wanted to put my family through that again. We didn't handle it the right way (during the investigation at Tennessee). We panicked going into our NCAA interviews without attorneys. Why? Because who does that?... We didn't tell the truth about that one incident. We all panicked. Came back, told the NCAA right away, man, 'You guys got to come back; we didn't tell you the truth.' At that point, it was too late."

Jacobs was determined to secure Pearl for Auburn. He flew to Knoxville on March 17 and gave the Pearl family a surprise visit in their home. After another conversation, they concluded the broad strokes of the coaching deal that night—the eve of Pearl's 54th birthday.

Looking back in 2022, Jacobs says, "Auburn was the right place at the right time, and Bruce Pearl was at the right place at the right time to lead this program."

John Ringer:

I was excited about hiring Bruce Pearl. He had delivered results in his previous jobs. He'd made Tennessee a perennial SEC contender and an NCAA Tournament team every year he was the coach there. They made the NCAA Tournament every year. So that told me he can do the job in this league.

He was working at ESPN as a broadcaster and was good at that, and it allowed us to see he was personable and funny and could do what was necessary to be successful.

We were willing to hire him when others were not, and that made him grateful to Auburn.

There were folks on the hiring committee who felt he was the only choice.

The show cause was short-term. We had a great coach and would be okay in the long term.

Van Allen Plexico:

I was definitely excited. I remember being impressed with him when he was at Tennessee. Bruce just brings energy and excitement with him. And he can recruit! Anybody who can make Auburn look like a great destination for 5-star basketball talent deserves a lifetime contract, in my view.

John Ringer:

The Bruce Pearl hire also impacts the legacy of Jay Jacobs at Auburn. Jacobs has mixed reviews overall from Auburn fans for his tenure as Athletic Director. But he hired Bruce Pearl and he got the new arena built, and those are things that I would describe as absolute successes. One of the best decisions Auburn athletics ever made was hiring Bruce Pearl.

And so Bruce Pearl packed up his bags and moved to the Plains.

To be fair, though, he carried metaphorical baggage with him as well; baggage from beyond just the events at Tennessee. Years earlier, there was another incident, this one involving recruiting at Illinois. Auburn fans need to understand all of this in order to fully appreciate what is true about the man, and what is a distortion by those determined to attack him.

THE ILLINOIS AFFAIR

In 1989, Bruce Pearl was an assistant coach at Iowa. He was lead recruiter that year for "Mr. Basketball" in Illinois, Deon Thomas. During the recruiting process, one of Thomas's teammates informed Pearl that University of Illinois assistant coach Jimmy Collins had offered Thomas $80,000 and a Chevy Blazer to join the Illini.

As the story goes, Pearl then secretly tape-recorded a conversation with Thomas (in which Thomas seemingly admitted the offer) and turned the tape over to the NCAA, which in turn launched an 18-month investigation into Illinois basketball recruiting practices.

The investigation ultimately could not prove the most severe charges related to the Thomas recruitment, but it did find other severe violations by the Illini, resulting in a "lack of institutional control" finding by the NCAA, and three years of probation.

To this day, Illinois fans remain hateful to the point of dementia toward Pearl for causing their sins to be uncovered by the authorities.

Despite that, Pearl took the opportunity a decade ago to try to make some amends with the former Illinois assistant coach he'd accused, 23 years after the incident occurred.

In an uncredited story in the April 3, 2012 edition of the *Alton (IL) Telegraph*, an unnamed Illinois fan reports that Pearl ran into former Illinois assistant coach Jimmy Collins and current assistant coach Jerrance Howard on Bourbon Street in New Orleans during the 2012 Final Four weekend in that city. According to the account given to the Telegraph, Pearl saw them as they all passed one another, and he went back and addressed Collins.

According to the alleged witness, Pearl "came right up to Jimmy (Collins) and extended his hand. And he said, 'I'm sorry, Jimmy. I was young. I was stupid. I was immature. Deon was the victim.'"

The witness noted that "Collins was a gentleman about the apology."

Moments later, after Pearl had moved along, Thomas himself came down the same street, and was told by Collins of the apology by Pearl.

"I was surprised," Thomas said later. "It's something I never thought he would do."

The article noted that Thomas felt Pearl owed him an apology, as well, but that he had "moved on."

"My grandmother used to say, 'When you're climbing the ladder, make sure you don't step on people on the way up because you might have to come back down,'" Thomas told the *Telegraph*.

Despite all of this, the article refers to Pearl as "the most reviled opposing coach in Illinois basketball history."

A 2019 story on the *SBNation* site, as Auburn was on its way to the Final Four, quoted an unnamed D-1 head coach: "You can be a cheat or a snitch and still get respect in this sport. Being both makes that a lot harder. (Pearl) can get away with it because he's charming and, you know, a hell of a coach."

It seemed a number of people, for whatever reason, had made up their minds about Bruce Pearl back when he was, as he himself put it, "young" and "immature." Few of those people seemed interested in revising their attitudes, despite all later evidence indicating that they should.

Van Allen Plexico:
I live in Illinois. I have good friends who graduated from the University of Illinois ("the U of I," as they call it). They appreciate my rabid Auburn fandom and, for the most part, are fine with it.

But they hate our basketball coach, John. They despise him. It's truly remarkable how much they still carry a grudge over all that. And it mystifies me.

Think about how we used to feel about Eric and Twilitta Ramsey (the former Auburn DB and his wife, who got Auburn in trouble in the late 1980s and early 1990s by claiming Pat Dye was paying players and giving them free food). Now imagine Ramsey had been one of the Mississippi State football coaches or boosters who tried to get Auburn investigated over the Cam Newton recruitment. Now multiply that by four or five. That's how Illinois people come across today over this incident from 1990. It's astounding to me.

But, in any case, we were able to get Bruce–and we all know what kind of person he really is and what he's accomplished on the Plains. I enjoy living in Illinois, but–in this particular case–"the U of I" can kiss my butt.

So, there was the Illinois incident. Then, years later, there was the infamous "barbecue incident" at Tennessee.

THE BARBECUE

In 2005, Bruce Pearl's long climb back up to the top ranks of coaching culminated with his hire by the University of Tennessee. Within three years, he led the Vols to the 2007-08 SEC regular-season championship, the program's first-ever No. 1 ranking in the AP Poll (sounds familiar, doesn't it?) and one of many visits to the NCAA Tournament.

A few years later, however, reports emerged of Pearl inviting top recruits to his home in Knoxville during the fall of 2008, against the rules. Pearl denied the reports, but then photos came to light that showed recruit Aaron Craft at a barbecue at Pearl's home. At first, Pearl continued to deny the allegations to NCAA investigators. Then, realizing the mistake he'd made, he called them back in 2010 and asked them to return, so that he could tell them the truth.

The University of Tennessee penalized him but did not fire him at first. Four days later, however, Pearl and an assistant committed a "bump rule" violation of the type pioneered by Alabama's Nick Saban, bumping into a recruit at an event. Pearl did not self-report the incident immediately, earning an eight-game suspension from SEC Commissioner Mike Slive.

On March 22, 2011, Tennessee fired Pearl. On August 25, the NCAA added a three-year "show-cause" penalty for Pearl, along with one-year penalties of the same type for three former UT assistants. The NCAA pointed out in the report that the violations would have been viewed as less significant if not for the evasiveness on Pearl's part.

Auburn hired Pearl to a six-year deal, four months before the end of his three-year show-cause penalty, making him the first coach in college basketball history to be hired by one school while still under show-cause from another. That penalty ended on August 24, 2014.

Van Allen Plexico:
I have said this over and over: Having that barbecue, and misleading the NCAA about it, was wrong. But it was also one of the best things that ever happened to Auburn athletics. Because if Bruce's career had continued on as it was then going, either Tennessee would have continued on an upward trajectory and become one of the "blue blood" powers of the SEC, if they could've held onto him, or Bruce would've moved on a true "blue blood" program like Kansas or UCLA, and that's where he would be today.

The only way–the *only way*–he ever could've ended up at Auburn is if he did something he himself would admit was incredibly dumb at Tennessee, and got himself fired over it. And he did. And now he's at Auburn, building our team into a dominant "blue blood" program. And we're incredibly fortunate it all worked out that way.

John Ringer:
What he got in trouble about was lying about it at first. If he'd admitted he'd done it, it would've been a slap on the wrist. The lying was the bad part.

So I think it's the kind of thing where we've come a long way with how we view this kind of thing. A coach giving a kid a sandwich outside of the recruiting window is not that big a deal. He should've said, "Yes, I gave the kid a hamburger."

But I also agree it made a huge difference because he never would've been available for Auburn to hire otherwise.

Van Allen Plexico:
We are put in the position of being glad our current coach did something bad before he was our coach. How should we feel about that?

John Ringer:
NCAA violations are not a moral quandary. Athletes should be rewarded for the benefits of their labor. The NCAA makes a fortune off their labor and (at least until recently), they don't get anything. So my view is, athletes should be getting a cut. And this stuff's been going on all the time, forever. We're bringing it above board now, doing it the right way and paying taxes on it now.

I'm not going to take up for the NCAA. I think the idea that Bruce Pearl is some kind of pariah for this stuff is silly. He's a good human being who cares about other people and does a lot for them. The idea that he's somehow sleazy because of this stuff is just nonsense to me.

A lot of it goes back to 2010 football for me (and how Auburn was treated by the NCAA during the Cam Newton investigation). As far as I'm concerned, the NCAA can kiss off.

THE 2014-2015 SEASON
15-20 (4-14, 13th in the SEC)

K.T. Harrell (G)	Cinmeon Bowers (F)
Tahj Shamsid-Deen (G)	Antoine Mason (G)
T.J. Lang (G)	K.C. Ross-Miller (G)
Jordon Granger (F)	Alex Thompson (F)
Malcolm Canada (G)	Trayvon Reed (C)

Pearl went to work immediately, rallying fan support across campus by dropping into classes and bringing Aubie and some of his players with him. He also did his best to bring in new players to bolster the team's depleted ranks–despite having to defer direct recruiting of players to the assistant coaches until August. As a result, in addition to stalwarts K.T. Harrell and Tahj Shamsid-Deen, inherited from the previous regime, Pearl added notable transfers Cinmeon Bowers (from Chipola College) and Antoine Mason (from Niagara University), among others.

His senior leader on that team was Harrell, a 6-5 guard who would average 18.5 points per game in his final campaign. Harrell was joined by fellow senior Mason, junior Bowers at forward and sophomore guard Tahj Shamsid-Deen, a talented player with nagging shoulder injury issues throughout his career.

The 2014-15 season ended up slightly worse than Tony Barbee's last season, in terms of their position in the final SEC standings. The Tigers dropped from 12th to 13th in the league, and lost two more conference games.

After trading wins and losses early on, Auburn lost four straight to end January. They managed 2-2 early in February, with wins at LSU and at Georgia. But then they finished the regular season with a six-game losing streak, including a horrific 110-75 defeat at the hands of No. 1 Kentucky in Rupp Arena. Entering the SEC Tournament in Nashville as the 13-seed, no one could've expected much from these Tigers.

What they did next shocked everyone.

They beat 12-seed Mississippi State on Wednesday night, 74-68, on the strength of K.C. Ross-Miller's 21 points and 7 rebounds. The next night, they defeated 5-seed Texas A&M, 66-59, as K.T. Harrell poured in 25, to go with Bowers' 8 rebounds. On Friday night in the Quarterfinals, they faced 4-seed LSU and took them to overtime before winning, 73-70, with Harrell and Bowers again leading the stat lines, scoring 29 and grabbing 10 rebounds, respectively. Suddenly the lowly Tigers found themselves in the Semifinals of the SEC Tournament–a spot they hadn't occupied in quite a while.

Unfortunately, an Auburn squad missing two key pieces was not able to go toe-to-toe with the Wildcats. The Tigers fell, 91-67.

Bowers was not available for the Kentucky game, due to an unspecified "rules violation" that Bruce Pearl was made aware of just after the LSU game the day before.

"It's obviously in the very early stages," Pearl said. "We hope that when we finish looking into the matter, everything is okay... It was enough that we felt like we wanted to be on the safe side."

This was far from the first time Bowers had flirted with controversy. He'd been shot multiple times in high school during a car robbery, then arrested for allegedly eating marijuana to conceal it from police. Florida State released him from his scholarship after that incident. He then tweeted about his visit to Auburn in 2014, which coaches retweeted, somehow causing an NCAA violation involving "creating public electronic messages to a prospect." During the 2014-2015 season, however, he had shown signs of maturing and had emerged as a key player for the team.

"It would have been a lot different (with Bowers)," said K.T. Harrell after the game—his last as an Auburn Tiger. "He's a tough matchup, and the way he's been playing defensively has been really good. We knew we would have to play ten times better without him, and we gave it all we could."

The Tigers were also playing without Jordon Granger, suspended due to a Flagrant 2 foul in the LSU game.

"Not having both of them made it really difficult to win," Pearl said afterward. "We had both (at Kentucky in the previous meeting) and got beat by five touchdowns, so it wasn't like..." He trailed off. "I just think from a team standpoint it's tough to have this be your last game and not be able to play and we would have loved to be able to go into this game as a unit."

"We made it all the way to the semifinals," said Harrell. "To play against the No. 1 team in the country in my last game, it gets no better than that."

About four hours after the Kentucky game ended, Auburn received a commitment from Atlanta's Jared Harper, a 3-star point guard. He was the first commitment to Auburn's 2016 class, meaning he would be arriving after the upcoming season ended. Suffice to say, Auburn fans would be seeing a lot out of this young recruit in the future.

Senior K.T. Harrell was named second-team All-SEC despite leading the league in scoring and in 3-point shooting. The mystery was how he missed making the first team. (As of this writing, he is back at Auburn, serving as a graduate assistant with the basketball program.)

John Ringer:
That season and the tournament run at the end gave us all a dose of hope, after not being "fine" for a long time. It made us feel we could get there, and could be competitive.

Despite their late-season success, this was a bad defensive Auburn team. They were 306th in the country in points allowed. When they lost, they tended to get blown out a lot, by 20 or more points. It didn't help that the average height on the roster was 6 foot 4.

After this season, Bruce knew he needed experience and he needed size.

One player that would be joining the Tigers very soon, and adding quite a bit of offense and defense, was one Bryce Brown of Decatur, Georgia. On September 21, 2014, the 3-star shooting guard committed—to UNC-Charlotte.

In October he visited Auburn, and promptly decommitted from Charlotte.

On November 14, he signed with Auburn, joining New Williams, Danjel Purifoy and TJ Dunans in the 2015 signing class. Later they would be joined by Horace Spencer.

Brown averaged 18 points and 5 assists per game as a junior in high school, and was ranked the No. 86 shooting guard in the nation by 24/7 Sports. He was also being recruited by Kennesaw State, St Peters, Georgia Southern and Florida International. At 369th nationally overall, he was the lowest-ranked recruit in the Tigers' signing class.

Those other programs were probably not heartbroken to lose such a player. It's doubtful they expected him to light up the SEC with 3-point shooting, or make it to the Final Four someday.

In his junior year, 2018, in the final game of the regular season, against South Carolina, Bryce Brown would make 8 of 12 3-point shots to help the Tigers win the SEC title.

In his senior season, Brown would have 21 games in which he made four or more 3-point shots. Seven of those games came in the postseason. Against Kansas in the Round of 32 of the NCAA Tournament, Brown would make 7 of 11 3-pointers.

This from the 369th ranked player in the country.

Yes, help was definitely on the way.

THE 2015-2016 SEASON
11-20 (5-13, 13th in the SEC)

Tyler Harris (F)
Kareem Canty (G)
Tahj Shamsid-Deen (G)
T.J. Lang (G)
Jordon Granger (F)
Cinmeon Bowers (F)

Bryce Brown (G)
T.J. Dunans (G)
Horace Spencer (F)
New Williams (G)
Cole Blackstock (F)

2015-2016 was unfortunately another forgettable season for the Tigers. They won only 5 SEC games and lost quickly in the postseason.

The year started out very promising, with buzz around junior guard Kareem Canty in particular. But, as Walt Austin put it, in the *College and Magnolia* blog, "As the team got into its preseason practice, things turned a bit sour. Tahj Shamsid-Deen hurt his shoulder again. New Williams tweaked a knee. All of a sudden things weren't looking quite as rosy."

Probably the bright spot of the season came the week of January 16-19, 2016. Over the course of four days, the Tigers beat No. 14 Kentucky and then Alabama, both in Auburn Arena. The Wildcats fell to Auburn, 75-70, and the Tide was defeated, 83-77.

"In those games, Kareem Canty rained three-pointers like sweet summer afternoon storms," said Austin.

On the day before the Kentucky game, Cinmeon Bowers stated that Auburn would win and that the Tigers' guards were better than Kentucky's guards.

It's no exaggeration to say few people believed him. But he was right.

Indeed, Auburn guard Kareem Canty led all scorers with 26.

"Cim says a lot of things but I was happy he said that," Canty stated. "When I heard about what he said, I thought, 'Wow—now I really have to come with it.'"

"I had talked to Cim about no bulletin board material. Do you now understand my pain?" Pearl said, joking. "At the same time, you love him for what he is and who he is."

"Anyone want to talk to me now?" Bowers growled after the win. "Growing up and coming from where I came from (Harlem, New

York), there's two things you always want to do in college basketball and that's either going to Kentucky or playing against Kentucky. I knew I had all my people in the neighborhood watching today. All the world was watching today."

"We weren't intimidated by the moment," said Pearl afterwards. "This gives us hope. ...It sends a message to recruits that we warranted their belief.

"I'm happy for our students because I haven't been able to provide that return on the investment yet. I wanted to see (the celebration on the court afterward) and I wanted to see the players enjoy themselves in it."

"We're not a vintage Auburn team," said Canty. "We have a chance to build this program with Bruce and it feels great."

After the final buzzer, Auburn fans swamped the court. It was Auburn's first win against Kentucky in 16 games and only their second in 34 tries. It was their first win over a ranked opponent since 2012.

Wildcats assistant coach Tony Barbee was not in attendance at his old stomping grounds for that game. According to Kentucky officials, he was on a recruiting trip.

Sadly, no sooner were those two games in the books than the Tigers suffered a 7-game losing streak from January 23 through February 13, followed by a 3-game losing streak to close out the regular season schedule. They lost the away leg of the two games against Alabama. The sole bright spot there–if it could be called one–was that it was their only SEC loss all year that didn't come by double-digits.

They then lost their opening game in the SEC Tournament to Tennessee, and in devastating fashion, 97-59, to end the season.

John Ringer:

That Tennessee game in the SEC Tournament was a beat down. Bruce needed to continue to improve the talent level on the roster.

We had no doubts about him as a coach. We just needed players.

Van Allen Plexico:
We had added a few, but they were still young. More help was coming!

And games like the one against Kentucky showed us all what was possible, if we could just build up our roster a little more.

Just before the game against Georgia on February 6, Kareem Canty—who was rumored to be suffering from an "attitude problem"— was suspended. He had led the team in scoring, with 18 points per game, and that contribution would be terribly missed.

"Kareem has had some strong moments for our team this season," said Pearl in a statement. "He has demonstrated that at the highest level of competition, he can win his matchup. However, his effort and attitude have been extremely inconsistent, which led to actions that are unacceptable."

The Tigers would have to go on without him. As it turned out, his season—and his Auburn career—were over. He would not play for the Tigers again. On February 11, while still suspended, he announced he would enter the NBA Draft.

Three months later, he told reporter James Crepea, "I said a lot of things, I got into an altercation with Steven Pearl that I regret and I learned from, which led to my suspension. That was a mistake that I made on my part that I should have just finished out the season. I just decided to leave after my two-game suspension because of my frustration with the season, and I handled that all wrong instead of just sticking it out and riding with my teammates."

"It wasn't just a run-in with my son, Steven; there was a series of run-ins," said Bruce Pearl. "Kareem is passionate and he's intense and there were times where he was as good as anybody out there on the floor. Had we had more success, had I had a little bit more depth, had we had some better players to play with, I really think he could have survived it and not made some of the mistakes that he made."

"I'm in the real world now," Canty told Crepea, "so a lot of the things that I got away with before or that I didn't think were a big deal, it's kind of a big deal to me now. The things that I was taking for granted, I don't take for granted as much anymore. That situation at Auburn really changed how I view things in life.

"I went to Auburn as a boy from the city that didn't have a clue about Auburn and I left as a boy still, but I'm transitioning to a man," Canty said. "I look back at it like, 'I really love Auburn and miss everything that they did for me.'

"(I learned to) listen to the coaches. All they ever tried to do was help me and I wasn't trying to buy all the way in like I should have. All they ever tried to do was make me a man and I was too focused on other things that caught my attention."

As of the 2021-22 season, Canty was playing with the Windsor Express of the Canadian pro basketball league.

THE 2016-2017 SEASON
18-14 (7-11, 11th in the SEC)

Mustapha Heron (G)	Bryce Brown (G)
Jared Harper (G)	Horace Spencer (F)
Danjel Purifoy (F)	Austin Wiley (C)
T.J. Dunans (G)	LaRon Smith (F)
Ronnie Johnson (G)	Will Macoy (G)
Anfernee McLemore (F)	Cole Blackstock (F)
T.J. Lang (G)	

Coming into the 2016-2017 season, Bruce Pearl signed what was to that point the highest-regarded player he'd brought on board yet, and possibly the highest-rated recruit in Auburn basketball history, to that point: Mustapha Heron, a 5-star guard from Waterbury, Connecticut.

Heron became the first 5-star player to come to Auburn since Rivals began ranking prospects in 2002. He was the 26th best player in the country that year.

Pearl was enthused to have him aboard. "He's a program changer. Not just because he's a five-star and probable McDonald's All-American, probably the third one we've ever had here at Auburn, but he's an incredible young man.

"The combination of seeing historically how my wings have scored, particularly like K.T. Harrell as a senior, and our system of playing fast, (plus) Chuck Person getting to coach him at his position...was very attractive to Mustapha."

The Scout web site was quite impressed with Heron's signing. Evan Daniels, their director of basketball recruiting, said, "When Bruce gets a Mustapha Heron from New York (where he was playing AAU basketball), that's a program changer for Auburn. The reason I say that clearly Bruce is going to take this nationally with recruiting."

Along with Heron, the Tigers also welcomed aboard point guard and long-time commit Jared Harper. They also signed forward Anfernee McLemore, who would go on to become another big-time contributor.

And finally, about the same time Pearl was welcoming Heron aboard, he received a verbal commitment from Spain Park 5-star center Austin Wiley, son of former Tiger Aubrey Wiley and Auburn All-American superstar Vickie Orr. That gave the Tigers two 5-star McDonald's All-Americans on the same roster–something no Auburn team had ever been able to claim before.

The Tigers finished higher this season than they had before under Bruce Pearl, winning 7 SEC games and rising to 11th in the conference.

Unfortunately, they won only 2 games after February 7 and lost in the first round of the SEC Tournament (again)—this time to Missouri, 86-83, in overtime.

One bright spot this season was a rare sweep of Alabama. The Tigers beat the Tide by 20 at home on January 21, 84-64. On February 4 they achieved a similar result in Tuscaloosa, taking down Alabama, 82-77.

"They count the same, but sometimes these types of wins mean more," Pearl said after beating Alabama in Coleman Coliseum. "Even when I was at Tennessee, winning here mattered more because of the rivalry with football."

"How many 3-pointers did they make tonight? Fifteen? Come on, man," said Tide guard Corban Collins afterward. "Sometimes shooters just need to see one or two go down and then it's all she wrote."

Six different Auburn players made 3-point baskets for the Tigers during the game, with the team going 15 for 27 overall. Bryce Brown broke out of a mini-slump to hit 3 of his first 4 3-point shots. Mustapha Heron made four free throws at the end to stop an Alabama comeback attempt and seal the win.

It was the Tigers' first sweep of the Tide since 2009.

Heron was named to the 2017 SEC All-Freshman team, after leading Auburn in scoring (15.2 points per game) and rebounding (6.1 rebounds per game). He was also named to the SEC All-Community Service team for his work in encouraging academic success for athletes at his high school in Connecticut, and for promoting a weapons buy-back program there.

John Ringer:
This is the core of the Final Four team, but still young and inexperienced.

Heron was 18th overall in the country in recruiting, one of the highest we'd ever had. It proved Pearl could go out and get players like that. He was from Connecticut–not a legacy like Austin Wiley and not from down the road like Chris Porter. He could've gone anywhere in the country he wanted to go.

He was a good player, the leading scorer on this team as a true freshman, and again as a sophomore. Especially offensively. For whatever reason, after two seasons he was gone. A lot of those shots he was taking went to Bryce Brown and others.

Van Allen Plexico:
There were medical issues with his mother, and he wanted to be closer to home, so he transferred to St John's.

Were we better without him?

John Ringer:
It's a good question. What the team needed was experience, and they got that. And we kind of replaced him later with Samir Doughty.

We've been able to change out players pretty successfully, year to year, under Bruce Pearl. His ability to bring in new talent, and adjust and adapt when players leave for any reason, has been impressive. He brings in more talent year after year and keeps it going.

Van Allen Plexico:
How did you feel about the program after three years under Bruce?

John Ringer:
In Bruce Pearl's first three seasons, we finished 13th, 13th and 11th in the SEC.

It was similar to the first few years with Sonny Smith, and in both cases you had to feel like things were bound to improve. This is unlike how we felt with the first few seasons of Tony Barbee.

I felt we were moving in the right direction, we just needed to get there.

THE CHUCK PERSON INCIDENT

In September 2017, the FBI revealed that it had been investigating shady practices by a number of college basketball programs. They arrested four assistant coaches on the day of the announcement, one of which was Auburn assistant coach and former star player, Chuck Person.

Person had joined Pearl's Auburn staff at the very beginning, bringing with him Auburn connections and NBA success. The events of 2017 would bring that job to a very sudden end. Person was hit with six federal charges including bribery, fraud and conspiracy.

Shortly after the Person arrest, Auburn put two other coaching staff members on leave, and was told by the NCAA that Danjel Purifoy and Austin Wiley had to sit out the entire 2017-2018 season.

Said Auburn's then-president, Steven Leath, "There is no rush to judgment here and we have been working with the coach for weeks to find a solution to this difficult situation. Having three of his employees suspended or terminated is troublesome at best. His unwillingness to even talk to me about it is particularly troublesome."

In January 2018, Pearl was asked by ESPN's Jimmy Dykes what he had learned from this latest controversy. "That my faith in God has never been stronger and that my faith in man has never been weaker — including myself," Pearl replied.

Auburn imposed penalties upon itself for the 2020-2021 season, including a postseason ban on both the SEC Tournament and the NCAA Tournament.

"I hate it for our current players," Pearl said at the time. "They lost the opportunity for the postseason last year because of COVID, and now they will miss the postseason again. It's a two-year postseason penalty for them. However, we need to take this penalty now to put it behind us."

On December 10, 2021, the NCAA delivered its final judgment on the Chuck Person affair. Person was found guilty of accepting bribes to attempt to lure players away from Auburn and into deals with agents. (This was a particular point of interest to Auburn fans, as it showed Person had *not* been engaged in violations in recruiting players *to* Auburn—quite the opposite, in fact—a distinction unfortunately missed by many in the sports media and fans of other programs.)

Auburn had fired Person in November 2017. In 2019, he was sentenced to community service and two years of probation.

Auburn was hit with four years of probation and a reduction of two scholarships over that time, and Pearl was suspended for two games in the 2021-2022 season—a suspension he served immediately, with his son coaching one game and assistant Wes Flanigan coaching the other.

"We are pleased that a conclusion has been reached in this case," read a statement issued by the university. "For the last four years, Auburn has been proactive and cooperative with the NCAA enforcement staff and Committee on Infractions. We have been and will continue to be committed to NCAA rules compliance. As such, we accept all penalties and are ready to move forward."

John Ringer:

This (violation) was not something that was done to benefit Auburn's basketball program. Person wasn't trying to attract recruits to Auburn. It was more about helping an agent and Person enriching himself in the process. This was driven not by a desire to make Auburn basketball better, but by Chuck Person having made poor financial decisions.

The other thing about the Chuck Person scandal at Auburn is that many other schools were caught by the FBI wiretapping stings and had much worse charges from an NCAA perspective—see Will Wade at LSU. But because all the stories broke at once Auburn got lumped in with those schools (Arizona and LSU in particular) who committed more egregious NCAA infractions.

There was a brief moment when this story broke, during Steven Leath's time as president of Auburn University, that he felt he couldn't get Pearl to speak with him (about the situation). It looked for a minute like Pearl's job might be in danger.

Van Allen Plexico:
In hindsight, Leath is the one whose job was in trouble. Soon enough, he was gone.

John Ringer:
He didn't need to be interfering. The (decision to give a) big contract to Gus Malzahn (after the 2017 Iron Bowl) goes back to him, too.

There were people writing that Pearl was in trouble or should've been in trouble for not speaking enough to Leath about it. This is another case where Rich McGlynn, Auburn's compliance officer, deserves credit for giving Pearl and company good advice on how to handle things, and in the end, we were and are okay.

THE 2017-2018 SEASON
26-8 (13-5, 1st in the SEC)
SEC Regular Season Champions
NCAA Tournament: Round of 32

Mustapha Heron (G)
Bryce Brown (G)
Jared Harper (G)
DeSean Murray (F)
Anfernee McLemore (F)
Chuma Okeke (F)

Davion Mitchell (G)
Malik Dunbar (G)
Horace Spencer (F)
Will Macoy (G)
Cole Blackstock (F)

The Tigers roared out of the gate to start the 2017-2018 season, winning 16 of their first 17 games. After an 88-74 loss to Temple in the Gildan Charleston Classic tournament (a game in which Anfernee McLemore scored a team-high 19), Auburn didn't lose again until their trip to Tuscaloosa on January 17.

Quickly turning things around again, the Tigers ran off five more wins before a home loss to Texas A&M on February 7. That would be their only home loss of the season.

Auburn led the SEC down the stretch, but a combination of injuries (including a devastating leg injury to McLemore) and a back-loaded slate of away games in late February allowed Tennessee to catch up in the race for the regular-season title. After falling at South Carolina, at Florida and at Arkansas in three of their last five games, the Vols pulled even with them. A gritty win at home on March 3 in the rematch with South Carolina, 79-70, assured them of a share of the championship. Having beaten then-No. 23 Tennessee in Knoxville, head-to-head, 94-84, on January 2, the Tigers and their fans made it clear they felt *they* were the true SEC champs.

The Tigers had indeed limped across the finish line, however, and it was clear things were not working at anything like peak efficiency as the postseason got underway.

As the No. 1 seed in the SEC Tournament, played this year in St Louis, Auburn faced 9-seed Alabama on Friday, March 9. The Tigers were dominated by the Tide, losing 81-63.

Van Allen Plexico:

I was at that game. I was so excited to have the SEC Tournament in St Louis, and I made sure to get tickets. But as time for the tournament rolled around, I could see we were a damaged team and we probably weren't going to make it far in the tourney. I did hope we would at least beat Alabama in our first game. But it was ugly, ugly, ugly.

The best thing about that game was, there weren't many Alabama fans in attendance to give me trouble after it was over. That's one more thing to recommend about having the SEC Tournament in St Louis–Tide fans aren't going to travel all the way up here to support a mediocre team (or basketball in general). It's nice!

The Tigers were made a 4-seed in the NCAA Tournament and sent to the Midwest Regional, where they defeated the College of Charleston, 62-58, in the opening round. Going up against 5-seed Clemson in the Round of 32, however, all their problems were exposed, and they got blasted out of the building, 84-53.

In his freshman season, Chuma Okeke averaged 7.5 points and 5.8 rebounds per game. He grabbed 197 rebounds in the season, the most by an Auburn freshman since Jeff Moore in 1984–85.

Austin Wiley and Danjel Purifoy were on the team this season, but had to sit out all year, due to NCAA eligibility issues.

Following the season, Mustapha Heron was named to the AP All-SEC Second team. On April 4 he declared for the 2018 NBA Draft, but did not hire an agent, allowing him to maintain his amateur status. Shortly afterward, he changed his mind and instead transferred to St John's. He was granted a hardship waiver (allowing him to play immediately there) by the NCAA in October, on the grounds that he needed to be closer to his mother, who was ill.

In the summer of 2019, Heron was a part of the US National team that competed at the Pan American Games in Peru, winning the bronze medal.

Heron played his two remaining seasons of college ball at St John's, then signed with the Leicester Riders of the British Basketball League after not being drafted in the 2020 NBA draft or being signed as a free agent.

John Ringer:
McLemore got hurt against South Carolina. He was a very explosive player–one who played bigger than he was. He was just coming into his own as a player and then he had this devastating injury and he was never the same after that.

After the injury Horace Spencer was the only big guy left on the roster. Chuma Okeke was a freshman and needed to put on weight and bulk up. As a result, they had trouble against big players inside; against physical teams.

Van Allen Plexico:
This was a team that looked great early in the season, and won a bunch of games early in the SEC schedule. But by the

end of the season, kind of like in 2022, they were struggling. Just not playing up to the same level.

John Ringer:
They kind of limped to the finish.

Van Allen Plexico:
They did. They had led the league all season, but got caught by Tennessee at the end. After that, they got killed by Alabama in the first round of SEC Tournament, and it was embarrassing.

Then, after beating College of Charleston in the NCAAs, they got bulldozed by Clemson. I think, going in, we all suspected that could happen.

John Ringer:
Yes. We weren't playing up to our previous level, but Clemson was a matchup problem for us, too. They had experienced big guys and we couldn't defend that well. Especially without McLemore.

But it was great to win the SEC title, especially after finishing 13th, 13th, and 11th the three previous years. It was a huge improvement, and a "proof of concept" that Bruce could do it, and do it at Auburn. This began to build the base of absolute support from the alumni and fans the program has had since then.

"After doing my due diligence at Auburn, I have decided to further my academic studies and basketball goals elsewhere," wrote backup point guard Davion Mitchell on Twitter on March 28. "I want to thank Coach Pearl and the Auburn Family for the opportunity to play and embracing me and taking this young boy and shaping him into a young man. I want to thank Coach Bruce Pearl and staff for their guidance and giving me the opportunity to make this decision. I wish the program nothing but success!!!! War Eagle"

"Davion is one of the most coachable players I've ever had. He had a great freshman season at Auburn," Auburn head coach Bruce Pearl said in a university statement. "We wish him well moving forward."

Mitchell, a consensus four-star prospect out of high school and ranked 33rd nationally by 247Sports, averaged 3.7 points and 1.9 assists per game in 17 minutes of backing up Jared Harper.

With Mitchell gone, Auburn was left with only one point guard with significant playing time, and none committed for the 2018 class.

That being the case, Samir Doughty, a "combo guard" transfer from VCU who ran point for Auburn's scout team that year, looked to be getting minutes with the team going into the next season, possibly at point guard.

John Ringer:
Davion Mitchell barely played on this team, then transferred to Baylor. He helped them win the NCAA title, and became a top ten NBA draft pick.

Van Allen Plexico:
Bruce really liked him, right? I remember him saying how much he hated to see him transfer.

John Ringer:
Yeah, it was just that we had Jared and Bryce and other guards, and they took up most of the playing time at that position. It was hard to get Davion minutes and shots. But it also shows again that Bruce and his staff have a great eye for talent.

Meanwhile, Austin Wiley and Danjel Purifoy were officially (and finally!) reinstated to the team.

Despite the loss of Mitchell, the roster for 2018-2019 was shaping up nicely.

But—who could have imagined what was about to happen next?

THE 2018-2019 SEASON
30-10 (11-7, 4th in the SEC)
SEC Tournament Champions
NCAA Final Four

Bryce Brown (G)
Jared Harper (G)
Anfernee McLemore (F)
Samir Doughty (G)
Chuma Okeke (F)
Malik Dunbar (G)

Horace Spencer (F)
J'Von McCormick (G)
Austin Wiley (C)
Danjel Purifoy (F)
Will Macoy (G)
Cole Blackstock (F)

Talk about a team that absolutely caught fire at the right time–!

The 2018-2019 Auburn Tigers were enjoying a very good regular season as of February 20. Not *great*–not by any means–but very good, as Auburn fans tend to judge such things.

At that point, they had an overall record of 18-8. There was a serious question as to whether they were going to make the NCAA Tournament at all. Clearly, they'd need to close out the season in stronger fashion than they'd begun it, and they might need a decent showing in the SEC Tournament to give them a boost.

They'd lost to No. 1 Duke (and star player Zion Williamson) in a tournament back in November, but had shown glimpses of promise in keeping it close, before falling by the score of 78-72. They'd lost by 7 at Raleigh to a mediocre NC State team on December 19. They'd started off their SEC slate of games with a loss to Ole Miss in Oxford, 82-67. They dropped a tight game at home to No. 12 Kentucky, 82-80, on January 19–the first of three straight losses that also included South Carolina and Mississippi State. They lost two more, back-to-back, in mid-February, falling to No. 21 LSU and Ole Miss (again). Beating Arkansas at home on February 20–and in convincing fashion, with a score of 79-56–seemed to indicate they were ready to make the run most folks agreed they would need, to make it to the NCAA Tournament. Next up was Kentucky in Lexington. A win there would surely propel them to big things.

Instead, they fell on their faces.

The Wildcats steamrolled over Auburn, backed up, and ran over them again, to the tune of 80-53. It was brutal. It left them with an 18-9 record, with only four games left to go. Worse, it had the potential to be demoralizing. The season could very well have fallen apart right then and there, on the floor at Rupp Arena.

Instead, something truly remarkable happened.

The Tigers kept their heads up, pushed onward, and closed out the regular season with four straight tough wins–two of them on the road.

They beat Georgia at the buzzer, 78-75, on a Chuma Okeke 3-point shot.

They got past Mississippi State, 80-75, at home.

They traveled to Coleman Coliseum and beat the Tide, 66-60.

They finished out the SEC schedule at home on March 9 by beating No. 5 Tennessee, 84-80.

Now their record stood at 22-9, a much more attractive set of numbers as the postseason loomed. But they were just getting started.

Who could've imagined, after the debacle at Lexington on February 23, that the "9" there in the Tigers' loss column wouldn't change to a "10" for 13 more games? (Go back and read that sentence again. It's absolutely astounding.)

Who would've said these Tigers would win their final four regular-season games, then all four SEC Tournament games, and then four straight NCAA Tournament games?

Who could've possibly predicted this team—a team that, again, was 18-8 in late February—would not lose a game at all in the month of March, and wouldn't lose again until the Final Four in April?

How could any of this have happened?

Van Allen Plexico:
They barely won those last four games but, as we look back now, I think that Tennessee game at the end was where it really started to come together. The Vols were ranked fifth in the country and were very good; they'd shared the SEC title with us the year before. Slapping 84 points on them–which we'd turn around and do again in the SEC Tournament title game–was a statement. A statement to the SEC and to the country: This team had found the "on-switch" and was about to flip it. They were coming.

As fans began to grow excited about this team, we got perhaps the first glimpses of what this new Auburn fandom—the fandom that blossomed to full life during the 2021-2022 season—would be like. And it began with a song.

One of the great members of Auburn Twitter, "Son of Crow," wrote a song about this team. The song caught on, and was soon being shared by Auburn fans all over the world. It was catchy and it encapsulated the moment. Set to the tune of "Sugar Sugar" by the Archies, it was called, "We've Got Jared."

It was quite the hit among Auburn fans as the team advanced through the season and on into the tournaments. And it really did describe how we all felt about those players and that team. We embraced them and we just loved them.

John Ringer:
Here are the lyrics to the smash hit, "We've Got Jared," from Son of Crow:

Jared
Chuma Okeke
and my guy Bryce Brown
shooting that thing from way downtown

Jared
Chuma Okeke
and that dude Bryce Brown
shooting that thing from way downtown

I just can't believe that Coach pearl got us here
I just can't believe it's true
Beating Tennessee and Alabama twice this year
totally a basketball school

With Jared
Chuma Okeke
and that dude Bryce Brown
shooting that thing from way downtown

We've got jared
Chuma Okeke
and that dude Bryce Brown

shooting that thing from way downtown

Chuma and Bryce, Jared and McLemore
Doughty and Wiley too
Horace Spencer, Jvonn, and Danjel Purifoy

AND CLASSIC MALIK BUSTIN THROUGH
SHOOT IT FROM OPELIKA JARED
DUNK EM THROUGH THE BASKET CHUMA
CLASSIC MALIK 10 BUCKETS A WEEK
MAKE IT RAIN FOR ME
JARED
Chuma Okeke
and that dude Bryce Brown
shooting that thing from way downtown

We've got Jared
Chuma Okeke
and that dude Bryce Brown
shooting that thing from way downtown
WE'VE GOT JARED!

[Credit to College and Magnolia]

Auburn began play in the SEC Tournament in Bridgestone Arena in Nashville on Thursday, March 14, as the No. 5 seed. They'd tied South Carolina for 4th in the conference, but had lost the head-to-head matchup in January. To open play, Bruce's lads faced Missouri, the tournament's 12-seed team. They handled the other Tigers well enough, winning 81-71.

On Friday they faced 4-seed South Carolina and won by 9, 73-64.

On Saturday in the semifinals they faced old nemesis Florida, who was only the 8-seed but who had rallied in the tournament, knocking out 1-seed LSU, 76-73, to make it to the semis. It was a tough, hard-fought game. The Tigers prevailed, 65-62.

Now they were going to the finals, where they would play Tennessee again. The Vols had beaten 2-seed Kentucky by 4, 82-78, in the other semi, and were looking good behind the play of Grant Williams and Admiral Schofield.

This time the Tigers left no doubt in anyone's mind. They crushed the Vols by 20, 84-64. Bryce Brown went for 19 points, while Chuma Okeke pulled down 13 rebounds, and Jared Harper dealt out 6 assists.

Auburn's record now stood at 26-9, a much better total than what they'd had back in February. Of course, with the SEC Tournament title in hand, it didn't matter; the Tigers had earned an automatic bid to the NCAA Tournament. In the brief time between cutting down the nets in Nashville and learning where they'd be playing next, few could have imagined they would be about to face a gauntlet that would include Kansas, North Carolina and Kentucky–the three winningest programs in NCAA history.

Van Allen Plexico:
During the season, it didn't really look like this team was going to be all that special. They had the look of a good team, sure, but they had their share of losses.

And then something clicked. They did the opposite of 2018 and 2022–they got much better at the end.

John Ringer:
It was the experience–they were by then an experienced team. They had lots of juniors and seniors, and were a more talented team than before. Those two things together allowed them to grow over the course of the season and become more effective and better at what they were doing.

Some of the individual players–Bryce, Jared, Chuma–took big leaps forward. That all made a huge difference. Chuma's improvement had a lot to do with the team overall improving. In his freshman season Chuma averaged 7.5 points and 5.8 rebounds per game but in his second year he blossomed and emerged as a great player and averaged 12.5 points per game and 6.6 rebounds per game, with his best games happening at the end of the season when Auburn needed him.

Bruce Pearl's staff had helped these players develop individually—to become better basketball players during their time at Auburn. That, combined with the experience of playing a lot of SEC basketball games, together created a team that knew what to do and how to do it.

Auburn was designated a 5-seed—more of a commentary on their earlier regular-season performance than on their more spectacular play starting with the Tennessee game—and dispatched to the NCAA Midwest Regional, where they would begin play in Salt Lake City against New Mexico State.

The game against the Aggies very nearly derailed a miracle postseason almost before it got started.

The Tigers didn't play particularly well and led by only 3 at halftime, 32-29. In the second half, New Mexico State got going and poured in 48 points. It was almost, almost enough.

Auburn seemed to be pulling away in the final 10 minutes, going up 62-50 at the 8:36 mark. A Bryce Brown 3-pointer at the 7:50 mark kept the margin at 13, 65-52.

But the Aggies began pounding it inside, as well as hitting a few key 3s, and suddenly the momentum shifted. The margin between the two was only 5 points, 70-65, with just over two minutes left. After an exchange of goals, Jared Harper slipped and turned the ball over with 49 seconds to go. The Aggies cut the deficit to 4, at 73-69. A few seconds later, Harper turned it over again, and New Mexico State knocked down a very long 3-pointer to pull within one point, 73-72, with 29 seconds left.

Auburn was able to reel off 4 quick points, while holding their opponents to just 1, to push the lead back out to 77-73. But then the Aggies hit yet another clutch 3-pointer, making it 77-76, with less than 7 seconds remaining. Samir Doughty knocked down a free throw to make it 78-76, but then the Aggies' Terrell Brown was fouled by Auburn's Bryce Brown while shooting a three, with only 1.7 seconds left.

Auburn's Bryce Brown, so great at long-range shooting that some forget he was also an excellent defender, made a calculated gamble on the play.

"I didn't want him to make it," Auburn's Brown said of the other Brown. "What went through my mind was that (Coach Pearl) did tell us they were a bad free-throw shooting team. I didn't mean to foul him, but if I could get the hardest contest I could possibly get, it's better than a made 3-pointer. Because he's their best 3-point shooter. He shoots 42 percent. So I valued all that when I saw him (about to shoot the ball)."

Terrell Brown missed the first free throw, made the second–so it was now 78-77, Auburn–and then missed the third. Bryce Brown's gamble had paid off.

But in the battle for the rebound, the ball somehow came off Doughty and went out of bounds, giving the Aggies possession with 1.1 seconds remaining, and only down 1.

New Mexico State in-bounded the ball to a wide-open Trevelin Queen, who launched a 3-point shot at the buzzer. If it had gone in, they would've won by 2 and would've knocked the Tigers out of the NCAA Tournament on their first day. If he'd been fouled, the Aggies would have been back at the free throw line again, down only one and shooting three. Instead, Queen shot an airball and the Tigers had, some way, somehow, survived.

Even so, the rest of the team understood the bullet they'd just dodged.

"This win was a wake-up call," said Okeke afterward. "That wide-open shot he shot could've been a bucket. We could have been going home. I feel like we're going to come out and play better (against Kansas)."

Indeed they would. The wake-up call was received, and it was received loud and clear.

Van Allen Plexico:
It's amazing how close we came to losing that game, and to having our glorious NCAA run cut down before it really got started. It reminds me of the Clemson game in the 2010 football season, where they came within a hair's breadth of catching a pass in overtime that would've won the game for them, would have definitely kept us from going undefeated, and might have knocked us out of the national championship game later on.

Big things later often depend on little things early on, like one New Mexico State guy missing two of three free throws and another missing that wide open shot at the end of the game.

After somehow surviving the opening game, the Tigers' reward was to have to play basketball power Kansas just two days later.

Bruce Pearl had indicated his team was tired after playing four games in four days in the SEC Tournament and then a tough contest against New Mexico State. But if that was the case, the Tigers shook it off and looked very well-rested for the Jayhawks.

Bryce Brown scored 25, knocking down seven 3-point shots, as Auburn rolled over Kansas, 89-75. The game was not as close as the score indicated.

Kansas led, 2-0, but that was about it for the Jayhawks. Auburn led by 17 before 10 minutes were gone in the game, and they never let up. At the half, they were leading, 51-25. It was a rout. They made 13 shots from long range, and hit 53 percent of their shots overall.

"It doesn't even seem real right now," said Bryce Brown afterward, of the Tigers going to the Sweet 16 for the first time in 16 years, and the fifth time ever.

"The reality is our Auburn basketball team is a better team than the Kansas team," said Bruce Pearl afterward. "I think (Bill Self, the Kansas coach) will say that. So in some ways it really wasn't an upset. I thought the better team won tonight." He added, "You can't often say that when an Auburn team plays a Kansas team."

The game marked the second time Auburn faced Kansas for a spot in the Sweet 16, the previous time coming in 1985. Auburn won both games.

"We weren't too confident—we're not a cocky team at all—but we were ready to play," said Malik Dunbar. "It's a game, so you've got to have fun out there, sometimes find a way to have fun. If you're feeling good out there, you're going to play good."

"The whole game plan was to get out to the shooters," said Kansas's Dedric Lawson. "We did a pretty poor job really, getting back, and other guys getting out to the shooter. We let those guys get comfortable, and that's what led to the big deficit in the first half."

"We wanted to punch them in the mouth early," said Horace Spencer. "We're a veteran team. We ain't got no freshmen on our team. We knew how to come out of the gate and play hard."

"We basically hoped they missed and they didn't," said Kansas coach Bill Self, on his team's defensive efforts, afterward.

"We can go as far as this group takes us," said Okeke. "I just feel like this is a blessing. We're just going to keep playing hard."

"It's all about making a deep run in this tournament," said Brown. "It's a blessing to be here, but I want to be one of those people that makes a stamp on the tournament individually and as a team. I'm not satisfied with a second round or Sweet 16. I want to be a team that shocks the world."

Van Allen Plexico:
The guard play on this team was so good and so important. This team had really good guards, and that always matters in tournament play. I always say, having big guys and playing defense is great over the course of a long season, but when it comes to crunch time in the postseason, you'd better have some guards who can shoot, drive, penetrate, and create offense at critical moments.

John Ringer:
Jared Harper, Bryce Brown, Samir Doughty, Austin Wiley, Anfernee McLemore, Malik Dunbar, Horace Spencer, J'Von McCormick, Danjel Purifoy… The starters and the backups off the bench…Those guys were effective.

They still weren't a great defensive team, but they were a better defensive team than they had been. They had improved and were about 5 points a game better in points allowed than the previous year.

And the offense continued to improve, becoming one of the best in the country by the end of the season. That made them really hard to beat.

Van Allen Plexico:
And then there's being able to manufacture points at the end of a game, through multiple avenues, not just one person.

John Ringer:
This team was first in the country in 3-point shots made.

Van Allen Plexico:
That really kicked in during the SEC Tournament and then the NCAA Tournament.

Bryce especially was on fire. He was just unconscious at times, launching long-range shots.

John Ringer:
This team attempted more shots than any team in the country. Not just 3-point shots but shots in general. And they made a lot of them.

They were also fourth in the country in steals per game.

That shows you they created problems for the other teams on defense that led to baskets on offense.

Those veteran guards were good at anticipating what the other team was going to do and being ready for it.

Having gone 2-for-2 on the opening weekend, the Tigers now moved on to the Sprint Center in Kansas City, for their Sweet 16 game.

There awaited the No. 1 seed in the region: the North Carolina Tarheels. The team that had just annihilated Washington, 81-59.

Van Allen Plexico:
I'm not gonna lie; I thought we were going to have a very difficult time against North Carolina. I felt that we could win, especially with the way our offense was cooking as of late. But it's North Carolina, the No. 1 seed in the region. They bring a certain level of intimidation with them just because of all their history. You see that light blue color coming into the arena and you think, "Here we go."

I thought this game would be tough. In basketball terms, I was wrong.

But in terms of what happened to Chuma, unfortunately, I was right.

The game with UNC was even through the first 20 minutes, with Auburn making a coast-to-coast layup just before halftime to take a 41-39 lead into the locker room.

The second half would be a different story entirely.

The Tigers lit things up in the final 20 minutes, hitting twelve 3-point baskets in that half alone—19 overall for the game—and finishing with *five players* having made multiple 3-pointers. Austin Wiley also had a massive block on UNC.

With just 90 seconds gone in the second half, the Tigers had pushed the lead to double-digits. North Carolina pulled to within 6 at one point, but Auburn quickly corrected that situation with a massive run that saw them make 3-pointers on five consecutive possessions, to take a 76-57 lead late.

The score stood at 81-68 with five minutes remaining, and TBS helpfully pointed out that Auburn was 27-0 this season when leading with that much time remaining in the game.

Every time the Tarheels appeared to be getting themselves back in the game, Auburn would get a key steal or a 3-point shot and push the lead back out.

The Tigers indeed coasted home for the 97-80 win, and would be going to the Elite 8 for the first time since 1986 and only the second time ever.

But the victory was marred by the serious leg injury suffered by Chuma Okeke with eight minutes remaining in the second half.

He was taken off the court, and exams later revealed he had a torn ACL in his left knee. He would miss the rest of the tournament.

"I just hated to see my brother go down," said Bryce Brown after the game. "I saw how much pain he was in. It didn't only hurt me, it hurt the whole team. You could see it on all our faces. We got in here after the game and prayed twice."

"We're glad that we won, but we have that feeling like we lost, just knowing that we lost our most valuable player," said Harper. "We're a very close team. ... People don't understand how much of a close team we are. We're really close. We all love one another. When people (players) saw that he got injured, some were even crying, just that hurt for our teammate. We know Chuma wants to be there just as much as everybody and do all the things that he's able to do and provide for the team. It hurt us."

Okeke was helped by Anfernee McLemore in moving Auburn's name forward on the bracket board in the locker room. He would remain in town and come to the arena on Sunday during the Kentucky game, serving to inspire the team.

After the game, UNC coach Roy Williams was asked about two of his players being sick. "Those are just excuses," he said. "We've got to congratulate Auburn and Bruce and the job that he and his coaching staff did."

At the buzzer, Malik Dunbar ran across the court to where the Auburn fans were located, and shouted, "I told you!"

"I was just letting them know, 'I told you. I told you we weren't going to lose this.'"

"We were counted out," said Jared Harper. "We saw that we were supposed to lose by 12, by double digits. People just thought we didn't have the firepower, the depth, and blah blah, all that stuff. We don't let that (kind of talk) affect us too much."

"The issue for us earlier in the year is that if Bryce and/or Jared didn't play great, we had no chance," said another player (unattributed). "That's just not been the case in March. The other guys are stepping up and we're all relying on each other more, and those two guys don't have to carry us every night."

"Chuma offered us a lot of things this season and in this tournament," Harper said, "so, without him, it's going to maybe be harder. But if it was easy, anybody could do it. So we're definitely ready for the moment."

Van Allen Plexico:
Playing against Kentucky twice already that season, with Chuma in the lineup, we were 0-2. And they'd absolutely destroyed us in the second game, at Rupp on February 23, winning by 27. It was in fact the last time we'd lost. And this time we wouldn't have Chuma at all. So I didn't have a high degree of confidence coming into this game.

Add to that the fact that Auburn had never won a game in the Elite 8 round. Never. In fact, this was only the second time they'd had the opportunity to play one. (The other was the loss to eventual champions Louisville in 1986.)

I wanted to believe, but winning this game felt a lot like our chances of winning the 2013 Iron Bowl when Alabama was lining up to kick a last-second field goal to break the tie. Of course, we all know how that turned out, so...!

Kentucky came out strong to start the game, taking the ball away from Auburn and making transition baskets. Just over 3:30 into the game, Kentucky led 7-0 and Auburn was 0 for 6 shooting.

AUBURN BASKETBALL

The Tigers got things going finally with a combination of outside shooting—Danjel Purifoy made a critical 3-pointer—and Austin Wiley's inside power. But Kentucky remained hot, pulling out to a 17-7 lead with 12 minutes left in the first half. Bryce Brown's shooting kept the Tigers in the game as Kentucky continued to pour it on. To make matters worse, with four minutes remaining in the half, Malik Dunbar was on the bench with three fouls, and Austin Wiley and Horace Spencer—the inside men—had two fouls each. At that point, Kentucky had stretched the lead back out to 9, at 27-18.

In the final two minutes of the half, however, the Tigers flexed their muscles with guard play. Jared Harper was fouled shooting a 3-pointer that went in, and he converted the 4-point play to narrow the gap to 31-24. Then McLemore sank a short jumper to make it 31-26. Purifoy muscled his way to a rebound of a missed UK 3-pointer and the Tigers ran out on the fast break, at the end of which Jared Harper laid it in to cut the lead to only 3. After the Wildcats made a free throw, Auburn came right back with Harper knifing to the basket; he left the layup short but McLemore finished for him, and it was 32-30 Kentucky. The shell-shocked Wildcats managed a 3-pointer before the buzzer and took a 35-30 lead to the locker room, but they had to know they'd thrown everything they had at the Tigers in the first half and Auburn had absorbed it and thrown it right back, and UK were fortunate to be leading at all.

Chuma Okeke had planned to watch the game from his hotel room. He'd sent word to the team earlier in the day that he was in too much pain to come to the arena. At the half, however, he decided he couldn't sit idly by and watch as his teammates battled Kentucky. His mother and brother transported him to the arena, where he came out to the bench area in a wheelchair early in the second half. Seeing him, the crowd began to chant, "Chu-ma! Chu-ma!"

"That kind of put us into a whole other gear," said McLemore later. "We knew we had our last brother with us."

Wrote Jon Hale of the Lexington (KY) *Courier-Journal*: "Momentum seemed to crest for Auburn at the first media timeout of the second half when forward Chuma Okeke, who tore his ACL in the Tigers' Sweet 16 upset of North Carolina, was pushed onto the court in a wheelchair and stationed behind the Auburn bench. As the Sprint Center video boards showed the scene, Auburn fans, who were vastly outnumbered by Kentucky fans in the arena, reached one of their loudest moments of the afternoon."

The Wildcats looked to have regrouped at the half. They came out and knocked down a quick shot to increase their lead to 37-30, but then Auburn roared back with a 3-pointer by Brown, free throws and a short basket, and suddenly the game was tied, 37-37. At that point, Kentucky could have taken a time out, calmed themselves, and reminded one another that they had beaten this Auburn team twice already during the season. Instead, apparently, they only allowed themselves to become more flustered, throwing away an inbounds pass and giving Bryce Brown the chance to sink yet another 3.

Now Auburn had the lead for the first time, 40-37, and they started looking like the team that had run Kansas and North Carolina out of the gym. Jared Harper hit J'Von McCormick for an alley-oop dunk, an Auburn specialty under Pearl. It was 42-39 Auburn.

The lead swapped hands for a time after that, with a massive Malik Dunbar block of an easy Kentucky dunk shaking the rafters of the arena, while Bryce Brown kept pace with the Cats with his shooting on the other end. When Danjel Purifoy hit another 3 by banging the ball off the rim and sending it straight up into the air, only to fall directly down through the hoop, it started to feel like perhaps the Tigers were a team of destiny.

In the final six minutes, Kentucky went to a transition game and started forcing it inside again, and they pulled the score to 58-58 with a minute remaining, then took the lead, 60-58. Harper responded with his trademark hesitate-and-race-to-the-hole move, laying it in to tie the game yet again, at 60-60.

As the seconds ticked away in regulation, Kentucky tried again and again to score inside, only to have every shot blocked and stuffed and deflected by the Tigers. Auburn finally came away with the ball with less than 10 seconds left, when Brown nabbed the rebound and raced to the other end to attempt the game-winning score. Caught in traffic, he passed to Spencer, but clearly he intended for Horace to pass it right back to him as he broke open for the game-winner. Instead, Spencer turned to the basket and took the shot himself, just before the buzzer. The ball bounced harmlessly off the rim as the clock hit all zeroes, and Brown agonized visibly on the court at the missed shot and the missed opportunity. We were going to overtime to determine who would win the region and advance to the Final Four.

In overtime, it became the Jared Harper show, as the point guard scored the first 4 points, cutting to the goal and laying it in. After a UK goal, he drove down the lane again, but this time was cut off by a double-team. Instantly he fed the ball to McLemore, who laid in a short shot that took the long way around the rim before dropping. With two minutes to go, Auburn was up by 4, at 66-62.

McLemore wasn't done. Back on defense, he forced a Kentucky turnover and brought it back down the court himself, whereupon he promptly laid it in. Following one made Kentucky free throw, Harper again took the ball to the rack and laid it in, as everyone else on the court simply watched. 70-63, Auburn. Harper had 20 points on 7 of 18 shooting.

Kentucky kept fighting back, but Auburn kept making free throws, and the Wildcats were rapidly running out of time. Inside of 30 seconds left, Auburn led by 6, at 74-68. Kentucky needed a 3 in the worst way, and they got it, but then Auburn made its free throws to keep the pace. 75-71 with 10 seconds to go.

Inside of 10 seconds left, Auburn lowered the boom. McLemore wouldn't let their guard get a shot off, stuffing it back in his face. After more Auburn free throws and with the score now 77-71, Kentucky missed its final shot and Jared Harper grabbed the rebound, then took off for the other end of the court. Halfway there, he threw the ball into the air as the Auburn bench cleared in celebration.

The Tigers had done it. With a lineup less talented than the one they'd taken to Rupp Arena just over a month earlier, they'd gone toe-to-toe with the mighty Wildcats, with a trip to the Final Four on the line, and they'd won.

"They're always telling me to act like you've been there," said Bryce Brown after the game. "But I haven't!"

"Best backcourt in the nation," he added, referring to himself and Jared Harper, backed up by McCormick and Doughty.

"Definitely true," Harper agreed. "I've thought that since the jump."

"Jared Harper and Bryce Brown, at the end of the day they kind of got those (Kentucky) guys messed up," said Pearl. "Boy, they made plays."

Harper and Brown combined for 50 of Auburn's 77 points. Harper had 26; Brown had 24. The next highest scorer was McLemore with 8.

They made "tough twos," as Harper described it. The 3-pointers were great, but it was the ability of the guards to take the ball into the lane, into traffic, and put it in the hoop that proved the difference down the stretch. During tournaments, guard play usually dominates and determines the winners.

"We're not only a 3-point shooting team," Brown noted. "We're a dominant 3-point shooting team, but we do other things, too."

"We were able to get Jared downhill," Pearl explained. "Bryce made some huge plays. They took the 3-ball away, so Bryce went to his old-school, pull-up game. He didn't think he had it, but he got in the lane, rose up and them suckers were beautiful, great basketball."

Holders of the nation's longest winning streak, and now at 30-9, the Tigers had beaten the three winningest programs in college basketball history, in Kansas, North Carolina and Kentucky.

"I'm so happy for the people at Auburn who have been waiting forever to get to their first Final Four," Pearl declared, before cutting down the nets. "This one was for Chuma," he added. "The next two are for Auburn."

Van Allen Plexico:

We have to mention Charles Barkley again here. He was doing commentary work in the March Madness TV studio, and as Auburn progressed deeper into the tournament, his little section of the desk kept getting covered in more and more Auburn gear. By the time of this game, he had a large stuffed tiger, orange and blue balloons and an Auburn flag draped over the desktop. All of this to the chagrin of his broadcast partner, Kenny Smith, a former UNC player.

It felt like Charles was right there celebrating with the rest of us. It made it all even more special.

John Ringer:

I never thought I would see Auburn basketball in the Final Four in my lifetime. My goal for Auburn has always been, "Just make the tournament." I never thought we would get that far.

So getting to the Final Four was a dream. The way we did it, the run through the tournament, who we beat, again and again, was just one of the greatest months of Auburn fandom ever. It was pure joy.

I love this team, I love how hard they played, and the joy they played with; how they had no fear in how they did things. There was no shot Jared or Bryce wouldn't take. They were always in range. They had fun.

That's a recurring theme with Bruce Pearl's team: his teams have fun. It's not a grind. They aren't chess pieces executing his plan, they're having fun and enjoying the ride.

Auburn had won the Midwest Regional and was moving on to the Final Four for the first time ever.

Their opponent there would be the Virginia Cavaliers. The previous season, Virginia had become the first number 1 seed in NCAA Tournament history to lose to a 16-seed in the opening round. They felt they had a championship-caliber team and were looking for redemption after that humiliation the year before.

The Tigers came out a little stiff at first. Word before gametime was that Harper and Brown had picked up "the flu," which probably meant a cold, and weren't at a hundred percent. But nothing short of the bubonic plague would've stopped them from playing in this game.

After Virginia started strong, Auburn came back with a combination of inside and outside play and took the lead, 9-8, inside of 14 minutes remaining in the first half. By the time the first half reached the 10-minute mark, Auburn had made only 1 of 7 3-point attempts, and was trailing by 3.

Virginia was a strong defensive team; the danger was in allowing them to get far enough ahead that Auburn would not be able to score enough to come back. After missing their last 7 3-point attempts, they found themselves in a hole, 18-13. So they went back to the inside game, with Brown hitting McLemore for an alley-oop dunk, followed by McCormick driving the lane for a layup. This was an Auburn team that had matured over the past few weeks, and understood that if the outside game wasn't there or was being taken away, they had the ability to score inside, too. Just like that, the Tigers trailed by only one, and Virginia had to be thinking what

Kentucky had likely been thinking only a few days earlier: We're throwing our best stuff at these guys, and they just keep coming back!

After that, the two teams traded the lead back and forth, Virginia making 3s and Harper and McCormick driving in for layups. They went to halftime with Auburn ahead, 31-28. The Tigers were fighting their tails off out there, struggling to defend Virginia's odd cuts to the basket and deadly 3-point shooters, fighting to get to the rim and score in the paint. The second half was shaping up to be a war of epic proportions.

Van Allen Plexico:
One thing I've noticed going back and watching the 2018-2019 team is how flexible they were with their styles of play. Everyone remembers this team as "the 3-point shooting team," and they were certainly great at that. But when opponents worked hard at defending that part of their game, they could pound it inside, with Wiley and Spencer and Dunbar and McLemore, and they could also drive to the hoop. Nobody was better at that than Jared Harper, but McCormick and Doughty and even Brown were quite capable of slashing to the rim. They also excelled at the old "alley oop" play. They could play inside, outside, and a combination of both, and that's one big reason why they were so tough to defend, and why they made it as far as they did in March and April.

Virginia came out and made a run early in the second half, working the ball inside on offense while playing tough interior defense, largely due to the play of center Mamadi Diakite. They got a big block on an attempted dunk by Bryce Brown, then got a turnover as Harper was bringing the ball up. Nearly six minutes into the second half, Auburn had yet to score a point, and the Cavs were up by 5, at 36-31.

But then the Tigers rallied, with Harper nailing a 3-pointer to get things going and then Samir Doughty getting a rebound and score, and only seconds later they'd pulled even at 36.

Virginia was rapidly learning they would not take off and leave this Auburn team behind. The Tigers were going to scratch and claw and fight them all the way to the end.

Undaunted, Virginia began working the ball inside again, and the Tigers had no answers there. As the clock moved below 12 minutes remaining, the Cavaliers were back up by 4, with the score 42-38.

The two teams traded baskets for a stretch of the game, and then Virginia changed back to an outside shooting approach. Knocking down a couple of 3-pointers, they increased their lead to 50-43 with less than 9 minutes remaining. Again came the danger: Allow a good defensive team like Virginia to build a lead, and you may not be able to catch back up. The Cavs looked to stretch things out even further, but Austin Wiley violently rejected a shot and got the Tigers the ball back, whereupon Jared Harper hit a 3-pointer to cut the margin back down to 3.

Back into the paint the Cavaliers went, scoring 4 quick points on inside baskets, before they knocked down another 3 as the game neared the 5-minute mark. Suddenly the Tigers were down 10, at 57-47, and the game seemed to be slipping away.

But these Tigers were not done. They'd been through too much to give up now. They started chipping away, with a free throw and then a Bryce Brown 3-pointer to slash 4 points from the deficit. Now it was 57-51, Virginia—but Brown wasn't done. After missing a 3-pointer, he was given a second chance from the same spot when Doughty snared the rebound and whipped the ball out to Harper at the top of the key. Harper in turn fired it back over to Brown on the right side of the arc, and this time the sharpshooter in blue didn't miss. With 3:25 remaining, the score was now 57-54, UVA.

A Danjel Purifoy inside shot over two reaching Cavaliers somehow found its way through the hoop, bringing Auburn within 1 point. They stopped the Cavs on the other end and once again got the ball to you-know-who, at his favorite spot on the right side. Brown knocked down another 3 and suddenly the Tigers were leading the game with less than 2 minutes to go, 59-57. Suddenly it all seemed possible.

For the next minute, neither team could make a shot; even Brown threw up an airball from long range. Virginia got the rebound and moved into attack mode with 35 seconds left. They missed a long 3-point attempt and Auburn rebounded, followed by UVA fouling. The two free throws gave the Tigers a 4-point lead, 61-57, with just 12 seconds left. They made a 3-pointer over Samir Doughty to bring themselves within 1, 61-60, with 7.4 seconds left. Then they fouled

Harper and sent him to the line, where he made the first shot. It was 62-60. He missed the second and UVA rebounded. Doughty fouled their point guard but Auburn only had 4 fouls, so UVA inbounded the ball from the side in the backcourt with 5.4 seconds to go. Ty Jerome, the UVA point guard, was met by Bryce Brown as he attempted to bring the ball up the court. Jerome lost control of the ball, double-dribbled, and was then fouled by Brown (Auburn still had a foul to give) before attempting a desperation heave as the clock expired.

The referees ignored the blatant double-dribble, instead giving Virginia the ball back with 1.5 seconds on the clock.

Jerome inbounded the ball to their 3-point sharpshooter, Kyle Guy, who put up a shot in front of Samir Doughty.

Van Allen Plexico:
Doughty did not foul Guy. I know that, according to the letter of the rules, it could be seen as a foul. But plays like that had been happening the entire game and weren't being called. Samir's hands were straight up and he didn't touch Guy other than to bump him at the waist as he was coming down, after the ball was long gone. In any normal circumstances Doughty would not have been called for a foul there. But Guy put on an epic performance as he landed from his jump shot, falling over and acting like he'd been assaulted. It was an Oscar-worthy performance and it gave him the foul. It also made everyone forget—temporarily—how Jerome had double-dribbled a few moments earlier, and that Virginia shouldn't even have had the ball at that point in the game.

The referee blew the whistle and awarded three shots to Guy, an 82 percent free-throw shooter, with 0.6 seconds remaining. Guy calmly sank all three shots, putting Virginia ahead by 1, at 63-62.

Van Allen Plexico:
Doughty had to defend hard on the play, though. I don't blame him for what happened. If he just gives Guy the open shot, he probably sinks it. Doughty at worst put him on the line and forced him to make three consecutive shots. It's to Guy's credit he was able to do that, under incredible pressure.

But they never should have had the ball there to begin with, because the double-dribble wasn't called.

Purifoy inbounded the ball with a long pass to Brown, who spun around and attempted a sort of "Christian Laettner" shot even as Samir Doughty streaked under the goal to try for the putback in case of a miss. The shot did miss, as did Doughty's attempted shot just after the buzzer sounded.

Van Allen Plexico:
Lost in all of this was that Virginia's defender fouled Brown about as badly on that last shot as Doughty had "fouled" Guy a minute earlier. There was no whistle this time.

The game was over. It ended with the score 63-62, Virginia. The Cavaliers were advancing to the national championship game, having survived a 10-point Auburn comeback, a no-call on a double dribble, and a no-call on a foul on Brown, as well as being gifted a phantom foul for three foul shots.

Auburn held Diakite to just 2 points on 4 attempts; he'd scored in double figures the previous game, against Purdue. Samir Doughty led Auburn in scoring with 13, coming off the bench. Bryce Brown scored 12 points, all of them coming by way of four 3-pointers made out of 10 attempted. Jared Harper scored 11.

Van Allen Plexico:
Six of the Virginia players moved on to the NBA after their careers ended in Charlottesville. The only Auburn player on this team to play serious minutes in the NBA, Chuma Okeke, wasn't even able to play in this game. This Auburn team was the epitome of a great college basketball team. They were focused, dedicated to one another, and skilled in many different ways, and they took advantage of all of their various traits to make it as far as they did.

Sports are not always fair. This Auburn team should've gone on to face Texas Tech for the national championship. Instead, Virginia was allowed to play the Red Raiders and prevailed.

One interesting aspect of this matchup was that Auburn liked to create havoc and cause turnovers on defense, which they did at a higher rate than any other team in the country, while Virginia entered the game averaging the fewest turnovers per game of anyone nationally, at nine. During the game, Virginia committed only eight, leading to just 8 points for Auburn, including just 4 points off of fast break opportunities.

Van Allen Plexico:
We ended up playing Virginia's game more than we made them play ours. It was a slowed-down, grind-it-out affair for most of the time. Even so, we had the lead with just seconds remaining.

And while we the fans complained loudly and often–and still do!—about the double-dribble and everything else that went against us, the players handled it all afterward with nothing but class.

John Ringer:
What made the loss so much tougher to take was that the team came back at the end—we were down double digits and came back against this very tough UVA defense to make it a one shot game in the last minute. If this Auburn team had not made the big comeback, then the loss would be easier to accept and live with—but it did make the comeback and that is why this one hurts so much.

Everyone commented afterward on the utter class with which Bruce and the players conducted themselves after the game. The Tigers had every right to be angry and bitter. Instead, they were gracious and philosophical.

"It seemed like the ref wasn't about to call the foul, but I can't really tell you what's going on in these refs' minds," said Doughty afterward. "I'm pretty sure they're going to make the best decision to their abilities, so I can't really speak on what's going on in their minds or why it was (called) so late. I'm pretty sure he made the right call if that's the call he called."

"Controversial or not, we got the win," said Virginia's Guy afterward. "I could lie to you and say I knew I was going to hit (the three foul shots). But I was terrified."

"I thought we won it," said Pearl after the game. "The horn went off. I saw the shot miss. I saw the officials kind of looking at each other. I thought it was over, but obviously it wasn't."

From the NCAA's website:
Doughty, when asked about the foul, said, "They (the officials) do a great job at reffing and they're trying to the best of their ability to make the right call. I can't question none of that."

He had prepared for that moment, studying video of Guy and Ty Jerome that had revealed a pattern. Doughty had discovered that Guy and Jerome "like to kick their legs out when they shoot, so I just tried to be right there, let him shoot the ball and whatever happens, happens. He just hit a three the play before and I played defense the same exact way. I'm not really sure why they called that call, but I'm pretty sure the refs made the right decision."

Auburn coach Bruce Pearl said his response after the game was to focus on how his team would handle the defeat.

"My advice, as an administrator of the game, is if that's a foul, call it," Pearl said. "Call it at the beginning of the game. Call it in the middle of the game. Call it at the end of the game. Don't call it any more or less at any other time during the game."

In a corner (of the Auburn locker room), Bryce Brown sits in a chair. There is already a video making the online rounds of him shouting the NCAA needs new referees as the Tigers returned to their locker room.

"I regret saying that. I just got caught up in the moment. I apologize for that," he says.

"Our hopes were high at one point, we thought we had it in the bag. That's not where we lost the game, but that just made it hard for us. They let us play the whole entire game and I'm not going to hold back on what I feel. They let that play decide the game and I just didn't agree with that."

Bruce Pearl wanted something to be understood about his team that had beaten the odds to get here. "I thought we looked like we belonged."

And his first words to his team afterward were not about questionable whistles or no-whistles.

"We didn't focus on that. We focused on how we were going to handle the defeat at Auburn with class and dignity. There are lots of calls during the game and you're going to get some and some you're not going to get.

"But it won't, it can't, don't let it define the game, because you're taking away from Ty Jerome (and his 21 Virginia points) or you're taking away from Anfernee McLemore with 12 rebounds or Bryce Brown almost leading Auburn back to an incredible come-from-behind victory. I'd love that to be the story."

Van Allen Plexico:
I'm proud of how Bruce and the players handled it. I truly am.

But I'm not an official representative of Auburn University, and I'm under no obligation to be nice about what happened. And I'm never going to accept it.

"...One of the most controversial calls in Final Four history.

"The Auburn Tigers had only a devastated locker room to go. They may never accept that foul. Their fans won't. Whether it should have been called after a physical game, whether a Virginia double dribble was missed a few seconds earlier."

—*NCAA dot com*

"They hadn't been calling those fouls all game. There were plays where there were fouls on 3-point shots, when there was no calls. For them to call that foul was kind of surprising.

"I definitely feel like we deserved a better result, but it's always not going to be like that. I'm just going to allow God to take care of the decision."

—*Samir Doughty, after the game*

> "God's on our side, I guess."
> —*Virginia junior guard Braxton Key, after the game*

"We went through a lot of adversity (over the course of the season)," said Brown. "There's been a lot of times we could've given up as a team, and the season could've (gone) downhill easily."

"We made history," said Malik Dunbar, like Brown a senior who had just played in his final game as a Tiger. "We did something no Auburn team has ever done before." And then he added, "I still wish we could've brought that (champion)ship back to Auburn."

Van Allen Plexico:
I've always said that, of the various teams I follow in various sports, all trying to win their respective championships, Auburn winning the national championship in basketball was the least likely thing I'd ever see.

And we came so close.

John Ringer:
It's so difficult even when you have the players and the coach. How fortunate we were that season.

If Chuma doesn't get hurt, we win the national title.

Van Allen Plexico:
That's a bold statement, but I don't disagree. I'll also say, if we have a different referee in that last game against Virginia, I don't think Samir gets called for that foul at the end. Or maybe Virginia's double dribble gets called. Either way, we win, and go on to play for the championship.

And I'm confident we would have beaten Texas Tech in the finals.

Alas, Virginia's double-dribble was not called, and Samir Doughty was called for a foul, and the UVA player did make all three free throws. The Tigers would not get to play for a national championship. Still, they'd made the Final Four for the first time in program history. They'd taken the eventual champs right down to the buzzer. And they'd taken us all along for one of the most thrilling rides of our lives.

The 2018-2019 Auburn Tigers will live forever in glory—for who they were, and for what they accomplished.

They achieved what they set out to do: They did indeed shock the world.

THE 2019-2020 SEASON
25-6 (12-6, 2nd in the SEC)
Season ended prematurely due to Covid-19 Pandemic

Anfernee McLemore (F)
Samir Doughty (G)
Isaac Okoro (F)
J'Von McCormick (G)
Austin Wiley (C)
Danjel Purifoy (F)
Devan Cambridge (G)

Jamal Johnson (G)
Allen Flanigan (G)
Jaylin Williams (F)
Tyrell "Turbo" Jones (G)
Babatunde Akingbola (C)
Lior Berman (G)

It will forever be an unanswerable question: Just how far could this team have gotten in the SEC Tournament? In the NCAA Tournament?

They won 25 games without being able to play a single minute of postseason basketball. At 25-6 at the end of the regular season, they had a better record than the Final Four team had achieved by that same point.

Their guards, Samir Doughty and J'Von McCormick, had stepped up and were filling the roles vacated by the departed Jared Harper and Bryce Brown with supreme competence. No one could *replace* those two, but Doughty and McCormick were placing their own stamps on the team, and carrying them to victory after victory.

Austin Wiley was back, commanding the inside even more firmly than he had the previous season.

And while there was no Chuma Okeke available this time around, Danjel Purifoy and Devan Cambridge and Allen Flanigan were together approximating his impact.

And then there was forward Isaac Okoro, who was capable of dominating stretches of games. A true freshman, he already possessed the body of an NBA player and the power to impose his will on the game.

On November 25, the Tigers traveled to New York to play in the Legends Classic tournament in the Barclays Center in Brooklyn. They beat New Mexico on Monday night and Richmond on Tuesday to win the tournament, and to give Auburn its first 6-0 start under Bruce Pearl. It was Auburn's first win of an in-season tournament since 2004. Austin Wiley was named MVP of the tournament on the strength of his 14-point, 13-rebound double-double in the first game and his 18-point, 8-rebound effort in game two.

"BP said going into the tournament, during the week we had off, we had to work on our bodies, have physical practices and just focus in the weight room to get our bodies ready for this month because we were going to have two games in two days," Wiley said. "So I'm just proud of my team."

While they were in the area, they visited the 9/11 Memorial and attended a Knicks game at Madison Square Garden.

"(I wanted us to) go to New York and play good basketball," Pearl said after the New Mexico game. They scored 116 and 91 in their two previous games before the tournament, but Pearl understood that wouldn't happen often for this team. Indeed, against New Mexico they made only 13 of 42 attempts in the first half. "Our only chance (going forward) is to become a great defensive team," he said.

The team went on to sweep the non-conference portion of the season, winning their first 15 straight games, including their first three SEC games.

They first tasted defeat at the hands of their arch-rivals, on a trip to Tuscaloosa on January 15, falling 83-64 to the Tide. Three days later, they lost by a score of 69-47 at Florida–a place Auburn basketball hasn't had much luck in a very long time.

Those two defeats didn't get them down for long. They came back to win their next seven straight, including a big, 75-66 victory over Kentucky at Auburn Arena. The next three games, they beat Arkansas, LSU and Alabama in sequence–with all three wins coming in overtime. Taken along with their double-OT win over Ole Miss just before the Kentucky game, four of their last five games had gone to extra frames, and they'd won all four of them—a statistically improbable happenstance, to say the least.

The Tigers lost at Missouri and at Georgia in the middle of February, then beat Tennessee and Ole Miss at home, then lost at No.

8 Kentucky and at Texas A&M, before finishing out with their customary thrashing of Tennessee in Knoxville–this time by a score of 85-63. The final month of the season had been an up-and-down affair after the strong start, but they'd closed it out with a good win on the road.

Their final regular-season SEC record was 12-6, second only to Kentucky at 15-3. LSU also finished 12-6, but Auburn held the head-to-head tie-breaker for the second seed.

Van Allen Plexico:

I took my family to the game at Missouri, since that's only a two-hour drive for us. It was one of the last things my family did outside the house before the pandemic shut everything down.

We had fun there, but it was frustrating to see us lose, when we'd played so well for most of the season.

That was when I started to doubt that this team could achieve some of the things they'd managed the year before. They were very, very good, but they seemed to have lapses on offense or defense, and to lack that little something extra to get them over the hump. Of course, not many teams are as good as they were, anyway. And the team the previous year hadn't really turned things on until the SEC Tournament.

I think this team would've won at least a game or two in the SEC tourney–they would've played Missouri or Texas A&M– and ended up with maybe a 3-seed in the NCAA Tournament. Of course, we'll never know.

John Ringer:

I think this team would have been very dangerous in the SEC and NCAA tournaments. They had veteran guards, a reliable low post scorer and a great defensive stopper who could go out and shut down any team's best player. And I think this team had a lot of big game experience from the last few years—they would not have been fazed by a tough tournament game. So it is a real loss that we were not be able to see what they could have done.

With the regular season over, the team traveled to Nashville for what they believed would be the 2020 SEC Tournament, where their 2-seed meant they wouldn't have to play during the first two days. They were set to play the winner of Thursday's game between 7-seed Texas A&M and 10-seed Missouri on Friday.

On the opening night, Wednesday, Georgia beat Ole Miss and Arkansas beat Vanderbilt.

And then…it all just ended.

The tournament, and soon after practically the entire world, came to a screeching halt.

COVID-19 had arrived.

The SEC Tournament was canceled. The NCAA Tournament was canceled.

Auburn's season was abruptly over, as sure as if they'd been on probation and had to stop play at the end of the regular season, as had happened a couple of times in previous years. This time, though, it wasn't just Auburn, it was *everyone*. As hard as it was to fathom, the 2019-2020 NCAA basketball season was done. The great Auburn players left over from the previous year's Final Four run, who were in their last years of eligibility, would never get another chance to play in the SEC or NCAA Tournament.

The Tigers said farewell to McLemore, Doughty, McCormick, Wiley, Johnson and Purifoy, and also lost Okoro early to the NBA. Clearly the 2020-2021 Auburn Tigers would be a very different team, built around Flanigan, Cambridge and Stretch Akingbola– they'd need a lot of help, and they'd need it in a hurry.

At the end of the regular season, Doughty was named first team All-SEC by the coaches and second team All-SEC by the AP. He had averaged a team-leading 16.7 points, 3.9 rebounds and 2.7 assists per game during the season. Following the season, he went on to play for several G-League teams.

Isaac Okoro was drafted by the Cleveland Cavaliers with the fifth pick overall in the 2020 NBA draft.

On January 2, 2021, Austin Wiley signed with the Basketball Bundesliga in Germany. As of 2022 he plays for the Gladiators Trier.

In July 2021, Danjel Purifoy announced on Instagram that he had signed with a pro team in Portugal.

J'Von McCormick signed with a Ukrainian pro team in 2020, then moved (perhaps just in time!) to Turkish Basketball's first division.

Anfernee McLemore left basketball behind and took a job as a financial advisor with Regions Bank in Birmingham. "I feel blessed to have been a part of that program at that time," he told the *Albany Herald*. "I did my best to do my part, and I feel like I couldn't have done it on any other team."

John Ringer:
The Doughty/Okoro team. We sicced Okoro on the other team's best offensive player and said, "Take that guy out of the equation." And he usually did.

They were as good offensively as the team the year before. Not as good at shooting 3-pointers, but very good in other ways.

Doughty and McCormick were excellent guards, and probably underrated.

There were lots of seniors on this team. And a bunch of freshmen that blended into the lineup.

Van Allen Plexico:
At the time, I didn't think they were as good as the year before. But, looking back, they had a better record in the regular season than the 2018-2019 team had. I think this team was underrated at the time, and probably (and unfortunately) always will be, because they never got a chance to demonstrate their quality on the big stage, either in the SEC Tournament or the NCAA Tournament.

John Ringer:
Experience and talented guard play in tournaments really matters. This team had that, plus the X-factor Okoro. This team could've won a bunch of games in the tournaments.

I understand why it happened like it did, but I'll always be disappointed they didn't get to show what they could do.

They led the country in free throw attempts, and were number three in free throws made.

On the other hand, they were way down at 309th in 3-point shooting percentage after losing Harper and Brown and Okeke. They were just a fundamentally different team. Instead of firing it up from outside, they did a lot of forcing the ball inside to Wiley to get the offense going. He had a good season.

Van Allen Plexico:
In some ways, this team looked more like the 1986 team than the 2019 team.

It's amazing how many players we lost at the end of this season. The next year would be a real rebuilding job.

Bruce Pearl wasted no time in going out and finding new players to complement the few he had returning. As usual, however, there were issues with getting them all eligible to play.

And then came a round of self-imposed penalties, as the Tigers continued to deal with the fallout of the Chuck Person incident.

The 2020-2021 season had turned out to be an odd one, and the next season would be odd as well.

THE 2020-2021 SEASON
13-14 (7-11, 10th in the SEC)

JT Thor (F)	Dylan Cardwell (C)
Sharife Cooper (G)	Chris Moore (F)
Devan Cambridge (G)	Tyrell "Turbo" Jones (G)
Jamal Johnson (G)	Javon Franklin (F)
Allen Flanigan (G)	Babatunde Akingbola (C)
Jaylin Williams (F)	Lior Berman (G)
Justin Powell (G)	

On paper, this team looked like one that had a chance to be very good.

The two major additions, point guard Sharife Cooper and forward JT Thor, brought big reputations with them to the Plains. In addition, freshman guard Justin Powell appeared to possess a deft touch at shooting.

Unfortunately, the totality of the team never measured up to the sum of its various parts.

Heralded freshman point guard Sharife Cooper was ineligible to play for the first fifteen games of the season. When he finally was allowed to participate, he struggled at times, as one would expect from a freshman.

After seven games, they lost backup "Turbo" Jones to transfer. That left freshman shooting guard Justin Powell handling some of the point guard duties, along with Allen Flanigan and Jamal Johnson. None of them ever seemed entirely comfortable in the role.

They survived an overtime game with St Joseph's to begin the season, 96-91, then got blown out by No. 1 Gonzaga, 90-67. After a few non-conference wins, they reconvened on December 30 to begin the SEC schedule of play, and promptly dropped their first four games, including a home loss to Alabama. They were able to score an upset of Kentucky at home on January 16, 66-59–their fourth year in a row to win at least one game against Kentucky. This Wildcats team came into the game with a losing record overall, and would go on to finish 8-9 in the SEC. Nevertheless, Bruce Pearl described any win over Kentucky as "Historic."

The game was played in front of an Auburn Arena crowd limited to just 20 percent capacity due to Covid-19 precautions. Auburn won despite shooting only 24 percent in the first half, and making just 2-of-17 3-pointers. In the second half, however, they shot over 50 percent, going 15-for-27, and attempted 15 free throws. They also outrebounded the Wildcats, 41-38. Coming in, Kentucky was one of the best teams in the country at rebounding.

Sharife Cooper, the 5-star point guard, made only 3 of 13 shots from the floor, missing all five of his 3-point attempts. But he drew nine fouls, visiting the free throw line five times, and scored 11 points, while only turning the ball over four times.

"I want him to carry us," Pearl said afterward, "but even when he doesn't, we can still win. That's a really good sign."

Auburn also beat No. 12 Missouri handily, 88-82, in Auburn Arena on January 26. Sharife Cooper had one of his better games for the Tigers in orange and blue, scoring 28 points, with 8 rebounds and 7 assists in the win. JT Thor added 12 points, while Allen Flanigan and Chris Moore rang up Mizzou for 11 each.

For the remainder of the season, however, these Tigers lost more than they won.

After a 12-point defeat at the hands of Alabama in Coleman Coliseum on March 2, they came home and finished out the season with a win over Mississippi State, 78-71.

They'd agreed to accept a self-imposed postseason ban for the year, but they wouldn't have gone beyond the SEC Tournament anyway, unless they'd somehow found a way to win it. The victory over the Bulldogs brought their season to an end, at 13-14. It was the first losing season for a Bruce Pearl-coached Auburn team in five years.

Van Allen Plexico:
This team never felt like it was coming together. They suffered injuries, took on a self-imposed postseason ban, and generally underachieved all season.

John Ringer:
They got off to a poor start, because Cooper wasn't eligible at first.

Then "Turbo" Jones transferred away after seven games. He went to South Alabama.

So we had really poor play at point guard before Cooper became eligible. That was a big problem.

Justin Powell and Allen Flanigan ended up having to play point guard. Powell wasn't ready for that; it was not what he normally did. It hurt him and it hurt the offense.

Powell averaged 12 points, 6 rebounds, and 5 assists per game, and shot 44 percent from 3-point range. That's just insane. He was a good scorer. Fans were right to be excited about him and his potential. But he ended up getting hurt—got a concussion—and missed a number of games. He only played in 10 games for Auburn, then transferred to Tennessee.

Sharife Cooper had to wait well into the season to be able to play, because of eligibility issues. Out of 27 games, he only played in 12. He had injuries, too.

JT Thor was an athletic, explosive guy who showed enormous potential, but he had a lot of room to develop. But his potential attracted the NBA, so he turned pro.

We were back this season to being a poor defensive team. We were also 16th in the country in most turnovers committed per game.

Van Allen Plexico:
This truly was a disappointing season. In a lot of ways, it was an anomaly; a blip. The team was hamstrung by a whole series of weird issues that pretty much derailed the season from the start.

John Ringer:
Yes. Injuries and eligibility issues really hurt this team.
During the off-season we started to hear about a big roster turnover coming.

Van Allen Plexico:
Bruce was basically bringing in a whole new team, through a combination of transfers and freshmen. The 2021-2022 team would be virtually unrecognizable compared to the previous season.

THE 2021-2022 SEASON
28-6 (15-3, 1st in the SEC)
SEC Regular Season Champions
NCAA Round of 32

Jabari Smith (F)
Zep Jasper (G)
K.D. Johnson (G)
Wendell Green (G)
Walker Kessler (F)
Devan Cambridge (G)
Allen Flanigan (G)

Jaylin Williams (F)
Dylan Cardwell (C)
Chris Moore (F)
Babatunde Akingbola (C)
Lior Berman (G)
Preston Cook (G)

The 2021-2022 Auburn basketball season unfolded unlike any other in history.
The Tigers were coming off a disappointing season in which a number of negatives had impacted the team's record and outcomes.

Bruce Pearl addressed that situation in recruiting and in the transfer market, bringing in almost an entirely new team of star players, including top freshman recruit Jabari Smith and star transfer Walker Kessler, along with three new guards. The only ingredient this new lineup lacked at first was chemistry, which would only come with playing time; with playing together as a team.

By January, it felt to fans as if the team had truly jelled and was playing their best ball. In the AP Polls of January 24, 31, and February 7, and for the first time in program history, the Auburn Tigers were the No. 1 team in the country. They moved to No. 1 two days after defeating 12th ranked Kentucky at home, and remained there until after a road loss at Arkansas on February 8.

Unfortunately, the team never quite played at that level again after the Arkansas loss. In some ways it seemed they had peaked during January–a very different situation from the 2018-2019 team they were often compared with, who had peaked in March and April during the tournaments. Even so, the things they accomplished and the elan with which they played will not be soon forgotten by Auburn fans. This was a truly special team and a very special season.

Walker Kessler came over to Auburn from North Carolina, where he'd been recruited by Roy Williams before his retirement. He was the son and nephew of two Georgia greats, Chad and the late Alec Kessler, respectively–both of whom became orthopedic surgeons after their playing time had ended. (Alec was a first round NBA draft pick.) Alec passed away at age 40 in 2007 during a pick-up basketball game, in a situation very similar to that of Tommy Joe Eagles. The young Walker had been unhappy with his situation at UNC and was glad to make the transition over to the Tigers, where he expected to be used in a different—and better—fashion on the court.

Joining Kessler in transferring to the Plains were guards K.D. Johnson (of Georgia), Zep Jasper (the College of Charleston), and Wendell Green, Jr. (Eastern Kentucky). All became instant-impact additions to the Auburn roster.

These transfers were joined by a true freshman stopping off in Auburn Arena for a bit before becoming an NBA lottery pick: Jabari Smith. The highest-rated recruit in Auburn history, at 4th nationally and 2nd at his position (forward), Smith emerged immediately as a silky-smooth shooter and rebounder with remarkable accuracy on his shots, even at 3-point range.

John Ringer:
Five new players came in, including the two highest-ranked recruits in Auburn history, Jabari Smith and Walker Kessler. Smith was fourth in the country, and Kessler was 18th.

When I heard about the players we were signing, I was thinking, "How are they going to put that roster together and who is going to play?"

Flanigan had been injured, but he had been very good the year before and was coming back. Jaylin Williams was coming back. Cardwell. Stretch. Chris Moore. Those guys had played a good bit in 2020-2021, but they weren't going to get a lot of playing time with the new guys coming in. That much was clear. They would probably have to accept a smaller role; a backup role. And they did. It made this team better. They all had unselfish attitudes. The existing players were welcoming of the new guys and wanted to win. Because of that, the team gelled together pretty quickly.

Van Allen Plexico:
The potential was there for this team to be a trainwreck of the older players resenting the new players and people being selfish. But they never were. The ones that ended up coming off the bench—guys like Wendell Green and Dylan Cardwell and Chris Moore—seemed perfectly happy with it all.

John Ringer:
Bruce finds ways to solve problems with the roster. He was not going to let point guard be a problem again. There were some moments before the season when it looked like the roster would be different even from what it became, but we lost a couple of guys we thought were coming, like Desi Sills, the point guard from Arkansas, who had issues with transfer credits in his major.

I think you have to give Pearl and staff credit for finding these guys and identifying them as players they wanted, and getting them to come to Auburn to play. They saw in those guys and the returning guys that we would be okay.

Van Allen Plexico:
You can tell they prioritized point guard during this offseason because we suddenly had Zep Jasper and Green and almost had Sills.

But this team never had a true shooting guard. KD Johnson was awesome for what he was and what he brought to the table, but he wasn't a traditional number two guard. He was more "Vinnie Johnson" than "Michael Jordan" (or Bryce Brown). Ultimately, despite some remarkable shots made by Green and Johnson earlier in the season, they lacked that Bryce Brown-type 3-point shooter guy. They had to rely on Jabari Smith to be the most dependable 3-point shooter, which was fine up to a point, but they really needed a shooting guard as a complement and to fulfill that role.

John Ringer:
The backups brought energy when they came into the game. Often you see a drop-off when backups come in, but many times when our backups came in, Auburn played better and increased the lead. Wendell Green, Jr, is a perfect example. He didn't start, but he had the ability to get the offense up into another gear when he came in.

KD Johnson was a welcome addition. He played his first year at Georgia but didn't like the coach.

Van Allen Plexico:
And neither did Georgia fans!
They fired him after this season.

John Ringer:
KD Johnson was generously listed at 6-1, 190 pounds. He was a bowling ball, a spark plug. An absolute maniac, all the time. He made plays everywhere. He had no fear. There were times in games when we had to have something happen on offense, and he would take the ball and make it happen. In the

Georgia game in Athens, he went out there and got it and did it. He brought home the win at the end.

He was emotional and expressive. Many players are coached to be unemotional. That's not his game; he feeds on emotion. He has the most expressive facial expressions I've ever seen. He brought emotional intensity to the game. He was never afraid of any situation.

I would also note the relationship of this team to the crowd, the fans. Very seldom do you see a crowd of fans and a team that love each other as much as this team and its fans. Jabari would walk over to Bruce during the games and point to the Auburn fans.

Walker Kessler was a backup at North Carolina as a freshman and barely played. He almost signed with Auburn out of high school. Playing for Bruce Pearl, he blossomed into the best defensive player in the country, and won the national defensive award. He really changed this team's identity with shot blocking and his inside presence. He allowed others to play better on defense because they knew he was behind them, ready to seat away anything that got past them.

The team stumbled only once before February: a 115-109 double-OT loss to UConn in the first game of the "Battle for Atlantis" tournament in the Imperial Arena at the Atlantis Resort in the Bahamas. The next day, Thanksgiving Day, the Tigers beat Loyola (IL) and began a winning streak that would extend all the way until their visit to Fayetteville, Arkansas on February 8. That game also went to OT, meaning it wouldn't be until February 19 at Florida that the Tigers would lose a game in regulation. They never lost at home the entire season.

Their biggest wins included defeating Kentucky in a massively-hyped game in Auburn Arena on January 22, and sweeping Alabama home-and-away.

The win over Alabama was the first in which the Tigers scored in the triple-digits since 1999. Wendell Green scored 23, his season high, while Walker Kessler finished with 14 points, 12 rebounds, 8 blocks and 4 steals.

The win also represented a somewhat rare sweep of the Tide in the regular season, Auburn having already beaten them in

Tuscaloosa earlier in the year. To celebrate, Bruce Pearl grabbed a broom from one of the fans and waved it, then joined the players in striking the "crane kick" pose (from Karate Kid) in front of the Auburn student section.

"I want to make one more comment about the celebration," Pearl said afterward. "This game matters to both teams. It's a great rivalry. I've got tremendous respect for (Nate Oats, the Alabama coach) and his program. This game matters to our fans. But I think because there's so much respect between the players and the coaches, I told our guys, if Alabama came in and beat us tonight, and they did whatever that crane thing is that we do, that we started doing, I said I wouldn't be upset by that. I would be disappointed if they didn't do it. That's kind of what a rivalry's all about. And I'm glad the students and the student-athletes are having fun with it."

Comparing the atmosphere of the Alabama game to what he experienced at North Carolina when Duke came calling, Walker Kessler remarked, "I think I like this (rivalry) better. We wouldn't be in the position we are without the fans. I think the Jungle is, if not the hardest place, one of the hardest places to play in the country. It's a lot of fun. You can tell the atmosphere is always electric. It doesn't matter who we're playing. So it was fun to sweep Alabama."

Eleven days after the win over Alabama, on Saturday, January 22, the Tigers welcomed the 12th ranked Kentucky Wildcats to Auburn Arena.

When Auburn plays Kentucky at home, it's always a big deal. This time, though, it was even bigger.

The Tigers came into the game riding high and playing their best ball, having lost only one game all season to that point: the UConn game back in November. That's right—they hadn't lost since *Thanksgiving of the previous year*. And Kentucky is always seen as the bully of the conference, so the Tigers relished the opportunity to go against them on even terms, and maybe knock them off.

The night before the game, Auburn students began setting up tents outside the Arena. Despite the cold January temperatures, they fully intended to spend the night there and be in line for the game at first light. Fans and the media began to refer to it as "Pearlville." Later, Coach Pearl came by to visit, and he told reporters it should instead be called "Jungle City." (The name would change again, more than once, as time went by.)

Van Allen Plexico:
My nephew, Matthew, was a senior at Auburn and was out there in a tent with the rest of them, freezing his tail off. But he was having a ball. He did some commentary for a podcast (not the AU Wishbone) and described for people who weren't there what it was all like. My favorite quote–and it may have been from him, but I don't remember for sure–was when someone who was camped out there said, "We are trying to convince ourselves this is fun."

Allie Davison, a noted Auburn Twitter personality who has worked in sports journalism, organized an effort to bring the students food and hand warmers during the night. They raised a ridiculous amount of money that evening, and I believe they ended up donating a lot of it to Coach Pearl's "AUtlive" cancer-fighting charity.

As they often did, Auburn started the game slow, turning the ball over and missing shots. Kentucky led by 4 at the half, 33-29. In the second half, the Tigers clamped down on defense–one of their trademarks this season–and found some offense. They pulled ahead and won, 80-71, after scoring 51 points in the second half, compared with the Wildcats' 38.

The win over Kentucky was huge–not just because it was over a traditional basketball power, but because of how they approached the game before it started and after it was over. The Auburn coaches and players took it in stride–a sign of maturity, and a sign that they had only done what they'd come into the game expecting to do.

"We held serve. We did what we were supposed to do," said Pearl after the game, minimizing the accomplishment as just another day at the office. "There wasn't a lot of water splashing around our locker room. We didn't win a championship. We're not cutting down nets. We were good enough today to beat a really good team."

Walker Kessler began to take control of the game just before halftime, getting four dunks in the last eight minutes. Two came in the last 45 seconds. He finished the game as the leading scorer with 19 points, to go along with 7 rebounds.

The Tigers were able to score 51 points in the second half, while controlling Kentucky's star center, Oscar Tshiebwe.

"He's a big strong dude," said Kessler of Tshiebwe. "But it was a lot of fun down there."

The *Montgomery Advertiser* called the Tigers' starting point guard, Zep Jasper, "Auburn's quiet glue," for the way he would go about his business while holding the team together—particularly on defense.

"He's so solid defensively," Pearl said of Jasper. "He's so unselfish."

Jabari Smith finished with 14 points, 7 rebounds, 2 blocks and 2 assists—all while making it look somehow effortless, magical.

"There are nine really good players out there, and there are times when we have No. 10 and you don't," said Pearl, referring to Smith's jersey number. "It was time for No. 10 to step up."

The win marked the fifth straight year that Auburn had beaten Kentucky in basketball at least once during the season.

After the game, Kentucky fans pursued two different paths toward minimizing Auburn's win in the game. On the one hand, they asserted that Auburn had turned out the big crowd and had students camped out the night before the game solely because the opponent was Kentucky. In other words, they felt it was all about them, not about Auburn. On the other hand, they argued the game shouldn't even count anyway, because one of Kentucky's starters was injured partway through the game.

Auburn fans shrugged both of these claims off. The idea that a game shouldn't count in the standings just because one player was injured was patently laughable. The other idea–that it was Kentucky basketball that turned out the crowd, not Auburn basketball–was lambasted as just as ludicrous.

"It wasn't about you, it was about us," came the overwhelming response from hundreds and maybe thousands of die-hard Tigers fans online, directing their sentiments at Wildcats supporters. The students weren't camped out to see mighty Kentucky, they patiently explained to their salty rivals. They'd camped out to see Auburn play. Kentucky was just the victim of the day.

The Tigers had been working their way up the AP Poll all season. Coming into the game against the Wildcats, they'd made it all the way up to No. 2. Afterward, they claimed the No. 1 ranking in the poll for the first time in program history.

The Tigers continued to win after the Kentucky game, but they started to look shaky. Faults began to appear, or to be exposed. Teams began to figure out how to defend against them, and to attack them. The high point of the season had perhaps been reached and passed—though fans wouldn't fully know that for a while yet.

Three days after taking down the Wildcats, Auburn traveled to Missouri, where they managed to eke out a low-scoring, last-minute, 1-point win, 55-54. After trouncing Oklahoma and laying a hundred on Alabama, they struggled to get past lowly Georgia in Athens, 74-72–and that on the strength of former Bulldog KD Johnson taking over late, determined not to lose to his old school. He finished with 20 points, leading all Auburn scorers. Wendell Green, Jr., scored on a last-second layup to secure the win, and scored 19 overall.

"I wanted the team to play a lot better," said Johnson after the game. "But we came in here and got the W in a tough Georgia stadium. So I'm feeling okay about that."

The situation was made tougher due to the absence of Auburn's starting point guard, Zep Jasper, due to a "non-COVID illness." Without him, Green had to carry the load at point guard for most of the game.

"I miss Zep," said Green. "Having Zep out there, sharing minutes with Zep, gives me a break. I felt it in my legs. All my jump shots were short. I couldn't move like I wanted to."

The game-winner by Green was his first made shot of the second half, after going 0-9 after the break.

At its peak in January, this team appeared invincible, with dominating shot-blocking by Kessler (who led the country at that statistic) and scoring by Smith, Johnson and Green, along with their cast of supporting stars. Johnson in particular endeared himself to fans with his brash, emotional play, his fiery, determined temperament, and his ability to take over games at key moments down the stretch.

Sonny Smith:
I think (Bruce Pearl) would be a good coach anywhere. (If you want) to see what a good coach he is, just go to practice. He covers every detail—every little thing. He has every player's full attention. When he got here he had a couple of players that no one could get their attention, unless you had a

gun. And now he has the players wanting to play for him. And he gets them ready for a game in practice. The best thing is how he handles practice. And this coaching staff is the best I have seen at scouting—the way they put scouting reports together and use them.

Van Allen Plexico (to Sonny Smith):
Is this the best Auburn team ever?

Sonny Smith:
I don't know. When you say forever you have to judge them against who they played. We have great teams in the league and they play great schedules because of television. This could be, but it is all based on how well the guards shoot. If the guards shoot the perimeter shot well, this could be one of the best ever. We have good depth. We need to get a few more points out of the post. The guys that play the post need to score a little more. We have the coaching, the height, the athletic ability.

You don't have guys that can't catch it on this team. You don't see guys that don't stop dribbling. Our best player is 6'10" and he can bring the ball up the court and a lot of times he has to bring the ball up the court. He can shoot, he can rebound.

This team, their attention span towards the coach is terrific. Their attention span for scouting reports is really good. They pick it up and handle it well. Now the rest of the teams that we are playing are pretty good too. They are. So you could get beat any night and it is not a coaching mistake. I would have five "mafias" and another guy that is almost there to go to Florida and play. It is hard to win there! A guy (jumping down out of the stands onto the court after the Florida win over Auburn, when the fans rushed the floor) knocked me out the other night. I guess I will be like the Wisconsin coach (who got punched after a game by the Michigan coach), just take a lick and keep going.

On January 28, 2022, Auburn University and Bruce Pearl agreed to what was called by some a "lifetime contract" to remain the Tigers' head coach for eight more years.

The $50.2 million contract amounted to $5.4 million per year, with a $250,000 escalator each year.

"By leading Auburn's men's basketball program to unprecedented heights, Coach Bruce Pearl has earned this contract extension that's commensurate with his level of achievement within the Southeastern Conference," said Auburn AD Allen Greene. "We are thrilled to agree on terms that will keep BP on the Plains for many years to come while investing in his assistant coaches and support staff. In addition to Auburn's remarkable on-court success under his leadership, Coach Pearl has tirelessly championed Auburn Athletics and Auburn University while serving our community in countless ways. This extension ensures that Auburn's commitment to Coach Pearl matches BP's commitment to Auburn."

"My intent when I came to Auburn was to have enough success for this to be my last coaching job," said Pearl. "My family and I love Auburn University, the proud tradition, our alumni, student and fan support, as well as the close-knit community we have here on the Plains.

"I am grateful to all of my players, coaches and support staff for making history. Auburn will be our family's forever home. I am humbled and blessed to be your head coach for a very long time. War Eagle!"

The new contract made him the fourth-highest-paid coach in college basketball, and second in the SEC only to John Calipari at Kentucky.

For a while, it seemed the 2021-22 Tigers might actually go undefeated throughout the entirety of league play. Three days after the Georgia win, however, it all caught up with them. They traveled to Fayetteville, Arkansas, to face the surging Razorbacks. Still playing without their starting point guard, they took Arkansas to overtime before falling, 80-76. That made two losses, both in overtime.

Van Allen Plexico:

On the one hand, the loss to Arkansas was a surprise, because the team had been playing so well during January and February. On the other hand, it wasn't surprising at all. Sometimes when you follow a team closely, you can just sense when things have started to derail a tiny bit. After the extremely narrow escapes at Missouri and Georgia, it seemed like we were due for a loss—especially going on the road to play a team that was red hot at the moment. And Arkansas at that time was playing extremely well; this game marked their ninth win in a row, going all the way back to January 12. After a one-point loss at Alabama, they'd go on to win five more straight.

So, for me, anyway, this one was disappointing but not shocking.

After three weeks at No. 1 in the AP Poll, Auburn's run at the top came to an end. They dropped to 2, then 3, then 5. By the end of the regular season, they were down to No. 8.

Following the loss at Arkansas in early February, the team never seemed quite the same–even after Jasper returned to the lineup. The outside shooting went cold, particularly from the guards, Green and Johnson. For all his defensive and rebounding prowess, Devan Cambridge's long-range shooting appeared to regress from earlier seasons. Walker Kessler had games where he was almost a non-factor inside, and often found himself in early foul trouble. Jabari Smith was being double- and triple-teamed from the moment he walked out on the court, denying him the quantity of shots he probably needed to be taking.

The Tigers returned to form somewhat with wins at home over Texas A&M and Vanderbilt, but then they traveled to Gainesville on February 19 and dropped yet another game at Florida, 63-62. A week later they fell at No. 17 Tennessee, again scoring 62 points, while the Vols managed 67.

Even before the Arkansas loss that seemed to have started the slide, the team had begun to rely more heavily on its formidable defensive abilities to keep the opponent within reach, score-wise, while searching for some kind of offense in order to make a comeback. Often that was enough, as happened at Missouri on

January 25 and at lowly Georgia on February 5. But it wasn't enough at Florida or at Tennessee later in February, where they fell, 63-62 and 67-62, respectively. With three SEC losses at that point, anxiety arose among the fans: Might Kentucky or another challenger surpass the Tigers and steal the conference regular-season title at the last minute?

The situation looked dire late in their penultimate SEC game on March 2 at Starkville. Auburn led early, but the Bulldogs came roaring back late, using a 32-10 run to take the lead. For a moment it felt as if the SEC title might be slipping away. But then Jabari Smith knocked down a last-minute shot to tie the game and force overtime (and barely missed another that would've won it at the buzzer). KD Johnson took over the game in the extra frame—scoring the first 10 points by himself—and propelled the Tigers to an 81-68 overtime win.

Auburn concluded the regular season with an 82-71 win at home over South Carolina, locking up sole possession of the SEC Championship—their second in five years under Bruce Pearl.

The team headed off to Tampa for the SEC Tournament with a coveted double-bye to the third round. Outwardly fans were still confident and hopes were high, but doubts had begun to creep in.

Those doubts were made manifest on March 11, as the Tigers were beaten soundly in their first game, 67-62, by a surging Texas A&M. Again the shots just weren't falling for Auburn. And again the defense had to carry the team—and again it almost succeeded. Almost. It was Auburn's third straight loss in which they were held to just 62 points. A plan had emerged among the Tigers' opponents for how to defend and limit this Auburn team, and the Tigers couldn't seem to find an answer for it.

The Aggies went on to the finals, where they fell to an improving Tennessee, giving the NCAA Tournament's automatic qualifier spot to the Vols. The Aggies had to settle for the NIT, where they would ultimately finish second overall.

Meanwhile, knocked out of the conference tournament after just one game, the regular-season champs returned home to the Plains to await the news of where and whom they'd be playing in the NCAA Tournament.

A sure-fire 1-seed if the season had ended in January, the Tigers fell to a 2-seed and were sent to the Midwest Regional—the same regional they'd won three years earlier—where they would face home-state foes Jacksonville State.

As tended to be the case later in this season, Auburn struggled early with the hot-shooting Gamecocks. But the Tigers' smothering defense held their opponents in check long enough for Jabari Smith to find his game—including a monstrous dunk that electrified the arena and everyone watching, including players and the media—and Auburn pulled away in the second half, winning 80-61.

Meanwhile, on the other side of Auburn's bracket, potential opponents Miami and USC battled one another through a strange game in which the Trojans played well and limited the Hurricanes to just one made 3-point shot, yet turned the ball over constantly—something Miami wasn't doing. The 10-seed Canes, riding their unorthodox offense and harrying defense, pulled out a 68-66 win and prepared to meet Auburn in the Round of 32 on Sunday, March 20.

Some fans saw that the Tigers would be facing the 10-seed and felt good about it. Unfortunately, Miami was not playing like the usual 10-seed.

Before the game, Bruce Pearl noted that the Tigers would be okay if they could limit turnovers—something USC had failed to do against this opponent on Friday. As it turned out, the Tigers could *not* limit their turnovers. Consequently, Miami pulled out to an early lead, while the Tigers looked flat and listless.

As had been the case most of the season, though, Auburn was able to reach down inside and lean on their smothering defense to get them back into the game. They valiantly clawed their way back. At halftime the Hurricanes led by only 1 point.

Continuing that monumental effort through the second half proved too difficult. Miami pulled back out into an even larger lead than the one they'd enjoyed earlier in the game, and then the teams traded baskets the rest of the way. Auburn seemed incapable of stopping Miami's guards from driving to the goal. Jabari Smith went cold again and Kessler was rendered ineffective, repeatedly pushed directly under the goal where he couldn't get off a decent shot.

Miami won, 79-61. It was every bit as bad as that score would indicate. The Hurricanes continued on, winning over Iowa State in the Sweet 16, before being steamrolled by Kansas in the Elite 8.

Meanwhile, Auburn's season was over.

"If we shot the ball better, we would have gone further in the tournament. We shot it like (expletive). That's something that has to improve."
–Bruce Pearl

John Ringer:
I was in shock when it ended, then sad, and it really bothered me.

I wanted (this Auburn team, and the season) to keep going. Not just for the fans but for the players and the staff.

It wasn't just that we lost, it was the way we lost. If we had lost and Kessler and Jabari Smith had had a great game, I wouldn't have been as upset.

Going in, I was a little more concerned with Miami as an opponent, because of their style of play. USC had a similar style of play to Auburn, and Miami took them apart (in the Round of 64). And USC had a good offensive game against them (and still lost). Miami plays a weird offense, a different offense, that we hadn't really seen before, and we didn't do a good job against it.

Van Allen Plexico:
I was not shocked or surprised. I was hopeful going in that we would win, but the way things had been going for us, ever since the Arkansas loss... It seemed like we had to fight a lot harder to win games. It seemed like opposing coaches had figured out how to defend us.

I knew going in that Miami was an odd duck, or an odd ibis, and when they said that Miami turned the ball over like three times against USC while USC turned it over a bunch, I said to myself, "Oh no," because we tend to turn the ball over a lot at times, too, and then have to play to overcome it. And then, when Jabari couldn't hit the broad side of a barn and Kessler's short shots wouldn't go in, I became even more concerned. But I kept thinking, "We're going to get it together, we're going to rally and make a run like we've done so many times."

But when it got down to five minutes to go and we were just trading baskets with them, I felt like it was over. We'd made a run before halftime and gotten it down to one, but then in the second half we immediately dug ourselves into an even deeper hole. We couldn't get stops or turnovers. They were driving and making layups any time they wanted to. It felt like our best lineup in this game, our most effective lineup, was Jaylin Williams and the guards. When we had our bigger players out there, it wasn't working at all.

John Ringer:
As the game went on, some of the players were trying to do too much, trying to save us, and things broke down even more.

Van Allen Plexico:
They were looking for a 20-point shot that could bring us back instantly. They fell apart as a team.

John Ringer:
They were each saying to themselves, "I have to do something. I can't let this happen."

Van Allen Plexico:
They started playing playground ball. Each individual was trying to do something on his own to find a way to win. I don't blame them for that.

Were they defending Jabari well, or was he having a bad night?

John Ringer:
Some of both. He wasn't having a good night, forcing shots, but they were all over him every time he got the ball, hacking him. And they did a good job of pushing our players off the spots they wanted to get the ball. Kessler got pushed underneath the basket a lot, instead of in front of it, where he has a better chance of scoring. They slapped at our players all game long, and the officials just let it go (and didn't call fouls constantly on them).

We thought our size would be a huge advantage on both ends of the floor, but Miami turned our size into a weakness on both ends. Their coach coached a great game, and their system gave us fits. They made three 3-pointers against us, after only making one against USC! I think Charles Barkley was right at halftime when he said we should go to a zone defense. Make them try to shoot 3s and don't just let them drive and get layups.

Van Allen Plexico:
The whole final third of the season, what happened to our offense? A lot of our best plays just went away in the final weeks of the season, and it turned into four guys standing and watching while one guy tried to make a play, one-on-one.

John Ringer:
I think teams just scouted us really well and figured out how to stop us. They kept our players from getting the ball in places where they were more comfortable scoring.
Miami's players were small but quick. They swarmed around like piranhas and nibbled us to death. We could've gone to a zone on defense and gone to a smaller lineup on offense, with three guards, but we never tried it.

Van Allen Plexico:
Jaylin Williams had a good game against Miami, and it might be because it was unexpected and that was the one thing Miami hadn't prepared for.

John Ringer:
I think it was. They knew what we liked to do. The pick and roll play we've run a million times with Kessler at the top of the key that worked so well—no team in this tournament was going to let us run that. They were all over it. The second they saw it coming, they were going to defend it and not let us have any success with it. We just needed to do different things.

Van Allen Plexico:
Guards guards guards.
I don't know if our 2019 team could've won a game in January against this Auburn team, but in tournament play, I'd take the 2019 team every day of the week, because of Jared

and Bryce. This team just didn't have the same consistency and accuracy at guard, the ability to create scoring.

John Ringer:
And we have a long way to go as a 3-point shooting team. It was a real weakness for this team.

The perception was, "Jabari and Kessler will get theirs inside, and the guards shooting from outside will be complementary pieces." But when Jabari and Kessler don't get theirs, the whole offense evaporates. That was the thing that shocked me—the two of them being non-offensive factors.

Also, there was the experience gap. Miami had a bunch of seniors that had played four or five years of college basketball, and we had a bunch of 18-year-olds. The Miami players weren't fazed in various circumstances, while we didn't have that experience to fall back on. And you mentioned Bryce and Jared—they were the way they were because they had a lot of experience; they'd gone through two years of up and down play to get to that Final Four season. This Auburn team was very young. They'd played some basketball together but not a lot. To me, that was the biggest difference in the game–the experience of the Miami players versus our guys.

Despite the way the season ended, accolades poured in for this team in the days afterward.

Jabari Smith averaged 16.9 points and 7.4 rebounds per game during his one and only season with the Tigers. He was named the nation's best freshman by the National Association of Basketball Coaches, as well as SEC Freshman of the Year (by the SEC coaches) and first team All-SEC. He was named second team All-American by *USA Today*, *Sporting News* and the US Basketball Writers' Association. He shot 42% from 3-point range for the season, with an effective field goal percentage of 52.1%.

On April 3, Walker Kessler was named the Naismith Award winner for Defensive Player of the Year. He'd already joined Smith on the AP All-American team.

Despite the disappointing ending, there were many unique moments and special things to cherish about the 2021-2022 season.

One truly memorable thing to occur was the emergence on social media of the Auburn deep-fried meme squad, a large group of Auburn fans who would create clever internet "memes" about Auburn's victories ahead of time—often very visually distorted and with "laser eyes" added to everyone in the picture—and then wait to pounce with them on the opposing team's Twitter account when the (losing) final score was posted there. An example would be an image of Shug Jordan, distorted and with "laser eyes," and with text that read, "Shug stormed the beaches of Normandy to bring you this L."

At the height of this phenomenon, opposing programs became reluctant to even post the final scores, knowing what would instantly result. Kentucky's account, for instance, was hit by over a thousand memes commemorating the Wildcats' defeat within the first minute of posting the score.

"The world has taken notice (of the tweet storms). And we won't be slowing down anytime soon. As this team goes, we'll go. All the way to the end."
—*"Pablo Escobarner," the unofficial head of the Auburn basketball movement on Twitter*

"It's really unprecedented. I don't think what Auburn does is something you could copy or replicate, but it's certainly inspirational in terms of they all speak the same language and the individual memes themselves are pretty creative and funny."
—*Cody Worsham, social media strategist for LSU*

"At first, I was thinking, man, I got to make sure the notifications on my phone are off. But I think any time you got a passionate fanbase like Auburn, it's something that if you work in athletics, you can definitely appreciate it. They're going to do it regardless of what you do, so can we look at it as a negative or can we have some fun with it? That's kind of the route we tried to go."
—*Brant Danals, Director of Basketball Operations, University of North Alabama (who experienced the phenomenon after their loss to Auburn on December 14, 2021)*

Yet another fan-driven aspect of this season was the use of the terms "Peacock" and "Peacocking" to describe the fans' embracing of Auburn having a quality basketball program. It began when the Auburn fan known on social media as "Son of Crow"—the same fan who had created the "We've Got Jared" song during the 2019 Final Four run—noted on a podcast that Auburn fans needed to stop being hesitant and tentative and just go ahead and embrace the team and its success, and stop worrying about any failures or bad things that might happen. The goal was to encourage Auburn fans to be confident and proud of their program, and not to wait around for the "inevitable collapse and disappointment," as had happened with many Auburn athletic teams in the past.

"Peacocking" meant embracing the joy the team was providing for the fans to the fullest extent. It was symbolized by fans across Twitter placing the "peacock" emoji next to their Twitter names and incorporating peacock imagery into their memes.

Van Allen Plexico

The meme storms and the "peacock" thing were both just added bonuses during this season; they represented more ways we could all be involved with the team and with the winning, and good advice about how we as fans should enjoy the good times rather than fretting about the possible bad times to come.

There was also the thing where Auburn fans started referring to our program with utter sincerity as a "blue blood," meaning a top basketball power. I can't imagine anyone truly believes that about our program over history—everything in this book so far has made the truth about it perfectly clear—but there's no doubt the past few years have seen Bruce Pearl lift Auburn to that level just in the present era. And it's fun to watch the Alabama and other rival fan groups go nuts when we do it.

I also want to mention the contribution made to Auburn's cause by our own Jarrod "the Yardsale Artist" Alberich. He discovered early on that Auburn tended to win when he didn't watch, and lost when he did tune into the games. So he chose to "take one for the team," over and over, by not watching, so that Auburn had a better chance of winning. It also turned out, oddly enough, that if he spent game time watching old

"Airwolf" reruns, of all things, that particularly seemed to help Auburn. So that's what he did.

I can testify to the power of his abilities: When he and I were in Los Angeles with the rest of our James Bond podcast team, late in the season, we took time out to all watch the Auburn-Tennessee game together—and Auburn lost. I was disappointed for the team but also for Jarrod. He just wanted to see the Tigers win.

Another significant change occurred during the season. The University announced that Auburn Arena would be renamed in honor of the Neville family, who had recently donated the single largest gift in Auburn Athletics history. The total amount remains undisclosed, but the donors—Bill and Connie Neville—are members of the Pat Dye Society, Tigers Unlimited's highest level of giving. Every member of that group has given at least $3 million to Auburn athletics.

The ceremony marking the official name change was held on March 4, with a special on-court recognition the next day during the South Carolina game.

This wasn't their first donation to Tigers athletics. Their previous support resulted in the naming of "the Bill and Connie Neville Lobby" in the east elevator lobby at Jordan-Hare Stadium.

"I really love the two hours of magic and chaos that we all create together in this beautiful arena.

"The fact that we can benefit so many student-athletes, students and members of the Auburn family was our primary inspiration. We're honored that Auburn would consider us."

—*Bill Neville*

The Board of Trustees also approved a project—possibly funded at least in part by this gift—to build an additional basketball practice facility at the arena, as well as to renovate team support spaces and allow more room for the other teams that make use of the arena, including women's basketball and volleyball.

"(The additional facilities) will permit Auburn's men's and women's programs to conduct practices at advantageous times and bring their facilities to Southeastern Conference competitive standards."

—*USA Today*

"Bill knew how much his father (who graduated from the University) loved Auburn and he's dedicated much of his life to honoring his father," said Bruce Pearl, at the ceremony. "That's how I look at this gift. I will always work hard to try to continue to bring championships to Neville Arena.

"This is a commitment to all four of the programs that call Neville Arena home. The fact that our guys will truly have a place they can call home 24 hours a day, seven days a week with the way they train, is very significant and will contribute to our ability to sustain success."

And so the future appeared bright: Bruce Pearl now had what was effectively a "lifetime contract" as Auburn's basketball coach, and the arena had new and upgraded facilities on the way, along with its new name. The pipeline of 4- and 5-star players continued, as Auburn basketball–and it's hard to believe we are saying this–*reloaded* rather than rebuilt.

While the 2021-2022 season hadn't ended the way Auburn fans would've preferred, it had been a joy overall, with a number of accomplishments and milestones reached. The Tigers were SEC Champions. They'd been the top seed in the SEC Tournament and a 2-seed in the NCAAs; only the 1998-99 team had done better in that regard. They'd won at least one game in that tourney. Jabari Smith and Walker Kessler both were named first-team All-SEC, among many other accolades, and Bruce Pearl was voted SEC Coach of the Year. This was the first time the Tigers achieved that trifecta since 1999.

Going into the following season, big-time recruits and transfers were already coming in, wanting to play for Bruce Pearl, in Neville Arena, before the best fans in the country. There could be no doubt: basketball on the Plains—once a joke or an afterthought at best, save for the odd year here and there—had arrived in full-force at last.

- AFTERWORD -

In 1986, as high school students, we were giddy with excitement over Auburn advancing to the Elite Eight, and fully expected the Tigers to return there—and advance even deeper into the NCAA Tournament—during our own years on the Plains. We could only imagine what successes lay beyond that, as the 1980s gave way to the 1990s.

For a couple of years the good times kept rolling. Ultimately, though, things didn't work out the way would all have preferred. Sonny Smith left for VCU as the recruiting dried up. Tommy Joe Eagles never quite got the program going again. As Kevin Scarbinsky had memorably predicted, the Auburn roller coaster was indeed headed downhill. Despite a few solid seasons under Cliff Ellis, years of wandering in the wilderness lay ahead—years of Jeff Lebo and Tony Barbee. Years of futility.

But with Auburn's 2021-2022 season completed, and despite lingering disappointment at what might have been, there was also *hope* again—not "pie in the sky dreaming" hope, but hope grounded in reality. *Hope*, as well as *potential*, and therefore *possibility*—all qualities often in very short supply around Auburn's basketball program in years and decades past.

As of this writing, in the summer of 2022, no SEC team has won more basketball games over the past five years than Auburn. Not Kentucky. Not Tennessee. Not Alabama. Not *anybody*. The Tigers stand astride the Southeastern Conference. And, perhaps unlike in years past, the fans are now entirely committed to them and are on board.

The Tigers and their fans know that, this time, they have the right coach—the coach who can keep that roller coaster from nose diving, and indeed take it to new heights. The coach who will not just rebuild but *reload*, again and again, cranking out first-round NBA draft picks while recruiting 4- and 5-star players to fill their spots. The same coach they just signed to a "lifetime contract."

No, Auburn fans in 2022 are confident that, unlike after 1984-88 and unlike after 1998-99, this time the Tigers have succeeded in becoming basketball royalty— "blue bloods," as the fans liked to say on social media. Opponents might scoff at such a notion, questioning how long it could possibly last. But the philosophy of the Peacock makes it clear: You don't ask silly questions like that. You don't wallow in worry and insecurity about what bad things *might* happen down the road. No–you ride that roller coaster *now*, for as long as the ride can last, and you enjoy to its fullest every single moment of that ride.

Tiger fans can look back with pride to the past. But now, after so many years in the wilderness, they can look to the present, and to the future as well—with all of its *possibility*, and *potential*, and *hope*.

Hope grounded in *reality*.

Believe it or not, and almost entirely through the efforts of one man—the coach named Bruce Pearl—the Auburn Tigers have become college basketball "blue bloods," reloading each year while proudly "peacocking" and "meme-storming" their way to conference titles and tournament wins, powering through the SEC schedule and into the NCAA Tournament on a regular basis.

Enjoy the present. Trust in the future. For the future is bright, and it's *real*.

Greatness awaits.

War Eagle!

—Van Allen Plexico and John Ringer
  Summer 2022

- SOURCES -

While this book was mainly compiled as an "oral history," the following articles and sources were consulted during its creation:

Anderson, Reggie. "Cliff Ellis Out as Auburn's Basketball Coach." *WLTX TV* Web Site, March 18, 2004

AP Wire Report. "N Carolina Height Overcomes Auburn" *The New York Times*, March 23, 1985

Asher, Mark. "Auburn Basketball, Tennis On 2 Years' NCAA Probation. " *The Washington Post*, November 19, 1991

Austin, Walt. "Auburn Basketball 2015-16 Season Review: Dissecting Bruce Pearl's Second Year" *College and Magnolia*, March 15, 2016

Baker, Chris. "Barkley's Bark." *The LA Times*, February 22, 1987

Blackerby, Zac. "Neville Arena: Auburn Trustees approve arena name change, basketball facility improvements"
USA Today, Feb 8, 2022

Blum, Sam. "Ex-Auburn basketball coach Cliff Ellis still adamant it was a mistake to fire him 15 years ago"
AL dot com, 2019.

Crepea,, James. "Kareem Canty opens up about his departure from Auburn, pursuit of NBA"
AL dot com, May 22, 2016

Deal, Nathan. "Auburn Gets Landmark Win for Coach Tony Barbee"
The Bleacher Report, January 29, 2011

Dodds, Tracy. "Wizards of Louisville Stop Auburn, 84-76, and again Final Four."
LA Times. March 23, 1986

Durando, Bennett. "Auburn basketball freshman Jabari Smith declares for NBA Draft"
The Montgomery Advertiser, April 5, 2022

Durando, Bennett. "Intimidation factor": Why Auburn basketball's smallest arena in SEC is toughest place to win
The Montgomery Advertiser, March 3, 2022

Ellis, Zac. "Auburn fires head coach Tony Barbee after four seasons"
SI.com, March 12, 2014

Erickson, Joel A. "Auburn hires Bruce Pearl as men's basketball coach"
AL dot com, March 18, 2014

Feinstein, John. "Auburn's Smith Agonizes: To Leave or Not to Leave."
The Washington Post. March 22, 1985

Green, Tom. "Bruce Pearl's contract extended for 8 years, $50.2 million"
AL dot com, Jan. 29, 2022

Green, Tom. "'This is next level': What it's like from the other side of an Auburn basketball Twitter storm"
AL dot com, Jan. 11, 2022

Hale, Jon. "Kentucky's season ends in crushing loss to Auburn in NCAA Tournament"
Courier Journal, March 31, 2019

Heisler, Mark. "'84 US Olympic Team May have been the Greatest Ever"
Los Angeles Times, Jul 10, 1988

Hyatt, Richard. "Memories of a college basketball coach who never got to coach"
AllOnGeorgia editorial, July 15, 2018

Inabinett, Mark. "NBA 75th anniversary team introduction emotional for Charles Barkley"
AL dot com, Feb. 21, 2022

Marshall, Phillip. "Sonny Smith's story: The Auburn years"
24/7 Sports, Oct 21, 2020

Marshall, Phillip. "Sunday Reflections."
Auburn Undercover, Feb. 22, 2015

McGuire, Kane. "Hall of Fame Feature: Tommy Joe Eagles."
Louisiana Tech Web Site, Sept. 18, 2017

Smith, Sonny. Interview with the authors, February 22, 2022.

Staff and wire reports. "Auburn signs Cliff Ellis to take over its basketball program"
AL dot com, April 5, 1994

Uncredited story. "23 Years Later, Pearl Apologizes to Illini."
The Telegraph (Alton, Illinois)

Uncredited story. "Eagles Named Auburn Basketball Coach."
UPI Archives, April 2, 1989.

Uncredited story. "Ex-SIU Coach Lambert Dies in Motel Fire."
Southern Illinoisan, June 6, 1978.

Wilbon, Michael. "Barkley: The Great Wide Hope."
The Washington Post. April 23, 1984

Woodberry, Evan. "Auburn fires basketball coach Jeff Lebo one day after his sixth season with Tigers ends"
Al dot com, March 13, 2010

Woodberry, Evan. "Auburn hires UTEP's Tony Barbee as new hoops coach"
The Birmingham News, march 25, 2010

Boris the Tiger, AU Wishbone patron
& 2021 Bowl Pick 'em Champion

ABOUT THE AUTHORS

Van and **John** have been recording episodes of the **AU Wishbone Podcast** almost every Monday since fall 2012.

Van Allen Plexico is an award-winning author who managed to attend Auburn (and score student football tickets) for some portion of every year between 1986 and 1996. He teaches college near St Louis, and also hosts a number of different podcasts, appears at pop culture conventions, and writes and edits novels, stories and articles for a variety of publishers. Find links to his various projects at *www.plexico.net*.

John Ringer graduated from Auburn in 1991 (which may be the greatest time ever to be an Auburn student – SEC titles in 1987, 88 and 89 and the 1989 Iron Bowl). His family has had season tickets every year since well before he was born and he grew up wandering around Jordan-Hare on game days. He currently lives in Richmond, Virginia where he spends way too much time reading about college football and basketball on the internet.

You can hear Van and John discuss the latest in Auburn Football— with lots of humor and fun thrown in—every single week: Just search "AU Wishbone" on your favorite podcast app, or go to **www.AUWishbone.com**

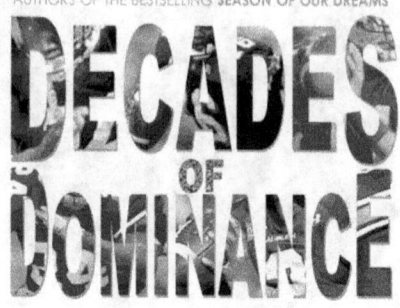

AUBURN FOOTBALL
IN THE MODERN ERA

VAN ALLEN PLEXICO
AND
JOHN RINGER

ALSO FROM THE AU WISHBONE CREW:

DECADES OF DOMINANCE:
AUBURN FOOTBALL IN THE MODERN ERA

The biggest games, the best bowls, the greatest players and coaches to ever wear the orange and blue—it's all here in this celebration of Auburn Football in the Modern Era. In its more than 300 pages of colorful memories, statistics, humor, Top Ten lists, and much more, DECADES OF DOMINANCE passionately argues for Auburn's greatness on the football field.

Only $16.95 in paperback, wherever books are sold.
ISBN: 978-0984139286
Only $4.99 on Amazon Kindle!
www.whiterocketbooks.com

WE BELIEVED
A LIFETIME OF AUBURN FOOTBALL
Vol 1: 1975-1998

Meticulously researched and created using the same style as AUBURN BASKETBALL: FROM BARKLEY TO BRUCE, WE BELIEVED Vol 1 dives deep into the Pat Dye era of Auburn Football. Filled with memories, full game descriptions, player stats and much more, it's the indispensable work on Auburn in the 1980s & 1990s. At nearly 500 pages, it's $19.95 wherever books are sold!
ISBN: 979-8536996751
www.whiterocketbooks.com

www.ingramcontent.com/pod-product-compliance
Lightning Source LLC
Chambersburg PA
CBHW050242010526
44107CB00032B/1378/J